Confucianism
in Context

SUNY series in Chinese Philosophy and Culture

Roger T. Ames, editor

Confucianism in Context

Classic Philosophy and Contemporary Issues,
East Asia and Beyond

Edited by

Wonsuk Chang

and

Leah Kalmanson

Published by State University of New York Press, Albany

© 2010 State University of New York

For information, contact State University of New York Press, Albany, NY
www.sunypress.edu

Production by Kelli W. LeRoux
Marketing by Michael Campochiaro

Library of Congress Cataloging-in-Publication Data

Confucianism in context : classic philosophy and contemporary issues, East Asia and beyond / edited by Wonsuk Chang and Leah Kalmanson.
    p. cm. — (SUNY series in Chinese philosophy and culture)
    Includes bibliographical references and index.
    ISBN 978-1-4384-3191-8 (hardcover : alk. paper)
    ISBN 978-1-4384-3190-1 (paperback : alk. paper)
    1. Confucianism. I. Chang, Wonsuk, 1966–   II. Kalmanson, Leah, 1977–
III. Title: Classic philosophy and contemporary issues, East Asia and beyond.
    BL1853.C73 2010
    299.5'12—dc22   2009051689

10 9 8 7 6 5 4 3 2 1

Contents

Acknowledgments   vii

Foreword   ix
    Youngjin Choi

Introduction: The Confucian Tradition—an Evolving Narrative   1
    Wonsuk Chang and Leah Kalmanson

Chapter 1
Transmitting the *Dao*: Chinese Confucianism   9
    John Berthrong

Chapter 2
The History of Confucianism in Korea   33
    Youngjin Choi

Chapter 3
The History of Confucianism in Japan   53
    Peter Nosco

Chapter 4
What Is Confucianism?   67
    Roger T. Ames

Chapter 5
Confucian Person in the Making   87
    Wonsuk Chang

Chapter 6
Confucianism and Democracy   103
    Sor-hoon Tan

Chapter 7
Confucianism and Human Rights   121
    Sangjin Han

Chapter 8
The Short Happy Life of Boston Confucianism   145
    Robert Neville

Chapter 9
A Feminist Appropriation of Confucianism   175
    Li-Hsiang Lisa Rosenlee

Chapter 10
Confucian Trajectories on Environmental Understanding   191
    Michael C. Kalton

Appendix I: List of Names   211

Appendix II: Historical Periods   215

Glossary   219

Bibliography   227

List of Contributors   235

Index   239

Acknowledgments

Chapter 1 was previously published as an article in the *Internet Encyclopedia of Philosophy*. Parts of Chapter 8 appear in Robert Cummings Neville's *Boston Confucianism: Portable Tradition in the Late-modern World* (Albany: State University of New York Press, 2008).

Foreword

About one hundred years ago, Park Ŭn-Sik (1859–1925), a Korean Confucian scholar and activist for Korean independence, warned of the decline of Confucianism and advocated reforms. He said: "The nineteenth and twentieth centuries have seen the enormous development of western culture, and the forthcoming twenty-first century will be a time when eastern culture prospers. Therefore, I am convinced that the way of Confucius will not decline. I predict that there will be a day when Confucianism will brilliantly shine throughout the whole world" (*A New Treatise on Confucianism*).

Now, at the beginning of the twenty-first century it is impossible to tell whether Confucianism will prosper as Pak Un-Sik predicted, or if it will decline. However, Confucian studies are spreading throughout the world as more scholars recognize Confucianism as a significant resource offering new approaches to contemporary issues. Needless to say, Confucianism does not presently function as a social norm in the areas of East Asia where it first developed. Nations such as Korea, China, Japan, and Taiwan, which formed the Confucian cultural sphere in the past, have accepted Western technology and capitalist culture as the means to becoming "successful." Of these nations, Korea and Taiwan have succeeded in establishing capitalism and democracy as norms, achieving both modernization and westernization in less than half a century.

Nevertheless, Confucianism has not disappeared from the minds of Asian people. Especially in the case of Korea, where the Confucian tradition is said to be now the strongest, Confucianism as a cultural grammar regulates the customs and the consciousness of the Koreans. Therefore, in order to understand East Asia societies, one must pay attention to Confucianism. However, confusion arises due to the many positive interpretations of Confucianism coexisting alongside the many negative ones. Until the mid-1990s Confucianism was appreciated as the motivating power for economic development in East Asia. However, during the 1997 Asian financial crisis, Confucianism was blamed as the main culprit behind the economic problems. Even now Confucianism is criticized as a form of authoritarian feudal ethics. Yet, at the same time,

Confucianism is recognized as a political ideal that can not only support democracy but that can supplement the shortcomings of liberalism. And, despite those who criticize Confucianism as oppressive toward women, many feminist scholars are reconstructing Confucianism as a theoretical basis for an ethics compatible with feminism.

I think we must try to understand Confucianism as objectively as possible before judging its positive and negative qualities. In order to do this, we must understand the essence of Confucian thought and how it has been accepted, developed, and modified in Korea, China, and Japan. Since Confucianism is a product of the premodern societies of northern and eastern Asia, it is only natural that it has premodern elements. However, Confucianism is not adverse to modern concerns such as the advocacy of human dignity and self-sufficiency and the rational approach to nature, humanity, and society. We may compellingly argue for continued studies in Confucianism as a part of our precious human heritage, which has contributions to make in planning our postmodern society.

The West pursued the discovery of natural laws to strengthen the power of humans over nature, with its sights on a seemingly limitless human empire. To the extent that the knowledge of nature leads to the control of nature, then indeed "Knowledge is power." With this power we have developed an industrial civilization, combining science, technology, and capitalism. We are living in an unprecedentedly affluent age of consumption. However, modern life is already pregnant with the seeds of contradiction. Atomistic views of the self have led to fractured identities, ecological destruction is rampant, and barbaric violence grows commonplace. Thus, we have arrived at the point when we have to fundamentally revise existing concepts and values. Human civilization has been exposed to the limits of modernity and is now entering a new phase. Therefore, it has become inevitable that we must reevaluate Western civilization, with its emphasis on scientific rationality and technological dominance, its mechanical view of nature, and its unbridled industrialization. Just as humanity once developed from a premodern society into a modern society, we now face the historic transformation from modern society to postmodern society.

For this reason, postmodernization resists westernization and promotes the development of a multifaceted civilization. This is evident in the aspirations of postmodernist scholars who deny totalitarian politics and promote a politics of difference, who recognize the variety of individuals and the variety of worldviews. Their work is prompted by the principle that the world is a display of "differences." Humans and nature are different, men and women are different, races and the colors of skin are different, and languages, customs, and cultures are different. However, in human society now such differences are the causes of discrimination, oppression, and antagonism. Seen from this angle, the postmodern society must evolve from human-centered thinking to ecological thinking that seeks harmony with nature, from Western-centered civilization to multiple civilization centers, from closed societies to open societies that respect individuality and variety. But how will we find a model for this postmodern society?

Just as Greek civilization provided a model for early modern thinkers working to overcome their medieval past, now the traditional thought of East Asia, centered on Confucianism, presents itself as a possible model for postmodern society. In this spirit, the present book addresses the questions "What is Confucianism?" and "What implications does it have today?" We hope this book will be a guide for English-speaking readers to understand Confucianism and East Asian society. Furthermore, readers may come to value Confucianism as a part of our human heritage relevant to the creation of a new civilization in the twenty-first century.

Finally, I am grateful to Sungkyunkwan University for generous financial support, to Dr. Wonsuk Chang who is responsible for this project, and to State University of New York Press for the publication of this book.

Youngjin Choi
June 2008

Introduction

The Confucian Tradition— An Evolving Narrative

Wonsuk Chang and Leah Kalmanson

One of the most renowned philosophers of ancient Greece, Parmenides, theorized that all reality is eternal, unchanging being and that change itself is only an illusion. In contrast, one of the great philosophical classics of ancient China, the *Yijing* or *Book of Changes,* devotes itself to the study of the changing world. Such contrasts arise between many of the great minds of Greece and China. Whereas Socrates searches for absolute definitions of concepts such as goodness and justice, Confucius takes a more aesthetic approach to the question of defining humaneness (*ren* 仁). In answer to Zhonggong's question of what *ren* is, Confucius describes it as behaving prudently, as though receiving important visitors. Yet when dealing with Sima Niu, known for being tiresomely talkative and impulsive, Confucius defines *ren* as "slow to speak" (*ren* 訒). And when Fan Chi repeatedly inquires into *ren*, Confucius gives a different response each time. At first *ren* means to love others, but at other times *ren* is deference at home, respectfulness in handling public affairs, or doing one's utmost in relationships. In every case, Confucius seems to be concerned more with the constant negotiation of meaning necessary for dealing with varying circumstances and less with establishing a determinate definition of the term.

The differences between Socrates and Confucius reflect two distinct cultural approaches to the shaping of philosophical narratives. Admittedly, Confucianism cannot be adequately characterized as a science in the Greek sense, in which inquiries must be based on clear and distinct definitions, or a religion in the Abrahamic tradition, which is grounded in dogma and faith.

What, then, is Confucianism? Responding to this question is the daunting task of the present volume.

As the following chapters show, Confucianism is a set of evolving philosophical narratives, which can adapt themselves to address any number of unique circumstances. As is the case with *ren*, ideas in the Confucian tradition are indirect yet productively vague, allowing interpreters from various philosophical eras and cultures to elaborate Confucianism differently in different contexts. In this tradition, philosophical narratives do not start from axiomatic certainties but rather are elliptical, often requiring a leap of the imagination to understand how their meaning is relevant to specific conditions. Confucian intellectuals continuously engage in hermeneutic negotiations, including the interpretation and arrangement of the Confucian classics as well as the appropriation of vocabulary from other traditions.

Recurring hermeneutic negotiations in Confucianism may serve a conservative purpose, namely, the maintenance of an enduring tradition. But they may also serve the creative purpose of producing novelty. These two aspects do not contradict each other. The Confucian version of the hermeneutic circle might be better termed a "hermeneutic spiral." Many Confucians, if not all, employ this hermeneutic spiral when they return to ancient sources in order to simultaneously create novel ideas. For example, the Southern Song philosopher Zhu Xi (1130–1200) productively focuses on ideas in the canonical Four Books—*Analects, Great Learning, Zhongyong*, and *Mencius*—through his compilations and annotations, while selectively emphasizing the notion of coherence (*li* 理) and locating it at the center of a new Confucian narrative. And while the Korean Confucian scholar Chŏng Yagyong (1762–1836) insists that authentic learning should return to the early teachings of Confucius pre-dating neo-Confucianism, he goes on to develop a unique theistic Confucian philosophy in dialogue with Roman Catholicism.

Confucianism, in its philosophy as well as its art, often describes this complementary hermeneutic process through the metaphor of water and mountains. Water stands for indeterminacy, fluidity, and the inexhaustible source of creativity. Mountain imagery expresses determinacy, endurance, and the paragons of cultural achievement that serve as models for the common people.[1] Water, as the uninterrupted flow of changeability, can be regarded as constituting the very wrinkles of mountains, which are like the enduring patterns of Confucian teachings (the Confucian "way" or *dao* 道). As an inexhaustible fund of immanence, water allows mountains to constantly renew themselves, like the living tradition of Confucianism. Not in spite of variance, but because of it, this enduring tradition is able to flourish. The Confucian narrative unfolds the way along which tradition never ceases to change in order to continue its existence.

In the present volume, Robert Neville engages in this hermeneutic spiral when, in spite of his fear of heterodoxy, he opens a debate over whether *Xunzi* should be included in the primary texts of what he calls Boston Confucianism—his vision for a self-consciously non–East Asian form of Confucianism. As he says, nothing is more orthodox in the Confucian tradition than disputes about the canon, which stimulate the emergence of novel interpretations. This evolutionary process is that of an advancing spiral that produces novelty while simultaneously returning again and again to nascent sources. Indeed, our book as a whole illustrates this interpretative give and take between past and present as it seeks to situate the wealth of the Confucian intellectual tradition within various contemporary contexts, thereby showcasing its relevance as a world philosophy.

The first three chapters of the text approach the Confucian narrative from a historical perspective, showing how the roots of Confucianism have branched out through the soils of East Asian countries such as China, Korea, Japan, and Vietnam.[2] In the first chapter, "Transmitting the *Dao*: Chinese Confucianism," John Berthrong provides an informative account of the history of Confucianism within China. He introduces and explains many terms that the reader will encounter in subsequent chapters and summarizes of the works of major philosophers from Confucius himself to the "new Confucians" of the contemporary era. As Berthrong states, and as the later chapters demonstrate, Confucian history is still in the process of unfolding. His account of this history is unique in comparison to other standard accounts by Angus Graham or Frederick W. Mote, because he attaches significant importance to the writings of Xunzi in the development of Confucianism. He pays careful attention to Xunzi's ideas concerning human disposition, psychology, language theory, ritual action, and society as evidence of a form of secularized Confucianism flourishing in the classical period.

The second chapter addresses "The History of Confucianism in Korea." Youngjin Choi gives an account of Korean Confucian philosophy, which is largely ignored in Western academia and is noticeably absent from other histories of Confucianism. Choi argues that indigenous Korean culture had contact with Confucianism since ancient times, making Korean intellectual history an integral part of the development of Confucian philosophy. He discusses famous intellectual debates occurring throughout the Chosŏn period (1392–1910), such as the Four-Seven Debate, the Ho-Rak Debate, and various Buddhist-Confucian dialogues. In trying to determine the place of Korean Confucianism in the pan-Asian Confucian orbit, Choi highlights modern Korea's unique answer to the dilemma of how to reconcile Confucian values with Western influences.

In the third chapter on "The History of Confucianism in Japan," Peter Nosco examines the complicated relationship between Confucianism and Buddhism in Japan. Rather than occupying strictly defined realms, the two traditions have often overlapped, as in the cases of Buddhist priests who were also committed Confucian scholars. The Japanese had access to the writings of both Chinese and Korean Confucian philosophers, and Nosco offers summaries of the positions of various Japanese thinkers within the broader, pan-Asian Confucian discourse, revealing in the process the indelible marks of Confucianism on Japanese culture today.

The fourth chapter provides a bridge from the historical material to the contemporary philosophical issues dealt with in subsequent chapters. In "What Is Confucianism?" Roger Ames delves into the interpretive context within which the Confucian philosophical narrative evolved, appealing to the prominent historian and scholar of Chinese archeology David Keightley and the preeminent philosopher Tang Junyi. Ames argues for revised interpretations of enduring Confucian terms such as family reverence (*xiao* 孝), consummate person or consummate conduct (*ren* 仁), harmony (*he* 和), natural tendency (*xing* 性), exemplary person (*junzi* 君子), and propriety in ritualized roles and relationships (*li* 禮). For example, he suggests that it is better to understand human disposition (*renxing* 人性) in terms of relationships and processes rather than discrete individuals. Given that the Confucian sense of order is aesthetic, harmony is not expressible in the language of quantity and closure but in that of quality and disclosure. In the latter part of the chapter, Ames invites us to revisit an issue long under consideration: the ambiguous role of family in the Confucian tradition. The family is both the primary site for the growth of truly robust democratic values, as well as the root of the excessive intrusion of personal relationships into public areas—an intrusion that potentially compromises the democratic principles of fairness and objectivity.

Wonsuk Chang, in the fifth chapter, titled "Confucian Person in the Making," articulates a Confucian response to the perennial philosophical question: What does it mean to be human? Unraveling the complicated fabric of core Confucian values relevant to the self, such as heavens (*tian* 天), propensity (*ming* 命), and natural tendency (*xing* 性), Chang exploits the Confucian legacies of China and Korea, as well as pertinent Western philosophies. The Confucian answer to the question of humanity seems to be formulated as follows: our aim is to achieve the most productive harmony between heaven and the human world, that is to say, the "continuity of heaven and humans" (*tianrenheyi* 天人合一). According to Chang, heaven, or *tian*, provides persons with a context for their growth and in turn increases along with the full growth of persons. Whoever attains excellence in self-cultivation becomes an integral part of *tian* by focusing the whole field of *tian*. His explication of the productive connectivity between the self and its larger environment as a core Confucian value serves as an opening for the next two chapters, in which the discussions hinge on Confucian notions of self, society, and politics.

In the sixth chapter Sor-hoon Tan explores the possibilities for dialogue between "Confucianism and Democracy." She examines and eventually rejects the extreme position that Confucianism and democracy are simply incompatible. She also warns against the assumption that democracy is necessarily tied to the Western value system. Moreover, she points out that many Western nations today may not provide the best examples of functioning, healthy democratic communities. Relying on the writings of John Dewey on democracy, Tan shows that Confucian values coupled with alternative visions for democracy within the West can offer the global community better examples of democratic potential.

In the seventh chapter, "Confucianism and Human Rights," Sangjin Han revisits an incident from contemporary Korean history to explore human rights in the context of Confucianism. The Kwangju uprising of 1980, a trauma for contemporary Koreans, is the account of a community's resistance to military rule. Despite the breakdown of governmental rule and the seeming "anarchy" that existed during the days of the uprising, the people of Kwangju maintained a communal cohesion that allowed them to successfully resist unjust military authority while at the same time caring for the needs of individuals injured or otherwise affected by the uprising. Han sees the Kwangju uprising as an example of spontaneous, communal democratic self-rule, not imposed on people through a top-down power structure, and he asks whether Confucian values could ever sustain such a community on a larger, long-term scale. His interpretation of Confucianism may be properly called a communitarian approach without authoritarian consequences. He proposes testing this interpretation against the historical development of South Korea, one of the most democratized countries in Asia as well as one of the most strongly Confucian.

In the eighth chapter Robert Neville tells the story of "The Short Happy Life of Boston Confucianism." He challenges the notion that only those people who are products of an East Asian culture can rightfully be called Confucians. His title refers to the coincidental concentration of Confucian scholars in Boston-area universities, but Neville extends the idea of "Boston Confucianism" to include a detailed analysis of the possibility for a flowering of Confucian values in a Bostonian culture. While Tu Weiming's prominent thesis of "the third wave of Confucianism" sees contemporary Confucianism as an extension of tradition, Neville's Boston Confucianism is an attempt to utilize this emerging, portable tradition from the standpoint of the intellectual needs of an American philosophical context. His intercultural philosophical adventure between American philosophers such as Charles Peirce, John Dewey, and A. N. Whitehead, and Confucians such as Xunzi and Wang Yangming is nothing less than a transformation of Confucianism in American soil that aims to create an inclusive world philosophy.

The ninth chapter proposes "A Feminist Appropriation of Confucianism," in which Li-Hsiang Lisa Rosenlee demonstrates the potential for a feminist critique arising within the Confucian tradition itself, not imposed from the outside as a harbinger of westernization. Rosenlee resists both the Confucians who reject feminism as an intrusion of Western values as well as the Western feminists who reject Confucianism as irredeemably patriarchal. These Western feminists fail to note that the forefathers of Western philosophy were often no less dismissive of women's intellectual capabilities. In her feminist appropriation of Confucianism, Rosenlee preserves core Confucian values, especially those that emphasize social and familial roles, while showing that they need not be interpreted either hierarchically or strictly in terms of gender.

Finally, in the tenth chapter Michael C. Kalton offers "Confucian Trajectories on Environmental Understanding." Confucianism has traditionally addressed itself to the question of the proper place of human beings within the natural world. Beginning with the assumption that humans are initially naturally integrated in their environments, Confucians then seek to explain the causes of imbalances in this relationship and how these imbalances may be corrected. As Kalton shows, the answers provided by Confucianism to this question are strikingly relevant to the contemporary environmental crisis.

What contributors in this anthology share in common is an understanding of the dialogical nature of Confucianism. Throughout different philosophical eras and distinct cultures, Confucianism is a product of its transactions with varying circumstances. What contributors do not share is a common focus; their interests range from the specific historical conditions of Confucianism in China, Korea, Japan, and the Western world, to significant contemporary cultural discourses such as philosophical anthropology, feminism, ecology, democracy, and human rights.

We first gathered this collection of essays as an introductory text to the world of Confucianism, intended for undergraduate students, both local and international, in the English-language general education program at Korea's Sungkyunkwan University. As more Asian universities seek to foster proficiency in English as well as encourage student participation in global academic exchanges, we hope that this text will be useful in a variety of classroom settings. We also hope that Western readers, both inside and outside the university, will enjoy this representative collection of articles showing the variety of important trends in Asian and intercultural philosophy today. It is our sincere hope that we have successfully exhibited the evolving Confucian narrative as it takes shape, modulates, endures, and thrives, through time and across cultures.

Notes

1. Water and mountains are recurrent images in the Confucian philosophical corpus and in artistic works such as landscape paintings. For water, see *Analects* 6.23:

"The wise enjoy water; the humane enjoy mountains. The wise are active; the humane are still. The wise find enjoyment; the humane are long-enduring"; and 9.17: "What passes away is, perhaps, like this. Day and night it never lets up." Confucius and his disciples occasionally refer to mountain or other celestial objects. For example, Confucius associates himself with image of high mountain in Kongzishijia. See 孔子世家 [*Biography of Confucius*] in 史記 *Shizhi* [The Record of the Historian] by Sima Qian.

2. We omit the Vietnamese Confucian tradition in this volume only because no specialist on the subject was available at the time of its compilation, not because Vietnamese contributions are negligible.

Transmitting the *Dao*

Chinese Confucianism

John Berthrong

What follows is a summary introduction to certain features of the historical development of Confucian philosophy in China, with an equal emphasis on the post-Song period, or what is called neo-Confucianism. Neo-Confucianism is the major form of Confucianism that dominated East Asian intellectual life ever since the fourteenth century and had a major impact on the lives of Korean, Japanese, and Vietnamese intellectuals. But before we meet with the remarkable group of scholars known as Confucians in East Asia, we need to outline the historical development of the various streams of thought and action that define the Confucian way in terms of the different epochs of its historical development.

The Six Epochs of the Confucian Tradition

During its spread throughout East Asia, there have been six paradigmatic historical transformations of the Confucian "way," or *dao* 道:

1. The classical period beginning in the Xia, Shang, and Zhou kingdoms, including the justly famous Warring States philosophers at the end of the Zhou kingdom (c. 1700–221 BCE);

2. The Han dynasty Confucians and the rise of the great commentary traditions on the early classical philosophical and religious texts (206 BCE–220 CE);

3. The renewal of the Daoist tradition and the arrival of Buddhism, roughly from the Wei-Qin period to the end of the Tang dynasty (or from about 220 to 907);

4. The Renaissance of the Song (960–1279) (also called neo-Confucianism), the flowering of the Yuan and Ming dynasties, and the spread of neo-Confucianism into Korea and Japan (960–1644);

5. The Qing dynasty's School of Evidential Learning, or School of Han Learning, and the continued growth of the movement in Korea and Japan (1644–1911);

6. Western impact and the rise of the modern world, involving the decline and then reformation of the Confucian way as New Confucianism (1912 to the present).

Such a historical analysis based on a review of paradigmatic changes challenges the hypothesis that the Confucian tradition was a perpetually rigid moral formalism of ritual and social domination—a philosophical tradition without transformation or significant change over time and place. The first or classical period began with Confucius (551–479 BCE), was reshaped by Mencius (371–289 BCE), and concluded by Xunzi (c. 310–298 BCE). In framing his vision of the *dao*, Confucius relied on a number of early traditions, including historical documents, governmental decrees, poetry, and ritual texts that were later given the title "classics." The number of classics grew from the initially recognized five to thirteen in their final canonization during the Song dynasty (960–1279). At that time, most of these texts were assumed to have been in existence prior to Confucius's lifetime. In fact, contrary to modern scholarly opinion, the early tradition maintained that Confucius was the first great commentator and editor of the Confucian classics. In terms of philosophy, Confucius, Mencius, and Xunzi are commemorated as the foundational masters, and indeed they do provide the basic structure for Confucian thought down throughout its long development in East Asia in one form or another.

The second epoch or transformation began with the founding of the great Han dynasty (206 BCE–220 CE). The second stage was marked by the formulation of a state-supported imperial Confucian ideology to replace the discredited Legalism of the Qin dynasty. This was also the grand era of commentary as the preferred technique for understanding the words and meanings of the sages. In one form or another, this Han mixture of Legalist realpolitik, Confucian ethics, and *yinyang* 陰陽 cosmology dominated the Chinese political, social, and intellectual world right up to the end of the imperial state and the founding of the Chinese republic in 1911. However, many Confucians were extremely disconcerted about the inevitable misuse of Confucian symbols by state authority. Balancing this fear of serving an unworthy prince was the perennial Confucian desire to bring good government and social order to the world through governmental service. The Confucians saw that this governmental service must be tied closely to the state for it to be effective. Three of the most representative of the Han Confucians were Dong Zongshu (c. 179–104 BCE), Yang Xiong (53 BCE–18 CE), and Xun Yue (148–209).

The third era began with the Wei-Qin period (220–420 CE) and the revival of a form of elite Daoist speculation called neo-Daoism or "abstruse learning" (*xuanxue* 玄學). Many of the greatest intellectuals of this era, such as the precocious Wang Bi (226–249), mixed their Confucian reflections with Daoist cosmology and metaphysics. Even more momentous was the arrival of Buddhism in China. The Chinese intellectual world was never the same after the impact of the Buddha's *dharma*. Although Confucianism never lost its pride of place in the Chinese state or family, it is accurate to say that the most acute religious, artistic, and philosophical mind-hearts in China from the third to the tenth centuries devoted themselves to the appropriation and Chinese transformation of the Buddhist *dharma*. Great temples were created; the huge Buddhist *sangha,* or monastic community, was formed; entirely new and elaborate schools of Buddhist thought such as Tiantai, Huayan, Pure Land, and Chan were created and sustained. The rise and flourishing of this great Chinese Buddhist world formed the background for new epochs of transformation of the Confucian way.

Toward the end of the Tang dynasty, a number of Confucian scholars saw their task as defending the Confucian way against the challenge of Buddhism. The three most famous of these scholars were Han Yu (768–824), Li Ao (fl. 798), and Liu Zongyuan (733–819). Along with continuing the Han Confucian interest in government service, commentary, family ritual, and historical writing, these scholars framed the major lines of the Confucian response to the Buddhist philosophical and religious challenge with a renewed interest in cosmology, self-cultivation, and social ethics.

The fourth stage in the development of Confucianism was the justly celebrated revival of Confucian thought known in the West as the neo-Confucianism of the Northern and Southern Song (960–1279). The Song scholars of the neo-Confucian revival invented a new name for their teachings, calling it the "learning of the way" or *daoxue* 道學. The revival itself began in the Northern Song period and reached its conclusion with the synthesis of Zhu Xi (1130–1200). Regarding the scope and influence of his work, Zhu has been likened to St. Thomas Aquinas in the West, and there is little doubt that except for Confucius no one has been more important in defining the course of the Confucian tradition. Zhu Xi's form of Confucianism—which he based on the writings of the Northern Song masters Zhou Dunyi (1017–1073), Shao Yong (1011–1077), Zhang Zai (1020–1077), Cheng Hao (1032–1085), and Cheng Yi (1033–1107)—was spread by his followers to Korea and Japan. Neo-Confucianism actually replaced Buddhism as the principal form of Chinese thought from the Song to the modern period.

According to Confucian scholars, the great neo-Confucian reformers of the Song, Yuan, and Ming dynasties are only second to the great classical Zhou founders in terms of their impact on Chinese culture. From the Confucian point of view, no higher praise can be given. If the classical Confucians—Confucius, Mencius, and Xunzi—defended the learning of the sages during the Spring and Autumn and Warring States periods of the late Zhou dynasty, the Song and Ming neo-Confucian masters did the same in countering the challenges of Daoism and Buddhism in their own ages. Even though there were great changes and transformations of the way after Zhu Xi, no one can deny the pivotal role that he played in the renewal and definition of the tradition. And although one might contest Zhu Xi's synthesis in the name of the tradition, one cannot overlook his contribution to it.

The most important challenge to Zhu Xi's summation of the way came during the Ming dynasty in the form of Wang Yangming's (1472–1529) epic struggle to come to terms with Zhu Xi's rationalistic study of principle. Wang Yangming is remembered as the founder of the School of Mind-Heart or *xinxue* 心學, in contradistinction to Zhu Xi's School of Principle, or *lixue* 理學. Wang Yangming, along with being a brilliant critic of Zhu Xi's thought, was also an outstanding general, civil servant, poet, and teacher. He held that principle, the rationale of *dao* in human nature, was in the mind-heart of the sincere student of the way. He further taught a doctrine of the unity of thought and action based on this understanding of true principle being in the mind-heart.

The fifth epoch of Confucian learning is itself a reaction to and transformation of the great neo-Confucian achievements of the fourth phase of the Song and Ming dynasties. I believe that the Qing School of Evidential Learning, also called the School of Han Learning or *hanxue* 漢學, is unique in its concerns and its self-conscious rejection of a great deal of Song-Ming scholarship. Its great leaders were thinkers such as Wang Fuzhi (1619–1692), Huang Zongxi (1610–1695), and Dai Zhen (1723–1777). By turns, these Qing scholars castigated the needlessly abstract thought of the Song and the equally debilitating subjectivism of Wang Yangming's thought in the late Ming as wrong turns for the Confucian way. They believed that Confucianism must be of some concrete, practical use for the people. Hence, they often stressed accurate, empirical, historical research. Likewise, they argued that much Song and Ming thought was infected with an unhealthy Buddhist and Daoist love of meditation without proper attention to what ought to be Confucian self-cultivation, namely, the practice of service to self and others in practical ways. They defended their empirical studies of the history of taxation and flood control as being more in tune with the true nature of Confucian thought than Buddhist or Daoist sensibilities.

The sixth epoch of the Confucian way differs dramatically from the first five. With the arrival of the expansive and aggressive Western powers, the Confucian tradition, like every other aspect of Chinese culture, was disrupted. This agitation continues today as Chinese intellectuals, along with their Korean, Japanese, and Vietnamese colleagues, struggle to come to grips with the interruption of the West and the modern question of "globalization." Although there is an early analogy to the arrival of the Buddhist *dharma*, there are profound differences because the Buddhists never arrived with such overwhelming military, political, and economic power.

East Asian Confucian intellectuals have responded to this great challenge from the West by searching for a modern identity for the Confucian way. This modern movement is called "New Confucianism" in order to distinguish it from the earlier neo-Confucian synthesis. The contemporary Confucian scholar Tu Weiming (b. 1940) often describes the New Confucian movement as the third wave of the Confucian tradition. He uses the metaphor of a great ocean wave to express the movement of the tradition within the East Asian cultural world and into the broader world of the modern global city.

Roots, Branches, and Flowers of Classical and Early Modern Confucian Discourse

According to Confucius, the *dao* is something as close to you as the palm of your hand. Moreover, he teaches: "It is the person who is able to broaden the way (*dao* 道), not the way that broadens the person."[1] Confucius would never let his students forget that they are responsible for their own conduct. In fact, one of the best ways to understand the Confucian project is to think of it as the steadfast quest to become fully human. Again, the Master himself describes the stages of the Confucian life as a series of steps toward the way:

> From fifteen, my mind-heart was set upon learning; from thirty I took my stance; from forty I was no longer doubtful; from fifty I realized the propensities of *tian* (*tianming* 天命); from sixty my ear was attuned; from seventy I could give my mind-heart free rein without overstepping the boundaries.[2]

The trick was to figure out what you were to learn along the way and then how to put your insight into service of yourself and others. Once you had found your stance, then the rest would come to you through continued self-cultivation and education. At the end you could roam free without worrying about offending heaven (*tian* 天) or other people. His disciples record this conversation about the Master's teaching: "The Master said, 'Zeng, my friend! My way (*dao* 道) is bound together with one continuous strand.' Master Zeng replied, 'Indeed.' When the Master had left, the disciples asked, 'What was he referring to?' Master Zeng said, 'The way of the Master is doing one's utmost (*zhong* 忠) and putting oneself in the other's place (*shu* 恕), nothing more.' "[3] Of course, the disciples realize that the Master is speaking of true humanity, or the virtue of *ren* 仁. Only a person of true humaneness could show the empathy and utmost courage to become a worthy person.

The modern scholar Mou Zongsan (1909–1995) defines this primordial Confucian ethical sensibility as rooted in "concern consciousness." He believes that Greek philosophy's root metaphors express analysis and wonder about the nature of being. This is why those touched by Greek thought always ask the question of why something is as it is. Likewise, the great religions of Christianity, Judaism, Islam, and Hinduism have metaphors expressing awe before the divine reality as the root of their spiritual experience. The characteristic mode of their experience is piety before the awesome character of the divine reality. Confucianism's root metaphor was and is a concern for the world. If we need to search for a Western analogy, the Quaker tradition surely provides one. Quakers speak of having a concern for the world; Confucians are taught that the Master's "one thread" is a constant and vigilant concern for self, family, community, society, nation, the world, and the beyond, the veritable *dao* of all that was, is, and can be.

If one asks how "concern consciousness" arises, the Confucian tradition always begins with the person as a social being, and the primal aspect of human social being is the family. Confucians have been accused of idealizing the family. However, Confucius knew that blind reverence for unreflective filial piety (*xiao* 孝) and respect for the elders could be a mistake. In a passage that some Confucians have found hard to understand, the Master even mocks an old man for his ethical failures. What could be more out of kilter with the stereotype of rigid Confucian morality that demands respect for family and the elders? But it is clear that Confucius meant just what he said. There is nothing intrinsically good about an aged person who is without virtue. Likewise, there would be something wrong with a young person if they failed to respect a worthy elder. But concern for each person demands reciprocity. An adult who is merely chronologically old does not merit reverence from the young. This is a hard teaching, but it fits with Confucius's persistent demand that we cultivate the way of virtue and recognize that this way is long.

Nonetheless, as countless generations of Confucian teachers have pointed out, for better or worse, we begin and are formed as human beings in our families. Xunzi, the third of the classical masters (after Confucius and Mencius), argues that human beings are unique because of their culture, which includes their use of language and their ability to transmit cultural distinctions based on ritual action from generation to generation in an orderly fashion. Xunxi does not mean that human beings are separate from nature. Human beings are part of nature but with the added dimension of culture, and culture is the gift of language. Human beings have the chance to embody the full range of virtues, according to Xunzi, because we are social animals with a sense of deference and social order. We become full human beings, fully ethical persons within the larger human family. It is here that we find language and learn about our traditions. Confucians emphasize the role of the family because they are "social" or relational philosophers. We become human in community; and community is worthy of being called civilized if and only if it is an ethical community of concern, reciprocity, and humaneness.

Confucius teaches that there is a single thread that unifies all of his thought. The highest virtue is, of course, *ren* or humaneness, but as stated earlier: "The way of the Master consists is doing one's best (*zhong* 忠) and putting oneself in the other's place (*shu* 恕), and nothing more."[4] In another section, Confucius defines *shu* by saying, "There is *shu* 恕: do not impose on others what you yourself do not want."[5] Other ways to translate *shu* include deference, altruism, reciprocity, and consideration. Hall and Ames summarize *shu*:

> The methodology of *shu* requires the projection or recognition of excellence as a means of eliciting or of expressing deference. *Shu* as a methodology requires that in any given situation one either displays excellence in oneself (and this anticipates deference from others) or defers to excellence in another. Again, *shu* is always personal in that it entails *zhong*: "doing one's best as one's authentic self."[6]

To actually defer to the *dao* in all things is something that Confucius himself had never seen nor expected to see, though he was convinced that it was possible for a sage to do just this very thing.

There is a gap of almost a century between the death of Confucius and the birth of Mencius, the second sage of the Confucian tradition. If Confucius believed that he lived in a world where the great cultural values of the early sage kings were in deep decay, Mencius lived in a world where these values were being destroyed by the ever-increasing warfare of the period the Chinese came to call, for good reason, the Warring States period (480–221 BCE).

The larger states were destroying and annexing the smaller ones, and all the rulers were claiming the title of king as they tried to replace the leaders of the Zhou dynasty. In fact, Mencius believed that there was no way to restore the Zhou leadership and that what must happen was for some state to reunite the Chinese world under the aegis of an enlightened ruler.

Philosophically, there was a great debate about the definition of *xing* 性, human dispositions, tendencies, or nature. On solid Confucian grounds, Mencius seeks to define what it means to be a human being in order to transform petty individuals into worthy members of the human race. After a person has discovered what it means to be human, then Mencius, like most Chinese thinkers, stresses a regimen for self-improvement that allows the person to be of service to the larger community. We must remember that for Mencius, self-cultivation is not merely a private enterprise but a public necessity.

Nonetheless, Mencius wants us to pay special attention to the social cultivation of the mind-heart (*xin* 心).[7] In fact, it is really with Mencius that the Confucian tradition begins to probe the various ways in which the mind-heart can be cultivated in order to achieve sage virtue. In debating with other philosophers, Mencius is particularly concerned with developing a theory of the mind-heart and explaining how the virtues can be cultivated within it.

The mind-heart is the repository of all the emotions, passions, appetites, and even reflective abilities that make us human if properly cultivated. The problem, as Mencius sees it, is that when we interact with our world without a properly cultivated mind-heart, this mind-heart is prone to wander about in all sorts of different directions. According to Mencius, there is nothing innately wrong with many of these emotions and passions, only that they can be misguided. Only the truly cultivated mind-heart can correctly guide the emotions and passions. This is why Mencius often uses the image of the unmoved mind-heart to speak about the kind of mind-heart that responds to the Four Beginnings (*siduan* 四端) of human nature and controls the passions and emotions. Hence, only the cultivated mind-heart can control both the senses and the *qi* 氣, or the matter-energy of the body.

Mencius rounds out the argument about the cultivation of the mind-heart and human nature by returning attention to the social dimension of Confucian thought. Accordingly, it is this mind-heart, informed by the manifestation of the Four Beginnings, that will recognize the rites as the right ways to act. And when these actions are the rites of a true king, the world will be well ordered. The final act of a cultivated mind-heart, the mind-heart of the cultured person, will be a benevolent government. One of the key features of Mencius's image of good government is merit for all. A government is only legitimate if it serves the people. Mencius, like his master, believes that heaven hears as the people hear and speaks as the people speak and that any ruler would be foolish in the extreme not to listen assiduously to what the people hear and say.

The third and last of the classical Confucian masters is Xunzi, who strenuously contravenes Mencius's theory that human nature or dispositions are good. Xunzi holds that our *xing* is odious, even potentially evil if it is not conformed to civilized conduct via proper education in Confucian ritual theory and practice. Although the argument about human nature is important, Xunzi still believes that education and ritual will allow for genuine human flourishing. This irreducible core of Confucian beliefs marks Xunzi as a Confucian, along with the fact that he saw himself as a Confucian, even if this did not constrain him to agree with everything in the tradition.

One of the common assumptions about Xunzi, and one that is probably true, is that he is the most secularized among the classical Confucians. For him the old religious concept of heaven clearly becomes a name for a natural process. Xunzi believes that the things of the world are created through the ceaseless activity of the *yin* and *yang* forces in the primal *qi*. For him there is no theistic intent for the notion of heaven beyond noting that "Heaven has the constant way; earth has the constant categories."[8] These are objective rules and regulations, indicating that perhaps there are laws of nature beyond even the power of social convention. But this is not a philosophic topic of much interest to him. As with all the Confucians, his attention is focused on human social relations.

Xunzi's epistemological stance is in line with his view of the cosmos. For him, why one knows is part of human nature, and what one knows is the pattern of things in the natural order. He starts with sensation and moves on to an analysis of the nature and function of the mind-heart. The real problem of the mind-heart for him is what he calls "one-sidedness." This is an improper fixation with only one aspect of human life or the world. So, for instance, he would argue that the early Daoist writer Zhuangzi knows the world and its *dao* but not the way of ritual or human government. To be a mind-heart capable of conforming to the way things are, Xunzi argues that the mind-heart must be "empty, unified, and quiet."[9] In essence, the mind-heart is empty of preconceptions and therefore able to entertain new ideas and data. It is unified in that it can compare different things or ideas without confusing their natures. And it is quiet because it is calm, dispassionate, and not deluded by any new data it may encounter.

Xunzi is also inordinately interested in disputation, logic, and language theory for a Confucian.[10] We will have to come to the much later Song, Ming, and Qing dynasties to see such clarity of thought about these matters. For him, concept formation arises from the labeling of things or events in order to fit reality as conventionally defined. We know that things and words fit because of empirical observation and the regulation of conventional naming.

He recognizes that names represent family types even if the proper names are unique. For example, the greatest common name would be "thing" (*wu* 物). Why do we use certain names and not others? He notes that we do so merely from convention and long usage over time. And the basis of human nature is that "We are happy and want to eat, cold and desire warmth, labor and desire rest, love profit and hate injury."[11]

Although I will not dwell on this aspect of his thought, we need to remember that Xunzi also sustains a passionate interest in ritual action. In this he is a good Confucian who is worried about *ren* and the other standard Confucian norms. In fact, he has a central place for ritual action (*li* 禮) as a way to make our natures conform to the way things really are. Even if we have powerful passions, he believes ritual can overcome or control these passions and will allow us to have a humane life together. What is critical for Xunzi is that these Confucian virtues are part of our learned or educated conduct and not something we have by birth.

The key to understanding Xunzi's hierarchical system is to understand the role of the sage. The sage is the person who is able to make constructive use of active reason. The mind-heart of the sage, having overcome error and illusion, can become a molder of correct social conduct. The real key here is Xunzi's belief that the mind-heart of the sage can have unrestricted vision. This vision is based on two things. First, there is historical learning, the dedicated struggle to examine and sift through all the accumulated wisdom of the past. The second pillar of the sagely mind-heart is clear, lucid insight. This is a topic we shall return to shortly. If the sage is going to do all of these wonderful things for humanity, then Xunzi will have to explain to us how it will be accomplished. A person must have the ability to overcome the common prejudices of the empirical mind-heart. We must learn to overcome our subjective limitations and yet remain passionately committed to the cosmic moral order. And what we shall see for humanity at the base of this cosmos is order and hierarchy. But unlike many later Confucians, Xunzi is not hostile to a complicated economy to create this good form of social order. In fact, he encourages all kinds of specialized industry: "Goods and grain shall be allowed to circulate freely, so that there is no hindrance or stagnation in distribution; they shall be transported from one place to another as the need may arise, so that the entire region within the four seas becomes like one family."[12] He goes on to say: "The farmers do not have to carve or chisel, to fire or forge, and yet they have all the tools and utensils they need; artisans and merchants do not have to work the fields and yet they have plenty of vegetables and grain."[13] Xunzi is unique among the Confucians in having something good to say about commerce and merchants: "This, wherever the sky stretches and the earth extends, there is nothing beautiful left unfound, nothing useful left unused. Such goods serve above to adorn the worthy and good men, and below to nourish the common people and bring them security and happiness."[14]

Having reviewed briefly Xunzi's notion of civilized human life, we need to examine more closely his theory of human nature. This is the most complicated and controversial part of his philosophy. The great opening line of Xunzi's essay on human nature, as I would paraphrase it, reads conventionally: "The nature of humanity is evil, our goodness comes from conscious human action."[15] Whatever else it means, it is clear that Xunzi, at least for the sake of argument, is seeking to contravene Mencius. He is picking a quarrel, and an important one. Hence, what Xunzi really means is something like, "Human dispositions are coarse and goodness comes from conscious human effort." Somehow it seems a bit strange to reduce one of the great quarrels in Confucian history to an exegetical flaw. What if this reading is correct?

The contemporary New Confucian scholar Xu Fuguan (1903–1982) makes the preliminary observation that Xunzi is more empirically inclined than either Confucius or Mencius. He quotes Xunzi's dictum that "if not heard and not seen, although certain, it is not humane (*ren*)."[16] Further, Xu Fuguan notes that Xunzi has very definite views about the relationship of heaven, earth, and humanity, which are rather different from other Confucian views. Arguably, Xunzi's notion of heaven has more in common with Zhuangzi than some other early Confucian texts. What this means is that Xunzi has a naturalist view of heaven as the *dao* of the cosmos.

In Xunzi's view, *xing* is what all human beings share in being human. There are three levels of nature: (1) the desire to eat when hungry, (2) the capacity to discriminate white and black or good and evil, and (3) the undetermined nature of desire, such that both desire and knowledge are essential features of nature. Xu Fuguan argues that Xunzi tends to conflate the empirical and the moral in terms of branches and roots of the same tree of being. Human nature can be fully cultivated when it accords with the way things really are. Nature responds to what we desire; hence nature is a kind of responsiveness within the general generativity of the *dao*.[17] But we need to remember that Xunzi believes that morality, too, is a part of the way things are. Had he believed that morality is pure convention, he probably would have gone even farther in his admiration of Zhuangzi's vision, which would have been too much for any Confucian. The trick is that nature is really a compound of desire and knowing.

Evil arises out of the capacity for or intensity of desire, not from the desire itself. Evil is therefore essentially a lack of control, not the natural responsiveness of human dispositions. "The nature of present day people is such that they are born having a liking for profit, and following this, the result is a life of struggle and contention wherein courtesy and humility is lost."[18] Basically, we need to remember that Mencius wants to reduce the desires to a minimum, whereas Xunzi takes desire to be natural. Hence, contrary to the rhetoric of the opening of the chapter, Xunzi is quite sanguine about the real nature of human nature: "Therefore the sage transforms nature and gives rise to conscious human action."[19]

Our intellectual capacity for good actions and dispositions arises from our ability to make selective discriminations or "to know the way." On the one hand, the human mind-heart is prone to obstruction by desire, but on the other, it is the organ of calculation and selection. The role of a good teacher is critical at this point as a person begins to realize that the criteria of choice are objective. The teacher provides the mind-heart of the student with something concrete, some ritual to which the student can respond. The ritual chosen by the sage gives the mind-heart something to recognize, an object of choice that helps the student begin to navigate the world in accordance with the *dao*. Once recognized, this kind of choice for ritual feeds back upon itself and strengthens the will for an even more determined attempt at overcoming human error.

Xunzi has what we would call now an ordering of the sciences, the famous "ladder of nature": (1) fire and water have energy but not life; (2) grass and trees have life but no intelligence; (3) birds and beasts have intelligence but no sense of duty; (4) human beings posses energy, life, intelligence, and in addition, a sense of duty. This means that human beings are unique in the sense that they can organize society and pass on culture from generation to generation.

Why is society so important for Xunzi? "Why can man form a society? I say it is due the division of society into classes. How can social divisions be translated into behavior? I say it is because of humans' sense of morality and justice. . . . Accordingly, form birth all men are capable of forming societies."[20] Our unique ability is to form social organizations and establish hierarchical order. And such hierarchical order is predicated on our ability to recognize pattern, or the rationale for the myriad things. While it is clear than human beings belong to the natural order, their distinctive features have to do with their sense of duty and their ability to make discriminations. In Xunzi's chapter "Against Physiognomy," he gives us the best account of human nature in terms of the ability to make distinctions: "Hence the path of human life cannot be without its distinctions; no distinction is greater than social division; no social division is greater than the rules of proper conduct; rules of proper conduct are not greater than the sage kings."[21]

But Xunzi was not just a cool rationalist. He was also moved by the great Confucian virtue of *cheng* 誠, or true integrity, a term that is crucial to his theory of self-cultivation. In his chapter "Nothing Unseemly" he offers a hymn to self-realization that demonstrates how much a true Confucian he really is:

As for the gentleman's cultivation of the mind-heart, there is nothing better than *cheng* 誠 (true sincerity or self-realization), for he who perfects true integrity/sincerity need do nothing else than allow humanity to be maintained and justice acted upon. With the realization of the mind-heart and the maintenance of humanity, they become manifest, and being manifest they are spirit-like, and being spirit-like they are capable of transforming; with the realization of the mind-heart and the practice of justice, there is order, and when there is order, clarity, and with clarity there is change. The transformations and changes act together and this is what is called the Virtue of Heaven. . . . Heaven and Earth are great, but without true integrity they cannot transform the ten thousand things; although the sage has knowledge, yet lacking true integrity, he is out of touch. The exalted ruler is indeed eminent, and yet, without true integrity, he is lowly. Therefore true integrity is what the gentleman seeks to approach, and is the root of the cultivation of affairs. Only when he rests in the perfection of true integrity will he assemble the like mind-hearted to himself. . . . After having succeeded [in perfecting true integrity] the character of the person is completed and has progressed such a long way that does not revert to its origins, and this is transforming.[22]

From the Classical to the Neo-Confucian World

While many creative Confucians polished and honed the legacy of the classical masters of the Warring States during the Han and Tang dynasties prior to the renaissance of the Northern Song dynasty, it is still true that most historians would agree, if pressed, that Confucian philosophy has two great flowerings: the first in the classical Zhou period and the second in the era of neo-Confucian thought from the Song through the Qing dynasty. Moreover, it is in its neo-Confucian form that Confucian philosophy has the greatest impact on the rest of East Asia.

Tu Weiming characterizes the history of Confucianism as a drama in three acts. The first act is the formation of the tradition in its Chinese homeland. The second act marks the passage of Confucian thought out of China into the rest of East Asia, such that many Korean scholars would later argue that Chosŏn dynasty Korea (1392–1910) was the most faithfully Confucian culture in East Asia. The third act marks the confrontation of Confucian culture with the modern West beginning in the nineteenth century. The outcome of the third act is still very much in question. Nonetheless, it is clear that the dominant forms of Confucianism in East Asia and the East

Asian diaspora are forms of neo-Confucian discourse. It is to the history of
neo-Confucianism that we now turn.

The characteristic Confucianism that developed from the Song to Qing
dynasties is modeled on what Zhu Xi (1130–1200) calls the transmission
of the *dao* (*daotong* 道統). By this turn of phrase Zhu Xi explains how the
teachings of his revered Northern Song masters were in direct connection
with the best teachings of the classical Confucians of the Warring States
period, with pride of place given to Confucius and Mencius as paradigmatic
Confucian philosophers and sages. Zhu Xi's notion of *daotong* is complicated,
because there is a break of more than one thousand years between the death
of Mencius and the beginning of the revival of Confucian learning by Zhou
Dunyi in the Northern Song dynasty—at least in Zhu's version of the story.

In the midst of the debate about the nature of the Confucian way, Zhu Xi
stands out as a defining force, both through the vigor of his own philosophical
synthesis as well as the persuasive power of his narrative of the histories of
his favored Northern Song masters: Zhou Dunyi, Zhang Zai, Cheng Hao,
and Cheng Yi (and Shao Yong, though Zhu Xi excluded Shao Yong from
the formal list for a number of reasons).[23] Zhu Xi's brand of Confucianism
defined neo-Confucianism as a philosophical movement and Confucianism
as a social ideology, because his philosophy served as the foundation for the
curriculum of the imperial civil service examinations from 1313 until 1905,
when the examinations were finally abolished. In short, mastering Zhu Xi's
philosophy was the price of entry into the world of the Chinese elite in late
imperial China; one could rebel against his *daoxue*, or "teaching of the way,"
as did the equally great Wang Yangming in the Ming dynasty or Dai Zhen
in the Qing dynasty, yet learning his interpretation of the Four Books was
something every student had to do before moving forward, even in rebellion
against Master Zhu. The great Korean and Japanese masters also entered
vigorously into the discussion of the formation of the Confucian way in the
post-Song period. Therefore, Zhu Xi's *daoxue* scholarship defines the world of
early modern Confucian discourse even when it serves as a negative model to
be rejected by great Confucians such as Wang Yangming and Dai Zhen.

Needless to say, there were many Confucian scholars even during Zhu
Xi's lifetime who rigorously disputed the particulars of his grand metanarrative.
How, they asked Zhu Xi, could something as important as the teaching of the
sages be lost for more than a thousand years until Zhu's favorite Northern Song
masters rediscovered the way? Both his contemporaries in Southern Song and
later scholars argue that Zhu Xi's tale of the *daotong* is much too restricted
in scope. Even among the Northern Song "philosophers" this tale excludes
Shao Yong from the charmed circle of orthodoxy for the simple reason that
Zhu Xi was nervous about Shao's elaborate cosmological numerology. Zhu

Xi tells an exciting tale, but it would have been even more exiting if he had
included the contributions of Northern Song masters such as Wang Anshi
(1021–1086), Sima Guang (1019–1086), Ouyang Xiu (1007–1072), and Su
Shi (1037–1101)—or someone such as Chen Liang (1143–1194), the great
utilitarian scholar of Zhu Xi's own age.[24] It is a sad fact, and perhaps one
that can be found in many different cultures, that great philosophers are not
always dispassionate intellectual historians.

In framing his metanarrative of the *daotong*, Zhu Xi includes a very
narrow selection of the great range of Northern and Southern Song Confucian
scholarship. Peter Bol has called Zhu Xi's favorites the "philosophers."[25] The
term *philosophers* is a good designation because it captures what Zhu was
looking for in his selection of the four Northern Song masters as exemplars
of the Song Confucian revival. Zhu Xi, following the younger of the Cheng
brothers, Cheng Yi, takes *li* 理 (order, pattern, rationale, or principle) to be
the defining character of the *daoxue* movement—therefore, to be a member
of the charmed group meant that you had to be a philosopher of principle
or rationale as Zhu Xi understood the term. He only does what so many
philosophers do; he selects his favorite root metaphor for reality and applies
it to the history of philosophy. In his case, it is a theory of *li* as the defining
characteristic of the world of objects and events. But his choice of *li* as the
root metaphor of *daoxue* obscures that fact that other Confucians during the
Song had alternatives to Cheng Yi, Zhu Xi, and their metaphor of principle,
pattern, rationale, and order.

Beyond Zhu Xi's construction of *daotong*, what were alternative models
for the reorganization and revitalization of the Confucian *dao* during the
Northern Song? One important aspect of the movement was a series of social
reforms. One of the most important early figures of the revival of Confucian
social theory was Fan Zongyan (989–1052). Although the Song government
did not implement the full range of his suggested political and social reforms,
such as changes to the civil service examinations and the foundations of public
education in general, it did start a movement toward the transformation
and expansion of the Song state. The general thrust of such political and
social reform was to encourage an active government in service to all the
people of the empire. Moreover—and this is what made it such a Confucian
enterprise—this reform of the government was to be coupled with a return to
Confucian moral learning with practical outcomes for the complete renovation
of society. It was to be a combination of practical programs and utopian
dreams of moral self-cultivation beginning with the emperor and ending
with villagers throughout China. Although Fan Zongyan was not successful
in implementing the full range of his proposals on a national level, he did
provide a set of rules for a charitable estate for his extended clan that set the

model for such local social reform. His clan protocols remained popular as prototypes for such forms of Confucian local self-regulation until the end of the imperial system in the twentieth century.

Born a generation after Fan Zongyan's pioneering efforts in social reconstruction, Wang Anshi (1021–1086) is forever remembered as the greatest political reformer of the Northern Song. Along with being a great Confucian scholar with a special love for the *Rituals of Zhou* among the canonical texts, he was an innovative reformer who had a plan for recasting the entire imperial government. Looking back, the argument between Wang Anshi and his interlocutors was a classic debate between the activist political factions within Confucianism that wanted to use a more energetic imperial government for rapid reform, as opposed to other scholars who were nervous about too rapid a pace for such drastic and dramatic social engineering. Wang Anshi fervently believed that if you reformed society via changes in the educational system and tax policy, you could then bring Chinese society back to the grand vision of the founding sages. Other scholars believed that this kind of institutional reform was backward; what needed to be done was to develop a new program of cultural and personal transformation and then seek institutional reform.

Other Northern Song intellectuals had different root metaphors. Ouyang Xiu (1007–1072), for instance, is remembered as a great classical scholar and historian. He wanted to use history as a mirror for reform in order to ensure that scholars and officials paid proper attention to the concrete historical development of the organs of imperial government. He believed that only by paying careful attention to the historical record could humane government flourish under the Song imperial house. If Wang Anshi appealed to classical models such as the ritual texts of the pre-Han sages and worthies, Ouyang Xiu cautioned that any such appeal needed to be based on an accurate historical account as to how these ideals play out in the political history of the Chinese state.

Along with Ouyang Xiu, Sima Guang (1019–1086) is remembered as another great critic of Wang Anshi's reform program. According to Sima Guang, the best metaphor for reform was to think of the dynastic institutions as a grand palace for the state. What was needed was the restoration of the various elements of the palace, to rebuild the edifice but still live successfully within it while the renovations were ongoing. Like his friend Ouyang Xiu, Sima Guang is best remembered as a historian with a political agenda. In contradistinction to Zhu Xi, Sima Guang had a very high regard for Xunzi and Yang Xiong in the Han dynasty. While morality was important to Sima, as it would be for any Confucian, he devotedly believed that even the most sincere reformer is constrained by the particular circumstances of history. Reform must be based on what history will allow at any point. In this regard Sima

Guang would take a different view of reform from either the social activism of Wang Anshi or the more introspective and personal *daoxue* program of self-cultivation.

Su Shi (1037–1101), in turn, provided yet another Northern Song model for Confucian revival. Su Shi was opposed to what he saw as the philosophical dogmatism of too many of his Song colleagues, especially Cheng Yi. Simply put, Su Shi defended a vision of the *dao* as a way of humane culture with a deep appreciation of the role of literature and poetry as germane to a genuine revival of Confucian culture. Befitting such a program for reform, Su Shi is best remembered as the finest poet among the Song luminaries. He believed that we inhabit an imperfect world and that even though we need to seek as best we can for a set of principles to guide our lives, we will never find a set of moral principles sufficient to bring perfection to the world. What we need to do is to try to become as impartial as possible in our search for humane perfection—we need to use whatever comes to hand to encourage genuine human flourishing. In order to find such a pattern, Su often wrote commentaries about the *Yijing* or *Book of Changes* as models for such suggestive patterns of social renewal. In the midst of the committed Northern Song search for political, social, and moral reform, Su Shi remained a staunch defender of the role of the arts. Beauty helps us to understand the spontaneity of the patterns of the cosmos as much as examination of the particulars for moral rubrics. I believe that Zhu Xi would have done better to find a more prominent place for Su Shi's defense of poetry than to merely dismiss this as an unworthy waste of time for someone in search of the Confucian way.

Of course, Zhu Xi's role was crucial in creating the paradigmatic neo-Confucian synthesis. By making the choices he did many other Northern Song thinkers were excluded from the list of teachers of the way. Such notables as the great politician and reformer Wang Anshi and the poet Su Shi did not make the list, along with the historians and classicists Ouyang Xiu and Sima Guang. Zhu Xi ultimately privileged one particular group of philosophers over all the other Confucian scholarly groups. Nonetheless, Zhu was sensitive to philosophical creativity in selecting Zhou Dunyi, Zhang Zai, and the brothers Cheng Hao and Cheng Yi as his paragons of Northern Confucian thought—with Shao Yong lurking in the background when the philosophical debates turned to epistemological issues.

Song and Ming Rebuttals of *Daoxue*

In terms of philosophical debate about the worthiness of *daoxue*, there was a great deal of argument about a variety of issues in the Song, Yuan, Ming and Qing dynasties. Although the Qing scholars were the most radical in their critique and merit a separate discussion, there were immediate Song dynasty rejoinders to Zhu Xi that argued against his synthesis on philosophical grounds. The first major rebuttal came from Zhu Xi's friend and critic Chen Liang (1143–1194), one of the great utilitarian philosophers of the Confucian tradition. What worried Chen Liang about Zhu Xi's *daoxue*, with its emphasis on rational analysis of the world through the examination of things in order to discover a universal order—all linked to a complicated process of moral self-cultivation—was that it was too idealistic and hence not suited to the actual geopolitical demands of Southern Song reality. While it is clear that Zhu Xi was passionately involved the politics of his day, Chen Liang contended that the world was a more empirically complex place than Zhu Xi's system implied: "I simply don't agree with (your) joining together principles and (complex) affairs (as neatly and artificially) as if they were barrel hoops."[26]

The nub of the debate revolved around the proper understanding of the notion of public, or *gong* 公, defined as public benefit, or *gongli* 公利. Here Chen Liang broke with Zhu Xi and suggested that what was needed for real, concrete reform were good laws as well as good neo-Confucian philosophers trained in a metaphysical praxis such as *daoxue*: "The human mind-heart (*xin*) is mostly self-regarding, but laws and regulations (*fa* 法) can be used to make it public-mind-hearted (*gong*). . . . Law and regulations comprise the collective or commonweal principle (*gongli*)."[27] Such arguments about pragmatic political theory and even an appeal to the beneficial outcomes of carefully constructed legal regimes were never well received in the neo-Confucian period, even if they did point to some genuinely diverse views within the Song Confucian revivals.

The most influential critique of Zhu Xi's *daoxue* also came from another good friend, Lu Xiangshan (1139–1193). The crux of the philosophical disagreement resides in Lu Xiangshan's different interpretation of the role of the mind-heart in terms of the common neo-Confucian task of finding the right method for evaluating the moral epistemology of interpreting the world correctly. In a dialogue with a student, Lu Xiangshan pinpoints his argument with Zhu Xi:

Bomin asked: How is one to investigate things (*gewu* 格物)?

The Teacher [Lu Xiangshan] said: "Investigate the principle of things."

Bomin said: "The ten thousand things under Heaven are extremely multitudinous; how, then, can we investigate all of them exhaustively?"

The teacher replied: "The ten thousand things are already complete in us. It is only necessary to apprehend their principle."[28]

There are two important things to notice about Lu Xiangshan's critical response to the question of the examination of things. First, in many ways he does not disagree with the basic cosmological outline provided by Zhu Xi. Second, his philosophic sensibility, however, becomes even more focused on the internal self-cultivation of the person. Many scholars have remarked upon the fact that we find a turn inward in much of Song and Ming philosophy, and none more so than in Lu Xiangshan's intense desire to find principle within the person. Of course, this is not to be understood as a purely subjective idealism. Rather, Lu Xiangshan contends that only by finding principle in the mind-heart can a person effectively comprehend the rest of the world. The point is not a solipsistic retreat into the subjective and relativistic reveries of an isolated individual, but rather a heightened ability to interpret and engage the world as it really is. The critical question is to find the proper place to start the investigation of things. If we start with the things of the world, we fall prey to the problems of self-delusion and partiality that infect the uncultivated person. But if we can find the correct place and method to investigate things and comprehend their principles, then we will understand the actual, concrete unity of principle.

Centuries later in the mid-Ming dynasty, Wang Yangming (1472–1529) sharpened what he took to be Lu Xiangshan's critique of Zhu Xi. Wang Yangming's philosophy was inextricably intertwined with his eventful life. He lived the richest life of any of the major neo-Confucian philosophers, being a philosopher of import, a poet, a statesman, and an accomplished general. Wang Yangming began as a young student by attempting to follow Zhu Xi's advice about the investigation of things, or *gewu* 格物. Once, he and a group of naïve young friends went into a garden to sit in front of some bamboos in order to discern the true principle of bamboo. The band of young scholars obviously thought that this would be an easy task. One by one they fell away, unable to make any progress in their quest to understand the bamboo's principle. Wang Yangming was the last to give up and only did so after having exhausted himself in the futile effort. He later recounts that he believed he lacked the moral and intellectual insight to carry out the task at hand; at that time he did not question Zhu Xi's master narrative about how to engage the world as a Confucian philosopher.

Later, during a painful political exile in the far south of China, Wang Yangming had a flash of insight into the problem of finding the true location of principle. As Tu Weiming writes: "For the first time Yangming came to the realization that '[m]y own nature, is, of course, sufficient for me to attain sagehood. And I have been mistaken in searching for the *li* [principle] in external things and affairs (*shiwu* 事物).'"[29] Wang Yangming clearly understood this enlightenment experience as a confirmation that Lu Xiangshan was correct in declaring that principle was to be found complete within the mind-heart of the person. In much greater detail than Lu Xiangshan, Wang Yangming then set about developing the philosophical implications of his primordial insight into the proper way to carry out Confucian moral epistemology and self-cultivation. And after having straightened out the epistemology, he then went on to explain how the Confucian worthy should act in the world. This strong emphasis on the cultivation of the mind-heart led to the categorization of Wang Yangming's teaching as a *xinxue*, or teaching of the mind-heart, as opposed to Zhu Xi's *lixue*, or teaching of principle. And in fact, this is the way later scholars often label the teachings of Zhu Xi and Wang Yangming.

In his famous doctrine of the unity of knowledge and action, Wang Yangming teaches about the task of realizing what he calls the innate goodness of human nature. He says: "Knowledge is the direction for action and action is the effort for knowledge"; and "Knowledge is the beginning of action and action is the completion of knowledge."[30] Wang Yangming expresses deep concern that Zhu Xi's method for examining things in order to cultivate the essential goodness of the mind-heart is too fragmented and that such epistemological fragmentation would eventuate in moral failure and cognitive incompetence. Real praxis and theory cannot be separated, and even if Wang Yangming acknowledges that Zhu Xi is a sincere seeker after the *dao*, he believes that Zhu Xi's methods are hopelessly flawed and actually dangerous to the cultivation of the Confucian worthy.

By the late Ming dynasty many of the followers of Wang Yangming severely questioned perceived negative Song teachings about the value of emotions and natural human feelings (*qing* 情). In fact, many of these thinkers made the bold claim that the emotions were just as important and valuable philosophical resources for authentic Confucian teachings as reflections on the themes of principle or vital force. In fact, they contended that it was a proper and positive interpretation of human emotions and even passions that distinguished Confucianism from Daoism and Buddhism. Whether or not these thinkers were correct in their interpretations of Daoist and Buddhist thought need not detain us here. What is more important is that these thinkers developed a more positive interpretation of *qing* than had been the case in earlier Song and Ming thought. It might be argued that such a concern for the emotions was just another marker of the neo-Confucian turn toward the subject, a flight to the contemplation of an inner subjective world as opposed to the much more activist style of the Han and Tang scholarly traditions. However, this speculation about emotion, even romantic love, had the unintended effect of allowing educated Chinese women to enter into the debate. Debarred, as they noted, from active lives outside the literati family compounds, the women observed that although they lived circumscribed lives compared to their fathers, brothers, husbands, and sons, they did know something about the emotions—and thus they had something positive to add to the debate.

Furthermore, in the Qing dynasty, there was yet another complete turning of the wheel of Confucian discourse, namely the justly famous School of Han Learning or the School of Evidential Research.[31] This school argued vociferously against all aspects of standard Song and Ming Confucian discourse as being itself hopelessly compromised by accretions of Daoist and Buddhist elements incorporated into the pristine body of Confucian thought and praxis.[32] According to the School of Han Learning, all of this Song and Ming talk about cosmological issues and meditation betrayed how badly these Confucians had strayed from the noble path of the pre-Han masters. What matters is not metaphysics but empirical studies that will bear fruit in furthering human flourishing. These kinds of debates about the true nature of the Confucian way continue in the contemporary world among scholars associated with the rise of the New Confucian movement.[33]

New Confucianism

In one of his last lectures, the great contemporary philosopher Mou Zongsan speaks of the necessity for the New Confucian movement to include all the great Confucians of the past in the contemporary renewal of Confucian philosophy. Xunzi and Zhu Xi need to be as much included as Mencius and Wang Yangming. In fact, a creative Confucian reading of Daoist and Buddhist texts is probably in order within the rich matrix of modern global philosophy. Of course, Confucians have always read Daoist and Buddhist texts; it was just that they were never supposed to proffer a good word about them or admit that they were stimulated by these alternative traditions in the construction of their own Confucian philosophies. Moreover, Confucianism is now becoming an even more global movement than it was in the past.[34] It is useful to remind ourselves that the history of Confucianism has included major contributions by Korean, Japanese, and Vietnamese scholars for centuries. Both the Koreans and Japanese can make strong cases that during certain periods in the sixteenth, seventeenth, and eighteenth centuries they, and not the Chinese, were pursuing the most creative Confucian philosophy.[35] The great Korean Four-Seven Debate about the relationship of principle and vital force is a perfect example of the superlative quality of Korean Confucian discourse. And now Confucianism appears to be making some kind of impact on the world of Euro-American scholarship along with its cousins, Daoism and Buddhism.[36]

Confucianism has now spread even farther from its traditional East Asian domiciles. New or renewed Confucianism needs not only to resurrect the rich diversity of its past Asian glories, but likewise must engage the best of global philosophy in fruitful dialogue. As Tu Weiming has argued, Confucian philosophy is new entering a new epoch, an era marked by its contact with and appropriation of modern Western philosophy. Only time will tell what the philosophical contributions of contemporary Confucianism will be to the global city of the twenty-first century.

Suggestions for Further Reading

For excellent overviews of Chinese intellectual history, one can consult such standard works as those of Fredrick W. Mote (1989, 1999) or Valerie Hansen (2000) for both the classical and early modern period. It is always salutary to remember that the history of ideas is located in the larger cultural, social, political, military, and economic history of East Asian culture. Four additional comprehensive and outstanding resources for the history of Confucian thought are *Sources of the Chinese Tradition* (1999–2000), *Sourcebook of Korean Civilization* (1993–96), *Key Concepts in Chinese Philosophy* (2002), *Sources of Japanese Tradition* (2001), and the *Encyclopedia of Confucianism* (2003). For shorter accounts of the history of Confucian thought, one can consult *Transformations of the Confucian Way* (1998), *Confucianism: A Short Introduction* (2000), and *An Introduction to Confucianism* (2000); all these works contain useful bibliographies for further study.

Notes

1. Roger T. Ames and Henry Rosemont, Jr (1998), 190 (passage 15.29).
2. Ibid., 76–77 (2.4).
3. Ibid., 92 (4.15).
4. Ibid.
5. Ibid., 189 (15.24).
6. Ames and David Hall (1987), 287.
7. Please note that other authors in this volume translate the same term *xin* as "heart-mind."
8. Ren Jiyu (1979), I:210.
9. John Knoblock (1994), 3:104.
10. A. C. Graham (1989).
11. Ren Jiyu (1979), I:225.
12. Knoblock (1990), 2:102.
13. Ibid.
14. Ibid.
15. This essay composes the Xunzi's chapter titled *Xing'e* (性惡). See D. C. Lau (1996), 113.
16. Xu Fuguan (1975), 223–62.
17. Ibid., 228–37.
18. Xu Fuguan (1975), 238.

19. Lau (1996), 115.

20. Knoblock (1990), 2:103–104.

21. Knoblock (1988), 1:206.

22. Lau (1996), 11. For an alternative translation, see Knoblock (1988), 1:177–78.

23. John Berthrong (1998b).

24. Ibid.

25. Peter Bol (1992).

26. Hoyt Cleveland Tillman (1994), 52.

27. Ibid., 16.

28. Huang Siu-chi (1977), 31.

29. Tu Weiming (1976a), 120.

30. Julia Ching (1976), 68.

31. Berthrong (1998b), Benjamin A. Elman (1984, 1990), Frederick W. Mote (1999).

32. Berthrong (1998b).

33. Umberto Bresciani (2001), John Makeham (2003), Liu Shu-hsien (2003).

34. Robert C. Neville (2000).

35. Berthrong (1998b).

36. Neville (2000).

2

The History of
Confucianism in Korea

Youngjin Choi
Translated by Wonsuk Chang

"Comforting the people through self-cultivation" is a definitive Confucian idea. It means that excellence must be pursued in both inner morality and outer achievements. Morality and practicality, the two pillars of Confucianism, are evident in the following phrase from the twenty-eighth chapter of the *Zhongyong*:

> Even if one has ascended to the throne, if he has not achieved the necessary excellence, he dares not initiate ceremonies and music for the court. If he has achieved excellence, but does not occupy the throne, he dares not initiate ceremonies and music for the court, either.[1]

During Korea's lengthy Chosŏn dynasty (1392–1910) Confucian ideals were deeply valued. Confucian literati in the early Chosŏn imported Confucianism from China, establishing it as the governing political ideology and further developing Korean-style neo-Confucianism. Modeling neo-Confucian ideals, they transformed Chosŏn into a thoroughly Confucian society during the seventeenth and eighteenth centuries. This is why the Chosŏn could last for more than five hundred years with political stability.

However, many historians claim that Confucianism was first introduced to the Korean peninsula more than a thousand years before the Chosŏn period. It became integrated in the indigenous Korean culture over the next thousand

years and had already affected the morality, norms, and social institutions of
the Korean people when neo-Confucianism arrived on the peninsula. This may
explain why Chosŏn could so readily transform itself into a Confucian society.
Even in contemporary Korea the Confucian tradition remains intact, more so
than in neighboring East Asian countries such as China and Japan.

The history of Confucianism in Korea can be divided broadly into two
periods: before and after the introduction of neo-Confucianism. Keeping this
broad divide in mind, I will explain the history of Korean Confucianism in
four sections:

1. The periods before the arrival of neo-Confucianism, comprising
   the ancient period of the Three Kingdoms and Unified Silla
   (first to tenth centuries) and the medieval period of the Koryŏ
   dynasty (tenth to fourteenth centuries);

2. The introduction of neo-Confucianism in the first half of the
   Chosŏn dynasty (fourteenth to sixteenth centuries);

3. The further development of neo-Confucianism in the last half of
   the Chosŏn dynasty (seventeenth to nineteenth centuries);

4. The modern period of the Korean Empire and Japanese
   occupation (twentieth century to the present).

As Confucian philosophy began to influence institutions and norms in the
earlier periods, it spread to all spheres of life: academia, daily etiquette,
society, and culture. While tracing these developments, I will focus on the
distinctive issues of Confucian philosophy in Korea, thus highlighting the
basic characteristics of a uniquely Korean Confucianism.

Korean Indigenous Thought and Confucianism
in Ancient and Medieval Korea

Confucius formed a philosophical school, compiling cultures and texts in
ancient China. Surely, the origins of Confucianism could be traced back
much farther than Confucius himself. In ancient East Asia, the Han culture
in central China flourished and interacted with peripheral "barbarian" cultures
in eastern China. The *Analects* 9.14 records: "The Master wanted to go and
live in the area of nine clans of the Eastern Yi barbarians. Someone asked,
'What would you do about their crudeness?' The Master replied, 'Were an
exemplary person to live among them, what crudeness could there be?' "[2]
This gives proof that the nine clans of Yi barbarians in sixth century BCE

were recognized as a civilization in which an exemplary person could live. The Kojosŏn or "Old Chosŏn" kingdom (2333 BCE–57 CE), the earliest state in Korean history (not to be confused with the Chosŏn dynasty founded in 1392), seems to be located in the lands of the eastern Yi barbarians. If Confucianism emerged in ancient times through the interactions of diverse cultures such as the Han and the other nine clans of Yi, then the culture of Kojosŏn should be included in the history of Confucianism. The following passage by Ch'oe Ch'iwon (b. 875), a prominent politician and philosopher of his day, confirms this point:

> The country has a way of mystery, *p'ungnyu.* . . . In fact, [*p'ungnyu*] includes the three teachings of Confucianism, Buddhism, and Daoism and transforms people in touch with it. Thus, filial piety at home and doing one's utmost for the country are teachings of the Justice Minister in Lu; non-verbal teachings with non-coercive action are the essential tenets of librarians in Zhou; and practicing what is good without committing wrongdoing is a precept of princes in India.[3]

This incomplete passage may be a noteworthy record describing the origins of Korean thought. In the paragraph, Ch'oe mentions that *p'ungnyu* as an indigenous philosophy shared core ideas with Confucianism, Buddhism, and Daoism, the three major philosophies of East Asia, long before their introduction to the Korean peninsula.

The founding myth of the Kojosŏn kingdom tells us about characteristics of indigenous Korean philosophy. Tan'gun is credited with founding the kingdom in 2333 BCE. According to legend, his father was the divine Hwanung, symbolizing heavens or light, and his mother a she-bear, symbolizing earth or darkness. The humans in the myth are defined as the integration of heaven and earth, or light and darkness. The harmony of opposites—the essence of Korean indigenous thought—is also explicit in the founding myth of Koguryŏ, another kingdom in ancient Korea. In the myth, the founder of the kingdom is Chumong (58–19 BCE), whose father is Haemosu, the son of the heaven, and whose mother is Yuhwa, the daughter of the rivers.

A written record of when Confucianism came to the Korean peninsula is not available. Many scholars speculate that Confucianism penetrated into Korea, along with the character of classical China, prior to the beginning of Three Kingdoms period (57 BCE–668 CE), which includes the Koguryŏ, Silla, and Paekche kingdoms. The Confucian moral sensibility embedded in classical Chinese character seems to have been assimilated into the indigenous culture of the Korea at that time. The National Confucian Academy was founded in 372 in Koguryŏ. During the reign of King Koi (234–286) in Paekche, the central government structure was established according to the *Rites of the Zhou*. During the reign of King Kŭnchogo (346–375), a scholar named Wang In of Paekche is said to have brought the Confucian classics to Japan. In the mid-seventh century, Confucian institutions, customs, and moral precepts such as filial piety and loyalty to the state were firmly entrenched through education of the National Academy in Silla.

Confucianism also played a role in political reforms in the Unified Silla period (668–935). One example is Ch'oe Ch'iwon's *Shimuch'aek* (Detailed Proposal for Dealing with Major Issues). Ch'oe melded in his proposal three philosophies, Buddhism, Daoism, and Confucianism, from a Confucian perspective. He claimed that while the study of heart-mind (Ch. *xin* 心) in Buddhism is mythical, Confucianism starts from empirical reality and aims to reach a level of heaven indescribable in words.[4] He emphasized familiarity with the *dao* 道 (Ch.) in saying that the *dao* is not far from humans, such that they need not seek *dao* in the distance.

Confucianism prevailed between the late Unified Silla and the start of the Koryŏ period (918–1392), or the transitional period from ancient to medieval society. King T'aejo, who ruled Koguryŏ from 53 to 146, had already declared in his *Hunyo sipcho* (Ten Rules of Governing) that government should be guided by benevolence, the practice of the kingly way, and Confucianism, along with Buddhism, Daoism, and indigenous religions. By 958 the growing infuence of Confucianism led to the establishment of the civil service examination. The *Samguk sagi* (History of the Three Kingdoms), written and compiled by Kim Pusik in the 1100s, also shows the maturity of Confucianism in Korea. He based the book on Confucian rationalistic historiography and recorded Korean history coherently, modeling his account on the historiography of Sima Guang and Ouyang Xiu in China's Northern Song period (960–1127). While Confucianism, Buddhism, and Daoism coexisted and developed during the Koryŏ, Confucianism functioned as a governing method, a political ideology, and an academic subject.

Introduction of Neo-Confucianism in the Early Chosŏn Period

The Introduction of Neo-Confucianism and the Criticism of Buddhism

In the transitional period from the late Koryŏ to the early Chosŏn period, Confucianism played a critical role as a catalyst for social reform. Confucian literati, the new elites of the time, attempted to change medieval aristocratic society into a modern Confucian society by importing China's advanced philosophy of neo-Confucianism. The literati were already familiar with Confucian philosophy, as seen in the case of historian Kim Pusik. New literati officials, such as Lee Chae-hyŏn (1287–1367), An Hyang (1243–1306), Lee Saek (1328–1396), and Chŏng Mong-chu (1337–1392), employed neo-Confucianism in order to reform the Koryŏ effectively after military rule. They used neo-Confucianism in resolving the pending issues of Koryŏ.

However, after the reign of King Kongmin (1330–1374), the literati officials split into two factions, the old and the new, due to differences in their understanding of current events, reform agendas, and interpretations of neo-Confucianism. Though both accepted neo-Confucianism as a philosophy for change, the two groups disagreed over how the government should solve social problems. Lee Saek, the central figure of the former group, tried to overcome the conflict by restoring the institutions and norms of Koryŏ destroyed during military rule and Mongolian occupation. He revived rituals of the former kings and ancient institutions as models for institutional reforms. In contrast, Chŏng Tojŏn (1337–1398), the major figure of the latter group, aimed to consolidate a centralized political regime with complete reformation of Koryŏ's laws and institutions. He attempted to enact laws and institutions grounded on neo-Confucianism, being flexible in his views on the rituals of former kings.

While the former group wanted to maintain the status quo and allow limited reform within Koryŏ society, the latter advocated rapid and radical change. While the old faction was conservative as well as reformative, the new faction, recognizing neo-Confucianism as authoritative, partially incorporated the national socialism of the *Rites of the Zhou* and the utilitarianism of Confucianism during China's Han (206 BCE–220 CE) and Tang (618–907) periods. The difference between the two factions is apparent in their understanding of Mencius's notions of "a certain amount of livelihood" (Ch. *hengchan* 恒産) and "fixed mind" (Ch. *hengxin* 恒心). The old faction considered the fixed mind, or inner morality, to be higher than social institutions. However, Chŏng Tojŏn suggested that maintaining a fixed mind is possible because of a certain amount of livelihood. He said that once people were well fed and clad, then they could feel a sense of shame; and once people's stomachs were full, then ritual action and rightness could arise. Accordingly, new literati officials created policies to guarantee in perpetuity to each peasant household the amount of land minimally necessary for its livelihood.

The philosophical differences between the two factions are also evident in their understanding of Buddhism. In his treatise *Yupul t'ongdoron* (Treatise on the Similarities of Confucianism and Buddhism), Lee Saek maintained the superiority of Confucianism over Buddhism while claiming that the goals of the two philosophies are essentially the same. For example, Zen meditation in Buddhism is similar to the practice of deference in Confucianism. On the contrary, Chŏng Tojŏn insisted in his *Pulssi chappyŏn* (Criticism of Buddhism) that Confucianism is based on efficacy while Buddhism envisages the world as illusion. He sharply contrasts Confucianism with Buddhism in the following:

> We (Confucians) say "emptiness" and they (Buddhists) say "emptiness." We say "quiescent" and they say "quiescent." But our emptiness is empty yet existent. Their emptiness is empty and non-existent. Our quiescence is quiescent yet responsive. Their quiescence is quiescent and negative. We say "knowledge and action," they say "awakening and cultivation." Our knowledge means to know that the pattern of the myriad things is replete within our own minds. Their awakening is awakening to the fact that the original mind is empty, void of anything whatsoever. Our action means to accord with the pattern of the myriad things and act [in harmony with] it, without any error. Their cultivation means to sever the connection with the myriad things and regard them as unconnected to the mind.[5]

Chŏng called Confucianism productive and Buddhism nonproductive. Park Ch'o (1367–1454), a later orthodox Confucian, praised Chŏng's anti-Buddhist assault and said that Chŏng clarified the sources of heaven, humans, and natural tendencies by arguing in favor of neo-Confucianism and resisting Buddhism, which had been spreading unabated for a long period.

The Emergence of Pragmatic Neo-Confucian Philosophy

Literati officials in the early Chosŏn saw themselves on a historical mission to establish new institutions and social philosophies. The *hungu* faction, consisting of meritorious elites and based on the philosophy of Chŏng Tojŏn, focused on the reform of institutions; the *sarim* faction were critical of Buddhism and Daoism and made great efforts to establish Confucianism as orthodox political thought. Just as neo-Confucianism in China's Song dynasty started as a critique of Daoism and Buddhism, neo-Confucianism in early Chosŏn followed a similar path. Due to political circumstances in Korea at the time, Chŏng Tojŏn's critique of Buddhism arose first, while Sŏ Kyŏngdŏk's (1489–1546) attempts to overcome Daoist philosophy followed later.

Sŏ Kyŏngdŏk dismissed concepts of emptiness and nothingness that the legendary Chinese sage Laozi defined as the basic categories of Daoist philosophy. According to Laozi, the world is generated from the nothingness. Sŏ Kyŏngdŏk comments as follows:

> If emptiness had given birth to vital energy, then before giving birth, emptiness would have had no vital energy and would have

been dead. Already not having vital energy, how could emptiness spontaneously give birth to vital energy? It has no beginning; it has no birth. Already not having a beginning, where can it end? Already not having a birth, where can it cease?[6]

He criticized Daoist cosmology from the standpoint of neo-Confucianism, in which vital energy (Ch. *qi* 氣) has neither beginning nor end. He defined vital energy as creativity residing in the process of the world and called it "vast tenuousness," which is "tenuous but not empty." Unperceivable vast tenuousness is the real "stuff" that fills the cosmos. The pattern (Ch. *li* 理) and the vital energy are both indispensable components constituting the world. For him, undifferentiated pattern is tenuous, and undifferentiated vital energy is coarse. Yet the coalescence of these is "mysterious and mysterious." Neither pattern nor vital energy alone constitutes the world. He saw that the mystery comes from a place where pattern is in harmony with vital energy.

Fellow-philosopher Lee Ŏnchŏk (1491–1553) replaced Daoist and Buddhist notions of emptiness and nothingness with the Confucian language of the "great ultimate" and pattern as the "real stuff" of the cosmos. As a result, Confucianism became associated with practical learning. Lee Ŏnchŏk annotated the first passage of Zhou Dunyi's (1017–1073) *Diagram of the Great Ultimate* to say that *dao* was the source of things and patterns, was incomparably high and subtle, existed near to us, and was in fact easy to practice. Searching for *dao* in the distance without inquiring into what is near and practical leads easily to entanglements with futility. Pattern is real stuff, because it is the source of the world's existence and is immanent in the world. The practicality of pattern is mentioned in Lee's letter to Cho Hanbo (c. fifteenth century):

> When it has not yet been aroused by any object, but is completely empty and still, as if without object, this is what is referred to as the wondrous condition with no sound or smell, or what your letter refers to as "quiescence." But in the midst of its perfect emptiness and total quiescence it is wholly present throughout everything; thus it is said that "when roused it pervades the universe to its source." If to the word "quiescent" you add "oblivion," then that's quiescent like wood and stone.[7]

The ultimate and the quiescent (Ch. *ji* 極 and *jing* 靜) are Confucian terms used to describe the transcendence of pattern as an entity. The great ultimate in the *yin* 陰 and *yang* 陽 (Ch.) is quite different from Laozi's nothingness or Buddhist quiescent oblivion. Thus, Lee claimed that the *dao* was the due course of practice in all the affairs of ordinary life and immanent in useful things and events. In other words, *dao* was merely a good way of settling up human affairs. If one pursues *dao* beyond human affairs, it becomes nonproductive and has nothing to do with Confucianism as a practical philosophy. Lee wanted to locate Confucian philosophy in practical learning, as opposed to the unproductive philosophies of Buddhism or Daoism.

The Four-Seven Debate

The Four-Seven Debate is one the most significant scholarly debates not only Korea's early Chosŏn period but in the history of neo-Confucianism. It arose among scholars attempting to the resolve social and political issues of Chosŏn society within the framework of neo-Confucian philosophy. The debate contributed not only to the development of Chosŏn neo-Confucianism in general, but also to the formation of different Confucian schools such as the Yŏngnam School and Kiho School. T'oegye (1501–1570), Kobong (1527–1572), Yulgok (1536–1584), and Ugye (1535–1598) were the important contenders in the debates.

In the Confucian tradition, the Four Beginnings (Ch. *siduan* 四端) were proof of the fundamental goodness of human natural tendencies (Ch. *xing* 性). As explained in *Mencius*, commiseration is the beginning of benevolence, shame is the beginning of dutifulness, modesty is the beginning of the observance of ritual propriety, and discrimination between right and wrong is the beginning of wisdom. The Seven Feelings (Ch. *qiqing* 七情) mentioned in the *Records of Ritual Propriety* include the natural human feelings of pleasure, anger, sorrow, joy, love, hate, and desire. The Four Beginnings and the Seven Feelings are all emotions, but they are not directly related to each other since they are presented in different contexts. The relation between Four Beginnings and the Seven Feelings became a central question in T'oegye's time due to a shift in interest from human natural tendencies as metaphysical embodiments to feelings as functions. Pressing social conflicts in Chosŏn society also were important factors provoking the debate.

From the beginning, T'oegye recognized the uniqueness of the Four-Seven Debate. Preceding Confucians, having clarified and analyzed human feelings and natural tendencies in detail, maintained that the Four Beginnings and the Seven Feelings were all feelings and did not refer to these feelings' relations in profound cosmic terms. In contrast, neo-Confucianism engaged in speculative philosophy, interpreting the human heart-mind, society, and natural tendencies based on the ideas of pattern and vital energy. Chinese philosopher Zhu Xi (1130–1200) made a great effort to provide a metaphysical basis for human morality, concentrating on natural tendencies other than the heart-mind and feelings. Unlike Zhu Xi, T'oegye focused on the notion of feelings.

In 1553 T'oegye rewrote Chŏng Chiun's (1509–1561) *Chŏnmyoungdosŏl* (Diagram of Heavenly Command) to say that the Four Beginnings issue from pattern and the Seven Feelings issue from vital energy. Yet in the wake of Kobong's criticism of the first revision in 1558, T'oegye again revised the text to say: "Four Beginnings issue from pure pattern and are entirely good; Seven Feelings issue from vital energy and pattern, and can be either good or bad."

When Kobong wrote his critiques in reply to T'oegye's revisions, the Four-Seven Debate commenced. Kobong said that T'oegye misconstrued pattern and vital energy as two separate entities by contrasting the Four Beginnings issuing from pattern with the Seven Feelings issuing from vital energy. Kobong claimed that the Four Beginnings cannot emerge apart from the Seven Feelings. He understood the Four Beginnings and Seven Feelings as inseparable feelings that are yet named differently, due only to "that with respect to which one speaks" (所就以言之). His theory of pattern and vital energy is based on the idea of a "mixed state." For him, pattern is the master of vital energy and vital energy supplies the material for pattern. These two are certainly distinct, but when it comes to their presence in actual things, they are mixed together and cannot be split apart.

T'oegye addressed his first reply to Kobong's remark about "that with respect to which one speaks." He claimed that pattern and vital energy may be interdependent, but nevertheless we can refer to them by separate terms. Regarding human natural tendencies, the point of reference is pattern, not vital energy, so tendencies can be described as purely good and not evil. The same logic can be applied to human feelings. Although the Four Beginnings are a mixture of pattern and vital energy, the point of reference is pattern, so it is plausible to say the Four Beginnings issue from pattern. He also acknowledged that the Four Beginnings and Seven Feelings are within the boundaries of pattern and vital energy, because the Four Beginnings come from the human tendencies of benevolence, rightness, observance of ritual propriety, and wisdom; and the Seven Feelings are caused by outside entities. He argued although neither the Four Beginnings nor Seven Feelings are separable from pattern and vital energy, each points to a predominant factor and emphasis on the basis of their point of origin, so there is no reason why we cannot say that one is a matter of pattern and the other a matter of vital energy.

In the second letter in the debate, T'oegye revised his position, saying, "In the case of the Four Beginnings, pattern issues them and vital energy follows, while in case of the Seven Feelings, vital energy issues them and pattern mounts them" (四則理發而氣隨之 七則氣發而理隨之); yet he did not change his basic position. According to T'oegye, despite the fact that pattern and vital energy are inseparable, the Four Beginnings emphasize pattern over vital energy, and the Seven Feelings focus on vital energy over pattern. Moreover, the Four Beginnings and Seven Feelings can be distinguished from two different points of view, "the mixed" and "the divided." T'oegye's theory of pattern and vital energy was built on the view of the divided.

While recognizing the interdependence of pattern and vital energy, he argued that pattern alone can issue the Four Beginnings by itself. In his arguments with Kobong, T'oegye himself seemed to be unclear on this. During the debates, he saw the Four Beginnings as a philosophical idea of highest importance. He attempted to establish pure goodness as the theoretical foundation of the Four Beginnings. His idea of pattern as "self-issuance" may serve this purpose better than an explication of pattern itself. The theory of the self-issuance of pattern is the argument that pattern in human natural tendencies arises by itself. In order to make a qualitative distinction between the Four Beginnings and Seven Feelings, T'oegye defined pattern and vital energy as the beginning and end. He thought that since the Four Beginnings issue from pattern, which is the pure goodness of human natural tendencies, there is a metaphysical ground for the pure goodness of the Four Beginnings.

Thus, he thought that the Four Beginnings and Seven Feelings were to be valued differently. The pure goodness of the Four Beginnings stems from the pure goodness of pattern, while the likelihood for good or evil in the Seven Feelings comes from the relativity of vital energy. Zhu Xi's remark that natural tendency is nothing but pattern is meant to give a metaphysical ground to the moral value of pure goodness in human natural tendencies. In the same manner, T'oegye's idea that the Four Beginnings issue from pattern is an attempt to secure the pure goodness of the Four Beginnings. By aligning the Four Beginnings with pattern, he wanted to secure their pure goodness at theoretical as well as practical levels. For this purpose, he maintained the self-issuance of pattern despite logical overstatement, in order to distinguish the purity of the Four Beginnings from anything contaminated with vital energy. This carries the strong moral implication that the pure goodness of pattern can be realized not only in the metaphysical sense but also in real life.

Confucianism aims to achieve harmony in the world. Mencius's argument for the goodness of human natural tendencies implies some basis for moral imperatives, and Zhu Xi's remark that human natural tendencies are nothing but pattern provides a metaphysical ground. In this context, T'oegye's theory of the self-issuance of pattern is significant in the development of Confucianism, as is his interpretation of feelings as issuing from human natural tendencies as patterns. His *ibal-sŏl* 理發說 (self-issuance of pattern) evolved into *idong-sŏl* 理動說 (self-movement of pattern) in cosmology and *ido-sŏl* 理到說 (self-realization of pattern) in epistemology. T'oegye's lifelong belief in the agency of pattern characterizes his philosophy in general and differentiates him from Zhu Xi, who tended to strongly deny the agency of pattern. According to T'oegye, pattern is highly noble, commanding things and events but never being commanded by them. This might be traced back to idea of *shangdi* 上帝 (Ch.) as "Lord on high" in classical Confucianism, and is related to *shangdi* as presented by Korean scholars Yun Hyu (1617–1680) and Hŏ Mok (1595–1682) in the later Chosŏn period.

T'oegye himself was aware that the excessive use of metaphysical terms in debates may lead to pedantic speculations that detract from Confucianism's value as a philosophy of practical self-cultivation. No matter how speculative his ideas may seem, T'oegye's scholarly goals were practical, seeking to establish a theoretical foundation for self-cultivation and social practice.

The next major contender in the debate, Yulgok, disagreed with T'oegye's assertion that the Four Beginnings issue from pattern and are mounted by vital energy, while the Seven Feelings issue from vital energy and are mounted by pattern. Of T'oegye's Four-Seven theory, Yulgok writes:

> What he says about issuing from material force [vital energy] and principle [pattern] mounting it is permissible. But this is not the case only with the Seven Feelings; the Four Beginnings are likewise a case of issuing from material force and principle mounting it. What do I mean? Only after seeing the child about to fall into the well is there the issuance of feelings of commiseration. Seeing it and feeling commiseration has to do with material force; this is what is described as issuing from material force. The root of commiseration is benevolence; this is what is described as principle mounting it. It is not only in the case of the heart-mind of humans that this is so; the transformative process of heaven and earth is completely a matter of material force transforming and principle mounting it.[8]

Yulgok claimed that all activities—including the Four Beginnings, the Seven Feelings, the human mind, and natural tendencies—can be explained as issuing from vital energy and pattern mounting it. He speculated that things issue from vital energy, and the ground for their issuance is pattern. Without vital energy, issuance is impossible. Without pattern, the ground of issuance is impossible. According to Yulgok, if like T'oegye one says that vital energy and pattern are identified as two things, one of which is anterior and the other posterior, then they stand in contrast as two distinct branches. This could mislead people to assume there are two foundations for the human heart-mind.

Yulgok's critique of T'oegye's Four-Seven theory came from his view that emotions in the Seven Feelings represent all kinds of human feelings, while the Four Beginnings are the good feelings among the Seven Feelings. Yulgok discussed these ideas in detail in his correspondences with fellow scholar Ugye. He denied that vital energy or the human heart-mind could have two origins.

He called this the subtle inseparability of pattern and vital energy, meaning that pattern and vital energy are neither separable nor intermixable—that is, neither two separate entities nor one unified entity. Instead, Yulgok described pattern and vital energy as subtle inseparability "one and many, many and one" (一而二 二而一).

His thesis that "pattern pervades" and "vital energy delimits" expresses the generality of pattern and the particularity of vital energy. Thus, his Four-Seven theory emphasizes the unity of the feelings while acknowledging the differences in their values. Futhermore, his ideas of "human mind" and "*dao* mind" assume that there is a channel through which the human mind can communicate with the *dao* mind. All these ideas stem from his philosophy of the subtle relation between pattern and vital energy.

Neo-Confucian Developments of the Late Chosŏn Period

During the seventeenth century, there were great changes in the geopolitics of northeastern Asia. In China, the Qing dynasty (1368–1644) replaced the Ming dynasty (1644–1911), and the Edo period (1600–1827) began in Japan. Chosŏn also experienced significant changes. The Japanese invasion of Korea in 1592 was the turning point at which the *sarim* faction, loyal to orthodox neo-Confucianism, replaced the *hungu* faction, which consisted of the meritorious elites who founded the Chosŏn dynasty. In economy, private ownership of land became more widespread partly due to the increase of land productivity. During this time, there were vast qualitative social changes in Chosŏn society, which brought about ideas of reformation in the state. Therefore, the later Chosŏn period following the late seventeenth century is sometimes defined as the quickening period of modern society. The philosophical landscape of the late Chosŏn can be categorized by several trends, including (1) neo-Confucianism, (2) Pragmatic School, (3) Wang Yangming School, and (4) Western Learning:

1. The followers of Yulgok's philosophy formed a neo-Confucian group known as the Kiho School. Their Ho-Rak Debate (discussed in detail below) opened a new horizon in Chosŏn neo-Confucianism and provided fertile soil for the growth of the Pragmatic School. T'oegye's followers formed the Yŏngnam School, which included the prominent seventeenth-century critic of Yulgok's philosophy, Lee Hyŏnil (1627–1704). Though many scholars consciously identified with neo-Confucianism, such as Chang Hyŏn-kwang (1554–1637) and Lee Chin-sang (1818–1885), the so-called Southerners in the Kiho and

Yŏngnam Schools, such as Hŏ Mok (1595–1682) and Yun Hyu (1617–1680), started to keep their philosophical distance from neo-Confucianism.

2. The development of the Pragmatic School shows remarkable intellectual progress in the late Chosŏn. The Pragmatic School was against useless learning and approved of practical, empirical studies. The later Pragmatic School was qualitatively different from its predecessors, a consequence of the critical developments in Chosŏn neo-Confucianism.

3. T'oegye attacked the doctrines of Ming dynasty Chinese Confucian scholar Wang Yangming (1472–1529), whose ideas subsequently disappeared from early Chosŏn neo-Confucianism. However, in the late Chosŏn, Chŏng Che-tu (1649–1736) began to study the philosophy of Wang Yangming and formed a school on the island of Kanghwa.

4. Western sciences and Catholic theology, which traveled to Korea via China, provided new paradigms different from the then-current cosmology and worldview. Ch'oe Han-ki (1803–1877) contributed to a creative reconfiguration of neo-Confucianism based on Western science, and Chŏng Yagyong (1762–1836) annotated the Confucian classics using Roman Catholic theology.

The Ho-Rak Debate

In the above categories, the Ho-Rak Debate may be the most important development. Like the Four-Seven Debate, this philosophical dialogue is significant in the history of neo-Confucian philosophy. The debate began among members of the school of Kwon Sang-ha, which developed from the Kiho School (the "Old Doctrine" faction), and involved the scholars Lee Kan (1677–1727) and Han Wonjin (1682–1751). Han Wonjin asked whether there is a physical nature in the state of non-issuance and whether humans and animals share the five constant virtues in common;[9] these issues are respectively called "discussion of the state of non-issuance" and "analytic discussion of the similarities and differences in the natural tendencies of humans and animals." Lee's denial of physical nature in the state of non-issuance is related to the idea of the continuity of the heart-mind between sages and common people. This led to the thesis that there is also continuity in the natural tendencies of humans and animals. Han's recognition of physical nature in the state of non-issuance developed into a theory of the discontinuity of the heart-mind

between sages and common people. On the basis of this he concluded that there
are discrepancies between the natural tendencies of humans and animals.

Concerning the debate over whether human and animals are basically
the same (because both inherit the same five constant virtues), or whether
they are different (because animals only inherit a part of the five constant
virtues), Han Wonjin said humans and animals are endowed with the vital
energy of the five phases, despite differences in partiality. Lee Kan claimed
that human and animals are different in physical nature but should possess
the same qualities of the five constant virtues because both are made of the
vital energy of *yin* and *yang*. Therefore, humans and animals have the same
natural tendencies but different physical natures.

Lee may have repeated Zhu Xi's ideas here, because Zhu Xi split human
natural tendencies into original nature and physical nature. The original nature,
in which pattern coexists with vital energy without being mixed, has pure
goodness and generality; while physical nature, in which pattern is delimited
by vital energy, produces various consequences depending upon the extent
that vital energy is involved. Ontologically they are not two entities. "Original
nature" is the term used with respect to pattern, while "physical nature" is the
term that equally emphasizes pattern and vital energy. Therefore, human and
animals have the same original nature but not the same physical nature. Lee's
sameness theory, stemming from Zhu Xi's theory of human natural tendencies,
shows that humans and nonhumans share the five virtues in nature.

Han argued that pattern, originally one, has two terms. One can be
spoken of as being beyond disposition (*chohyonggi* 因氣質), and the other can
be spoken of as being according to disposition (*ingijil* 雜氣質). The former is
the great ultimate, from the standpoint of which myriad things are the same.
The latter includes heaven, earth, and the five virtues, from the standpoint of
which myriad things are not the same. Here Han Wonjin's view of what is
"according to disposition" refers not to original nature but physical nature.

His argument is not in harmony with neo-Confucianism in general.
While neo-Confucianism uses contrasting terms such as sameness and
difference, or original nature and physical nature, his theory allows for the
threefold stratification of human natural tendencies into *chohyonggi, ingijil,* and
ch'apgijil. He argued that human natural tendencies are different from those
of animals according to their dispositions and that the natural tendencies of
each kind are separate, but this is alien to neo-Confucianism. It is as peculiar
as T'oegye's doctrine of the self-issuance of pattern.

Han Wonjin saw that human and animals, though different in their
intellectual capacities, both have the capability of cognition. However, he
maintained that they were fundamentally different in terms of higher moral
values such as benevolence, rightness, observance of ritual propriety, and

wisdom. In other words, these higher moral values are only possible for human beings.

Departure from Neo-Confucianism and the Growth of the Pragmatic School

In the Korean history of neo-Confucianism, the study of ritual propriety is discussed in the theories of the heart-mind and natural tendencies, and disputes over ritual propriety are of central significance. This developed extensively from the two debates, Four-Seven and Ho-Rak. The main issues of these debates concern explicating the Four Beginnings and Seven Feelings, *dao* mind and human mind, and the heart-mind and natural tendencies of humans and animals in terms of pattern and vital energy. No matter how speculative these issues may seem, these debates had clear the political implications. Neo-Confucian scholars, bureaucrats, and politicians were sensitive to contemporary social issues, and these social issues continuously influenced their philosophy, directly and indirectly.

On the one hand, neo-Confucian philosophers made scholarly progress on these philosophical issues, particularly in the Ho-Rak Debate, and on the other hand they made political claims on the reform of land and social class based on Zhu Xi's social philosophy. In the same era, Hŏ Mok opposed the Old Doctrine faction in power, which advocated orthodox Zhu Xi studies and attempted to restore the Six Canons of Confucianism.

In the dispute over the mourning rites, the Old Doctrine faction represented by Song Si-yŏl was in conflict with the Southerners' faction represented by Hŏ Mok. Eventually the Old Doctrine faction took exclusive control of power. Many neo-Confucian literati including Southerners were excluded from participation in the political process, which laid the foundation for their life and education in the countryside. Lee Ik and Chŏng Yagyong, the founders of Pragmatic School, emerged from this background.

Yun Hyu, who participated in the dispute over ritual propriety, departed from orthodox neo-Confucianism. Particularly, his comments on the *Zhongyong* and the *Great Learning* were substantially different from Zhu Xi's annotations. One difference is his emphasis upon *shangdi* in the *Book of Poetry* and *Book of Documents,* which Chŏng Yagyong later repeated in his commentaries on the Confucian classics. This indicated a return to the original teachings of Confucianism without recourse to the authority of Zhu Xi's annotations.

Many social and economic changes occurred in Chosŏn in the late seventeenth century. Large areas of land damaged by foreign invasions were restored, and a significant amount of commercial capital was accumulated through intermediate trade between China and Japan. These economic changes naturally induced social changes. Beginning in the late eighteenth century, there were signs of a transition from an agricultural society to a commercial and industrial one. These social and economic changes prompted a new philosophical movement led by the young scholars of the Old Doctrine faction, including Hong Tae-yong (1731–1783) and Park Chi-wŏn (1737–1805). The movement began with a new attitude toward the Qing dynasty in China. Hong and Park argued that Chosŏn should introduce advanced technologies from Qing and keep neo-Confucianism intact.

The philosophy of the Northern Learning School may derive from Lee Kan's sameness theory in the Ho-Rak Debate. It challenged the justifications for discriminating Chinese from barbarians, because natural tendencies cannot account for such differences. In the following, Hong Tae-yong portrays himself as the "Practical Old Man" and clarifies his position:

> Master Void said, "Amongst the organisms in this world only the human is noble. Animals and plants do not have wisdom, enlightenment, propriety, or appropriateness. Humans are more noble than animals and plants are more base than animals." The Practical Old Man said, "The five morals and the five events are the propriety and appropriateness of humans. To wander around in groups and feed one another is the propriety and appropriateness of animals, and to be born as buds but flourish together is the propriety and appropriateness of plants. Viewing things from the perspective of the human, the human is noble and things are base. Viewing the human from the perspective of things, then the things are noble and the human is base. However, from the perspective of nature humans and things are equal."[10]

For the Practical Old Man, difference does not necessarily mean inequality. The superiority of humans seems to be relative, because viewed from the perspective of nature humans and things are equal. An anthropocentric view that things are inferior to human beings prevents us from seeing this truth.

Hong Tae-yong thought that ultimate truth is embedded even in mathematics, economics, and military science, all of which were traditionally considered superficial. Hong Tae-yong and Park Chi-wŏn's Northern Learning is an attempt to reform Chosŏn society with advanced technology, but Korean orthodox neo-Confucians considered science from the Qing as barbaric. The Northern Learning School culminated with Kim Chŏng-hŭi (1786–1856). He conducted empirical studies on Confucian classics and ancient documents in the wake of the Evidential Studies proposed by Qing scholars in China such as Weng Fanggang and Ruanyuan. Kim Chŏng-hŭi was pragmatic, interpreting the Chinese classics and deciphering the ancient characters empirically. Park Kyu-su (1807–1876), the grandson of Park Chi-wŏn and a student of Kim Chŏng-hui, energetically implemented the reform policies. Some politicians of the regime were the followers of the Northern Learning School under the influence of Kim Chŏng-hui. This is proof that the school exerted influence on the rise of enlightenment thought, because enlightenment thinkers in Korea did nothing but replace the Qing dynasty with Japan and Western countries, as sources of advanced culture.

The Pragmatic School may be traced back to two sources: Southerners in the Kyŏnggi and Chungchŏng provinces, and the Northern Learning School in the Nak School of the Old Doctrine faction. Despite being two different or even opposite political factions and academic trends, they collaborated to give birth to pragmatic learning. In Seoul in the late eighteenth century, there was active scholarly exchange among intellectuals regardless of their political alliance, school, or social class. These scholars extended their interests from Zhu Xi studies to governance studies, literati studies, and encyclopedic studies. These scholarly trends accelerated among intellectuals as they gained fresh insights into their changing society and recognized their social responsibility.

In this scholarly and social environment, Chŏng Yagyong interpreted the Confucian classics under the influence of Roman Catholic doctrines and created his own philosophy. He wrote: "Humans endowed with acuteness can be superior to other creatures and explore the ten thousand things. Given that heaven, earth, and five virtues are equally endowed among humans and things, who is the master? How can it be that undifferentiated order is the due course of the cosmos?"[11] He saw that two different spheres could be distinguished: humans enjoy morality and independence, while animals and things are bound to inexorable laws without any moral sense. Here, animals and things seem to become objects of human desire and exploitation. In this way, modern consciousness is apparent in his thought.

The Challenge of Western Modernity for Korean Confucianism

With the opening of Korean ports in 1876 to the outside world, Chosŏn entered into the global capitalist economy. Yet, it was a "distorted modernity" because modernity was imposed by the coercive power of Western imperialism and its civilization. Intellectuals responded in various ways to Western impact. There was a move to defend orthodoxy and reject heterodoxy, or to protect orthodox neo-Confucianism and reject Western civilization as a whole. The Eclectic School tried to selectively introduce Western technology and science into traditional culture and philosophy. The enlightenment movement claimed that Confucianism should be replaced by Western science, technology, religions, and value systems.

I will first survey the movement to defend orthodoxy and reject heterodoxy, a position occupying an important position in the history of Korean Confucianism, and then examine the thought of Park Ŭn-sik (1859–1925), who pursued modernity independently.

The Self-Esteem of the Conservatives and Resistance against Foreign Invasion

Neo-Confucian scholars, in defending neo-Confucianism, tried to protect neo-Confucian orthodoxy thoroughly while oppressing their challengers, both domestic and foreign. Confucian scholars such as Lee Hangro (1792–1868), Ch'oe Ikhyŏn (1833–1906), and Yu In-sŏk (1842–1915) organized a militia against the West and Japan. Philosophically, they were engaged in issues of the mind. There was a heated debate over the nature of the mind and "illuminating excellence" within the Hwasŏ School. Yet there was an underlying agreement in the debate that the good life for human beings is possible only when we follow the ways of normative patterns without distortion. The idea was that one should obey normative patterns as pure human natural tendencies that reveal themselves in human consciousness and practice.

Due to the distinction between the Chinese and barbarians, the critique and rejection of Western civilization was possible. On the one hand, Chosŏn, due to her location on the periphery of China, could be considered one of the barbarians. On the other hand, some Confucians saw Chosŏn as a small Chinese civilization, because it had assimilated Chinese culture and even developed it further. Yu In-sŏk, a leader of the militia, proclaimed that Chosŏn was the only successor of orthodox Confucianism after the demise of the Ming dynasty. The rejection of Western culture as a reaction to imperialist invasion was possible because of such self-esteem. Since a partially successful reformation in the modernization of Chŏson could not have protected the country from foreign invasion, conservatives fought against imperialism. Although they failed, the resistance made it possible for anti-imperialistic people to unify. This was the historical significance of their failed resistance.

Park Ŭn-sik's Intepretation of Wang Yangming

While conservatives tried to preserve orthodoxy in the face of Western impact, other intellectuals, aware of problems in neo-Confucianism, responded in mainly two ways. Some sought a new Confucianism, while others accepted Western civilization as the *zeitgeist*. Park Ŭn-sik pursued the first option. For this, Park clarified the possible role of Wang Yangming's thought in the context of modernity.

At that time, the theory of social evolution gained popularity among East Asian intellectuals. But this theory, advocating competition and survival of the fittest, gave legitimacy to the imperial invasion and perpetuated the reality of colonization. Since the nation-state became the unit of the modern world, supporters of the "self-empowerment movement" (*chagang undong*) such as Park saw the world as a place where nation-states compete for their own self-interests. While recognizing that social development is a consequence of competition, Park advocated fair competition and morality as seen in Wang Yangming.

According to Park, Wang Yangming took historical situations into account and put them into practice without recourse to theoretical objectivity or traditional authority. Park applied Wang Yangming's ideas to his contemporary situation, accepting science and technology from the West on the basis of the theory of social evolution. But his interpretation of Wang Yangming can be seen as a critical reflection on neo-Confucianism as much as a complement to Western modernity. At the crossroads of traditional philosophy and Western theories, his philosophy was the outcome of an eclectic way of thinking.

Conclusion

The characteristics of Korean Confucianism lie in its emphasizing inner morality as much as practicality. Confucian literati in Chosŏn formed their unique Confucianism in the process of resolving social issues with neo-Confucian language and philosophy. The political issues of Chŏsun society were changed into seemingly pure philosophical debates. This was partly because Confucians in Chŏsun were bureaucrats and politicians. Yet it also shows that the indigenous Korean way of thinking—the harmony of opposites—is at work behind Korean Confucianism, whose ideal is to achieve the continuity of theory and practice, philosophy and real life.

Nowadays, in spite of many challenges, Confucianism is still meaningful in Korea, because many are actively pursuing Confucian resolutions to the social and cultural issues of postmodern and late-capitalistic society. In contemporary Korea, Confucianism is in the present tense.

Suggestions for Further Reading

For an excellent history of Korea, see Yŏngho Chŏe et al. (1996), *Sources of Korean Tradition Volume I: From Early Times through the Sixteenth Century*; and (2000), *Sources of Korean Tradition Volume II: From the Sixteenth to the Twentieth Centuries*. For more on the relationship between ancient Korean and Chinese cultures, see Seung-kook Lew (1973), "Introduction of Yin and Chou Thought and Ancient Korean Society" in *Korea Journal* 13, no. 6. The history of neo-Confucianism in Korea is detailed in Wm. Theodore de Bary and JaHyun Kim Haboush, eds. (1985), *The Rise of Neo-Confucianism in Korea.* For an overview of Confucianism and various religions in Korea, see Donald Baker (2008), *Korean Spirituality.*

To read more on individual Korean philosophers, see Sa-soon Yun (1991), *Critical Issues in Neo-Confucian Thought: The Philosophy of Yi T'oegye*; and Young-chan Ro (1989), *The Korean Neo-Confucianism of Yi Yulgok*. For a translation of T'oegye's writings, see Michael C. Kalton (1988), *To Become a Sage: The Ten Diagrams on Sage Learning.*

Finally, for more on the Four-Seven Debate, see Michael C. Kalton et al. (1994), *The Four-Seven Debate: An Annotated Translation of the Most Famous Controversy in Korean Neo-Confucian Thought*; and Edward Y. J. Chung (1995), *The Korean Neo-Confucianism of Yi T'oegye and Yi Yulgok: A Reappraisal of the 'Four-Seven Thesis' and Its Practical Implications for Self-Cultivation.*

Notes

1. Roger T. Ames and David Hall (2001), 109–110.

2. Ames and Henry Rosemont Jr. (1998), 129.

3. Kim Pusik, *Samguk sagi* [*History of the Three Kingdoms*], trans. Wonsuk Chang (unpublished manuscript). The passage comes from Part IV, Annals of Silla of the 37th year of King Chinhung.

4. While most of the terminology in this chapter appears in Korean, some Confucian terms appear in Chinese. These are marked with a "Ch."

5. Chŏng T'ojŏn, *Pulssi chappyŏn* [*Criticism of Buddhism*], Section 14, trans. Charles Muller, http://acmuller.net/jeong-gihwa/bulssijapbyeon.html.

6. Sŏ Kyŏngdŏk, *T'aehŏsŏl* [*Discussion of the Vast Tenuousness*], trans. Jeongyeup Kim (unpublished manuscript), in *Hwadamjip* [*Collected Works of Hwadam*].

7. Lee Ŏjŏk, "First Letter to Manggidang," trans. Michael Kalton (unpublished manuscript), in *Hoejaejip* [*Collected Works of Hoejap*].

8. *Yulgok chŏnsŏ* [*Writings of Yulgok*] 10.5b; see Kalton et al. (1994), 132.

9. What the author refers to as the "five constant virtues" are called the "five constants," or *wuchang*, in the glossary.

10. Hong Tae-young, *Ŭisan mundap* [*Dialogues at Ui Mountain*], trans. Jeongyeup Kim, (unpublished manuscript).

11. Chŏng Yagyong, *Chungyong kang'ŭibo* [*A Supplement to the Discussion of the Zhongyong*], trans. Wonsuk Chang (unpublished manuscript), in *Yŏyudang chŏnsŏ* [*Collected Works of Yŏyudang*].

3

The History of
Confucianism in Japan

Peter Nosco

The history of Confucianism in Japan began at a time when "Confucianism" meant something quite different from what it means today, and when intellectual circles in East Asia were dominated by thoughts and concepts identified with Buddhism. During the long years from the fall of the Latter Han dynasty in 220 CE through the Tang (618–907), the classics esteemed by Confucius remained an important part of the standard curriculum for those who either aspired or were expected to exercise authority over others, but there was little evidence of creative scholarship or of individuals championing Confucianism as a creed distinct from and on a par with Buddhism or Daoism.

The sixteenth year of the reign of Ōjin is often taken as the start of Japan's experience with Confucianism, with traditional dating assigning this to 285 but around 404 being the more likely. Reportedly, in that year a Confucian scholar from the Korean kingdom of Paekche, Wang In (known as Wani in Japanese), arrived in Japan to tutor a son of Ōjin, bringing along with him copies of the *Analects* and the *Thousand Character Classic*. This narrative, however, overlooks the likelihood that literate individuals familiar with traditional Confucian texts and cosmologies had already for some time been arriving in Japan, where their knowledge and skills earned them prominence in their new home.

Further, the "Confucianism" that this narrative speaks of was far removed from the ethical teachings and political theories of the sage Confucius and his early disciples, and instead was rooted in the study of court ritual, ceremonial divination, Chinese poetry and history, and cosmology. The earliest Confucian authorities on these subjects in Japan were immigrants from the mainland,

and especially individuals who came from the Korean peninsula. Their
services included divination and record keeping: the former associated with
astrologically identifying auspicious dates for important events, or determining
lucky and unlucky directions for travel on a particular day; and the latter
with ritually sacralizing early elites in Japan, especially the nascent Yamato
monarchy. However, the most basic Confucian advice on how to order the
affairs of state, or to regulate and cultivate the individual, would remain absent
from Japanese Confucianism for centuries to come.

Certain Chinese principles of statecraft and other policies often identified
with Confucianism proved useful to Japan's seventh- and eighth-century
monarchy. Principal among these were practicing equal-field land distribution,
imposing a single tax upon the people, having a single monarch whose rule
could unite spiritual and political authority, establishing a symmetrical central
bureaucracy, administering performance reviews to those in government
service, undertaking a census, issuing legal codes, participating diplomatically
in a Sinocentric international order, and constructing a capital region. To be
sure, these were as much Chinese as they were distinctively Confucian. Their
success in practice varied widely, and only the existence of a clearly defined
capital region survived beyond the early tenth century.

For centuries one found few recognizable Confucians in Japan, in the
sense of acknowledged authorities on the Chinese classics. Even though the
Song (960–1279) and Yuan (1280–1368) neo-Confucian innovations and
transformations of Confucianism were as a matter of course introduced in
Japan soon after their advent in China, these new teachings had very limited
circulation in Japan. For example, to the extent that the neo-Confucian teachings
of the Cheng brothers and Zhu Xi were found at all in Japan under the Ashikaga
shogunate (1338–1568), it was only either in select Zen temples associated with
licensed China trade, or from about the mid-fifteenth to mid-sixteenth centuries
in the noted academic institution, the Ashikaga Gakkō (or Ashikaga School).
It was within the walls of this exclusive academy that mostly Buddhist monks
and other members of the Ashikaga family—especially those who aspired to
high service in the Ashikaga government—studied Confucian classics, concentrating on the *Yijing* or *Book of Changes* (J. *Ekikyō*), which was prized for
its application to military science, a feature that resonated with the century of
civil war that provided the background for the Gakkō's heyday.

Besides having an important role in mediating Sino-Japanese relations,
Zen temples were also appropriate institutional settings for neo-Confucian
teachings in Japan, owing to the powerful conceptual resonances between the
respective teachings and traditions. As is well known, the similarities between
certain key concepts in Chan, Zen, and Son Buddhism on the one hand and
neo-Confucianism on the other was always an issue for neo-Confucians, who
even in China at times had to defend themselves against the charge of being

derivative of Buddhism and especially the Chan variant. Thus, for example in medieval Japanese Zen circles the neo-Confucian contemplative practice of quiet sitting (Ch. *zhengzou* 正座) was typically represented as an inferior variant of Zen sitting in meditation (*zazen* 座禅), the neo-Confucian idea of principle (*ri* 理) was understood to have its analog in *dharma* (*hō* 法), and so on.[1]

This situation changed utterly with the ill-conceived invasion of Korea in the 1590s, and Tokugawa Ieyasu's (1542–1616) establishment of the Tokugawa line of shoguns in the early seventeenth century. The initial successes experienced by the Japanese invaders resulted in an array of war booty that included Korean and Chinese neo-Confucian texts. Once brought back to Japan, these previously unknown texts were distributed to those same Zen temples where neo-Confucianism was already institutionalized, and within just a few years of the arrival of these new texts, one observes a number of Zen monks turning away from Zen Buddhism and to neo-Confucianism for both intellectual and spiritual succor.

The first prominent convert, and in many ways Japan's first committed neo-Confucian, was the Zen priest Fujiwara Seika (1561–1619), a descendant of the celebrated poet and arbiter of taste Fujiwara Teika (1162–1241). Seika found much inspiration in the new texts that had arrived from Korea, and after 1597 he received guidance in their interpretation from a Korean prisoner of war, Kang Hang (1567–1618), himself an authority on Zhu Xi. Thereafter, Seika quickly moved to sever his ties with Zen and to identify himself publicly as a neo-Confucian, something unprecedented in Japan. Intellectually, Seika was drawn to both the orthodox teachings of Zhu Xi as well as the heterodox interpretations of Wang Yangming; and personally he preferred the lifestyle of a semi-recluse to one of public service. In both these respects he differed from his most famous student Hayashi Razan (1583–1657), who was the Tokugawa period's first champion of Zhu Xi's teachings, and the first to place his teachings in service to the Tokugawa Bakufu (the Tokugawa government).

Hayashi Razan began training as a Zen priest at the Kenninji, where he came under the tutelage of Fujiwara Seika. Unlike Seika, Razan eschewed the heterodox interpretations of Wang Yangming and accepted only Zhu Xi's interpretations as correct, here aligning himself with prevailing Korean interpretations as well. Also, where Seika shunned the spotlight, Razan embraced it. In 1603 he gave public lectures on the *Analects*, a revolutionary act that broke the centuries-long tradition in Japan of esoteric transmission of scholarship. Then, after Seika apparently declined Ieyasu's invitation to lecture to him on the principles of Chinese dynastic change, Ieyasu turned to Seika's student and brought Hayashi Razan into his government, not initially as an advisor but rather as an authority and raconteur on Chinese history, ceremony, and culture generally.

This began a long association between the two families. Hayashi Razan actually served the first four Tokugawa Shoguns, being rewarded in 1630 with the land and funds to establish a school within Edo (modern-day Tōkyō). By the time of his death in 1657 Razan had solidified his position and that of his family as hereditary heads of this school, later renamed the Shōheikō, or School of Prosperous Peace, as well as hereditary interpreters of neo-Confucianism and related matters in service to the Bakufu. The school declined in prestige after the seventeenth century, only to reemerge in the spotlight during the 1790s at a time when ideological orthodoxy was being championed within the Bakufu as the cure to society's ills.

An even more ardent champion of Zhu Xi's teachings emerged in the person of Yamazaki Ansai (1619–1682), the son of a *rōnin* 浪人 or "masterless samurai" who was initially trained in Tendai and Zen Buddhism, and then gravitated toward the neo-Confucianism of the Southern School in Tosa on Shikoku, later converting wholeheartedly to the teaching. Ansai chose the phrase "inwardly reverent, outwardly righteous" (*naikei gaigi* 内敬外義) as his personal maxim, and acknowledged the influence of the Korean scholar T'oegye (1501–1570) on his views. Ansai and his school, the Kimon, came to be renowned for a spirit of moral rigor, whereby students were forbidden to read works of poetry, literature, or even history—even when these were included within the Confucian canon—if these were not seen to help the students advance on the path to moral perfection. Ansai's pietistic rigor eventually proved to be at odds with more liberal forces that were developing within Japanese urban society, and though his school endured into modern times, its popularity waned after Ansai's death in 1682.

In many ways Ansai seemed to pattern his career after Razan's, though of course they had differing respective strengths. Both were renowned for their broad learning, and both inaugurated ambitious Japanese historiographical projects. However, only Razan brought his to completion, and this only with the posthumous help of his descendants. Both sought opportunities to enter service to the state, with Ansai eventually catching the eye of Ieyasu's grandson, the Daimyo and Bakufu advisor Hoshina Masayuki (1611–1672). Further, both sought to reconcile neo-Confucian principles with beliefs rooted in the *kami*-worship of Shinto. Yamazaki Ansai's Suika Shinto was the better known of the two variants, though they shared much in common.

In addition to these pioneers of Cheng-Zhu teachings in Japan, the heterodox teachings of Wang Yangming also found articulate spokesmen in the writings of Nakae Tōju (1608–1648) and Tōju's student Kumazawa Banzan (1619-1691), who was particularly concerned with their practical relevance to the samurai class. Wang Yangming's teachings (*yōmeigaku* 陽明学) never enjoyed the same degree of following in Japan as in China, at least during the Tokugawa period's (1600–1867) early years, when the hostility of the Hayashi and Kimon Schools was sufficient to keep Wang Yangming's teachings at bay. They did, however, enjoy renewed popularity toward the end of the Tokugawa period, when they proved inspirational to several generations of activists who challenged the declining status quo.

During the seventeenth century, Japan's intellectual world was, in fact, transformed from one in which Buddhist assumptions were dominant, to one that partook of much the same neo-Confucian legacy as elsewhere in East Asia, a legacy that included humanism, rationalism, ethnocentrism, and historicism.[2] The humanism of this Confucian worldview rested in the assumptions that humankind is ultimately the key variable in an otherwise orderly cosmos, that the highest goal of humankind is good government, and that all have an opportunity if not an actual responsibility to engage in self-cultivation as part of a path toward human perfection. The rationalism that hereafter coursed through much of Tokugawa society was premised on the assumption that the world as a whole, its various rhythms, and even its minute specifics are all ultimately knowable, and while the interpretations of this knowledge of course varied from one scholar to another, the very assumption that the world was knowable invited a host of scientific and quasi-scientific speculation and other forms of skeptical enquiry.

The historicism of the Confucian tradition was rooted in the belief that the copious records of the past held sufficient examples to demonstrate the historical principle that ultimately good is rewarded and evil punished; remarkably, when transplanted into its Japanese context, under Chinese neo-Confucian influence, there were more works on Japanese history written during the seventeenth century than in all of Japan's history to that point. And, the ethnocentrism that characterized Chinese Confucianism—the chauvinism of China as the island Middle Kingdom surrounded by seas of the semi-civilized and barbarian peoples—inspired any number of ardent Sinophiles in Tokugawa Japan but also subsequently triggered the construction of new forms of Japanese identity. What is perhaps most remarkable about the Japanese example is that in Japan neo-Confucianism attained this measure of influence essentially on its own intellectual merits, and without linkage to an examination system, as in China and Korea.

Both the aforementioned broad learning and skeptical character associated with Japanese neo-Confucianism were personified in the career of one of the Tokugawa period's most richly gifted neo-Confucians Kaibara Ekken (also Ekiken, 1630–1714). Trained in Kyōto in both herbal medicine and the orthodox neo-Confucianism of Zhu Xi, Ekken went on to distinguish himself not only as a moral philosopher, but also as an authority on the taxonomy of flora and fauna, Japanese history and geography, native medicinal herbs, and even the principles of children's and women's education. Toward the end of his life, Ekken in a celebrated passage confessed to having grave doubts about a number of neo-Confucian assumptions, especially regarding the correct interpretation of the relationship between the key terms principle (*ri* 理) and material force (*ki* 気).[3] Nonetheless, at the same time his skepticism was itself part of the important neo-Confucian tradition in Japan as elsewhere of critical reflection and skeptical inquiry.

If in China and Korea the most spirited challenge to Zhu Xi learning was found in the teachings of Wang Yangming, in Japan the greatest challenge came from a number of schools collectively known as Ancient Studies or Ancient Learning (*kogaku* 古学). Though they each had a distinctive character, the leading Ancient Learning schools of Yamaga Sokō (1622–1685), Itō Jinsai (1627–1705), and Ogyū Sorai (1666–1728) all shared the perspective that the true messages of the sages were to be found not in the commentarial tradition of Zhu Xi and the Cheng brothers, but rather in a direct and unmediated examination of the ancient classics themselves.

Yamaga Sokō issued the clarion call to this movement in 1665 in a work called *Essential Teachings of the Sages (Seikyō yōroku)*, when he asserted that it was not until he stopped using the commentaries of later scholars and went directly to the works of the sages that he finally attained to the true message of the sages. These ideas, which sound so commonsensical, were sufficiently radical in the ideologically charged atmosphere of mid-1660s Edo—under the watchful eye of the Bakufu and the antagonistic gaze of the Shōheikō—that Yamaga Sokō was exiled from Edo for nine years, after which he dedicated himself to writing about Japanese history. Yet another figure of broad learning, Sokō regarded the paramilitary Bakufu as a perfect latter-day analog to the ancient Zhou dynasty state of Confucius, and he accordingly sought to apply the sages' teachings to the samurai class of his own day. By being the first to articulate its philosophical basis, he has come to be regarded as the founder of Bushidō, the Way of the Warrior, though Sokō himself never used the term.

Itō Jinsai was the first to demonstrate the popular appeal of such seemingly narrow study by opening his remarkably successful private academy, the Kogidō or Hall of Ancient Meaning, in Kyōto. Jinsai's parents had hoped for a more sensible livelihood such as medicine for their son, who gravitated initially to the teachings of Zhu Xi and Wang Yangming before formulating his own Confucian perspectives. Jinsai shunned the abstruse explanations of neo-Confucianism, insisting that it was fruitless to seek to explain the world with a single word such as *principle*. He instead sought a practical application of Confucian virtues in the world, acknowledging the supremacy of *jin* 仁 (humanity, love) but for practical reasons stressing *chū* 忠 (loyalty) and *shin* 信 (faithfulness) instead.[4] By the time of his death hundreds of students had registered in Jinsai's school, enabling him to pass on its headship to his adopted son Tōgai (1670–1738) under whom the school continued to grow, providing an institutional model for a host of rivals.

The success of the Ancient Learning challenge to the Zhu Xi orthodoxy has been seen as evidence of Japanese Confucianism's divergence from its continental counterparts, and its responding to quite different social and political conditions. Jinsai's private academy emerged at the same time as other self-funding forms of popular culture such as the plays of Chikamatsu Monzaemon (1653–1725), the fiction of Ihara Saikaku (1642–1693), and the woodblock prints Hishikawa Moronobu (d. 1694). It was also likely the inspiration for Kada no Azumamaro's (1669–1736) efforts in nearby Fushimi to found a nativist private academy to rival its Confucian counterparts. Jinsai's academy and the hundreds of competitors it eventually inspired also provided an important opportunity for voluntary association within the Tokugawa period's otherwise severely limited public sphere.

Perhaps the most radical innovator within the history of Japanese Confucianism was Ogyū Sorai, whose version of Ancient Learning moved sharply in a new direction. Generally speaking, Confucians of all stripes prior to Sorai had argued that the way was to be found in nature, and that it reflected natural principles. The way was thus understood to be the way of heaven, and in that sense ontologically prior to creation of earth. Ogyū Sorai, by contrast, argued that the way was merely a comprehensive term, a kind of shorthand for the rites, music, laws, and institutions of the early Chinese kings. This being so, the way was to be found not by observing nature or by looking inward for evidence of cosmic principles within one's inmost being, but rather within the texts that illuminate these ancient kings and their ages for us. These texts were not the Four Books of the *Analects, Mencius, Great Learning*, and *Doctrine of the Mean*, but rather the Five Classics and other ancient texts of all sorts, which were about things, that is, practical matters. These texts had to be deciphered if their secrets, that is, their way, was to be unlocked, and Sorai thus advanced the study of Chinese linguistics even farther than his earlier colleagues in Ancient Learning, insisting that his students not just learn how to read such materials but that they also compose in imitation of ancient styles. Significantly, for Sorai if the way was now essentially demystified and taken outside the realm of the cosmic, the sages too were now likewise just men. They were great men, to be sure, but they were great for what they created, and not in any cosmic sense.

Sorai was likely the most celebrated intellectual of his times in Japan. He advised the Daimyo Yanagisawa Yoshiyasu (1658–1714), himself an advisor to the fifth Tokugawa Shogun Tsunayoshi (1646–1709) for whom Sorai's father served as personal physician. The eighth Tokugawa Shogun Yoshimune (1684–1751) was likewise an admirer of Sorai, and Sorai dedicated a study of politics and administration to him. Sorai's ideas are said to have increased in popularity even after his death, making the mid-eighteenth century something of a zenith of Confucian and neo-Confucian influence in Japan, and thereby also signaling the start of its slow decline.

Some scholars, most notably Maruyama Masao (1914–1996), have seen in the historicist ontology of Ogyū Sorai the seeds of Japan's future modern transformation.[5] From Maruyama's perspective, by taking the way out of nature, Sorai briefly opened a space for human agency and politics in mid-Tokugawa Japan, with potential consequences for the Bakufu a century before its demise. By this argument, the eventual resurgence of naturalist ontologies by the end of the nineteenth century and their persistence into modern times had the effect of deforming Japan's modernity and neutralizing effective political action at a time when it was most needed during the first half of the twentieth century.

Sorai's success in attracting the attention of the highest rulers to his scholarship and views notwithstanding, Confucian advisors at the highest levels of government were less prominent in Japan than elsewhere in East Asia, and even the extent of the Hayashi family's influence, as opposed to their prestige, remains arguable. In the early eighteenth century Arai Hakuseki (1657–1725), a broadly learned orthodox Confucian who also wrote with authority on Japanese history and authored Japan's first autobiography (*Oritaku shiba no ki* or *Told Round a Brushwood Fire*), served as advisor to two particularly weak shoguns. As early as 1694 he won appointment as tutor to the future sixth Tokugawa Shogun Ienobu (1666–1712, shogun 1709–1712), and subsequently advised Ienobu's young son Ietsugu (1709–1716, shogun 1713–16).

Hakuseki's mission was to transform the Bakufu into a Confucian monarchy. The Bakufu had already lost much of its martial character and had acquired many of the trappings of a civilian government by the time of the fifth Shogun Tsunayoshi. Hakuseki sought to take this a step further, changing Bakufu structure and ceremony along Confucian models, and even asserting the Shogun as Japan's Confucian monarch (*kokuō* 国王) on the occasion of the reception of a Korean embassy in 1711. Hakuseki's Confucian program was entirely dismantled during the years after Ietsugu perished in 1716, but he nonetheless represents one of two paragons of Confucian advisors during Japan's eighteenth century.

The other, who came later in the century, was the equally learned Matsudaira Sadanobu (1758–1829). Sadanobu aspired to serve a similar function, hoping to rescue his age from its various ills by resurrecting the moral rigor which was believed to have prevailed during the Tokugawa's early years. Sadanobu was the grandson of the eighth Shogun Tokugawa Yoshimune, and in 1787 when not yet thirty he was appointed to the Council of Elders. From this position he began a systematic purge of the policies of the previous government, whose maladministration had compounded the devastating effects of famine in the early and middle 1880s. Among his reforms was the 1790 Ban on Heterodoxy, which demanded strict fidelity to the teachings of Zhu Xi within the Bakufu's own Confucian college, the Shōheikō, where a spirit of intellectual liberality had begun to appear as a violation of the policies and principles that informed the Tokugawa government during its successful first half-century.

Confucianism in Japan lacked much of the institutional support it received in China and Korea, most notably in the absence of an examination system, but in other ways Confucianism left its mark on Tokugawa Japan. For example, by the end of the eighteenth century, one finds remonstrance boxes proliferating under Confucian inspiration throughout Japan, allowing commoners an opportunity to voice complaint or to offer suggestions. These formed an important part of the limited public sphere available to non-samurai commoners.

Further, the Confucian academy became the vanguard for a broad spectrum of private and public educational opportunities for both samurai and non-samurai commoners. For samurai, credentializing oneself with knowledge of the classical texts of Confucianism, ideally instructed by one of the day's leading educators, was generally of vocational advantage within one's domain. Further, in an age when their martial services were no longer as relevant, becoming knowledge specialists of sorts provided an added measure of security in an uncertain time for many samurai. For commoners, by contrast, expertise in Confucianism was just another form of newly commodified knowledge that would have been inaccessible owing to the esoteric transmissions of just a century or two earlier.

The very way in which Tokugawa Japan conceived of itself as a polity was grounded in the Confucian concept of an organic society in which the state is both modeled on and comprised of family-households. Confucianism emphasized the individual and mutual responsibilities that attend to all relationships, as well as the duties that all individuals face in their everyday kaleidoscope of interactions. One's role is constantly changing—now a father, now a son, now a brother, now a husband, and so on endlessly—but in a perfect world one's obligations are always understood. Confucianism thus imagined an ideal society in which all persons not only have a precisely ordered place, but also attend precisely to the duties and responsibilities that attach to that place, neither exceeding nor falling short. And, when all are doing their individual parts in this organism-like society, the society itself can be said to have achieved a kind of heaven on earth, perfectly fulfilling the cosmic responsibility for humans to provide good government.

If intellectual arenas in seventeenth-century Japan were characterized by debates within the Confucian camp, in the eighteenth century they were characterized by debates between the Confucian camp and new fields of knowledge such as the nativists (*kokugakusha*) and Dutch Learning specialists (*rangakusha*). Like the Confucians, the nativists were looking to resurrect an ancient way, but for the nativists this was something Japanese and not Chinese. The leading lights among them—figures such as Kamo no Mabuchi (1697–1769), Motoori Norinaga (1730–1801), and Hirata Atsutane (1776–1843)—were unsparing in their criticisms of the Confucians and their way, but in both methodology and thematic content, the nativists owed much to their Confucian rivals.

Dutch Learning became a field of study following the relaxation of the ban on European books during the reign of the Shogun Yoshimune and referred to all forms of European knowledge, since of all Europeans only the Dutch were allowed to reside in Tokugawa Japan, on an islet in Nagasaki Harbor. Dutch Learning posed particular challenges to Chinese learning generally, especially in scientific fields of knowledge such as like medicine. With Confucianism again seen as one part of the broader Chinese learning, individuals in Japan began to question Confucianism's capacity to address the increasingly urgent problems of the day.

By the early nineteenth century, one finds an array of voices exclaiming the decline of those virtues essential to the polity's health, if not its survival, and Confucian voices were again among the most prominent in this chorus, though now these voices were realigned with the voices of nativists. In the Mito domain, where typically one-third of the domain's revenue was spent on scholarly endeavors, such as its massive Great Japan History (*dai nihonshi*) project, one found an effort to exalt the Confucian virtues of filial piety and loyalty as distinctly Japanese virtues, said to be represented both now and historically in a superior fashion in Japan by the people's unwavering loyalty to their sovereign and ultimately through him to the solar deity Amaterasu. This fusion of Confucian and Shinto elements and values provided a potent ideological mix that proved inspirational to many who began to question the Bakufu's legitimacy during the Tokugawa period's last decades.

The arguments that were used to justify the change in government were conservative ones rooted ironically in the very Confucian notion of an organic society that had provided so much of the glue that held Tokugawa society together. The Shogun, by this argument, was in fact formally the *sei-i tai shōgun* or "barbarian-subduing generalissimo." It was the Shogun's responsibility to manage foreign affairs, and the Bakufu's evident inability to manage foreign relations from the 1850s on effectively placed the Shogun in default of one of his most fundamental duties. Using arguments thus rooted in the Confucian rectification of names (*seimei* 正名, Ch. *zhengming*), and drawing inspiration from Wang Yangming's doctrine of the unity of thought and action, a coalition of the enemies of the Shogun succeeded in deposing him in a coup in January 1868, dismantling the Bakufu, and forming a new coalition around the person of the teenaged monarch, from whom the era took its new name of Meiji. Edo was renamed Tōkyō, and became both the site of Japan's monarchy, as well as its seat of government.

From the start of the new Meiji government (1868–1912), Confucian voices were increasingly on the defensive against the ideas that accompanied the industrially, technologically, and militarily advanced major European and North American powers. To those who advocated westernization, Confucianism, like feudalism, became almost synonymous with anything old-fashioned and hence bad. Nonetheless, the new generation that came to power during the early Meiji years and then eventually grew into its elders by period's end were typically cultural conservatives for whom a degree of westernization was the regrettable but necessary price one had to pay if Japan was to emerge from its subordinate status relative to the Western powers.

Confucianism remained prominent at the Meiji Court, where the young monarch was tutored by Confucian conservatives such as Motoda Eifu (also Nagazane, 1818–1891). In an extension of the synthesis forged at Mito during the last decades of the Tokugawa, Confucian conservatism was now melded with Japanese essentialism in a potent ideology intended to inspire self-sacrifice. Thus, at the same time that the Japanese government sought to impress the Western world with its newly promulgated constitution and Diet (parliament), its legal system, and its railways, one also saw a Confucian emphasis on loyalty to the monarchy and the importance of being good subjects in the era's most important ideological documents such as the Imperial Rescript on Education, recited each day throughout Japan's school system. Ironically, Confucianism, which throughout its history had never been attached to territorial expansion, now became an accomplice to Japan's imperial ambitions.

The legacy of Confucianism in the Japan of the last century is to be found in three areas: the high value placed on education, including the persistence of a kind of educational meritocracy; the enduring presence of high levels of trust in both horizontal and vertical relationships, along with the importance attached to relationships generally; and the organic conception of society designating a specific place for each individual in a coherent family-state.

Education has for centuries been an important priority in Japan, and one in which both individuals and their society have placed a heavy investment. One of the reasons for the success of Itō Jinsai's academy and the hundreds others that followed it was that they proved attractive to individuals across classes. Samurai soon found it vocationally advantageous to credentialize themselves in various forms of learning, but familiarity with the Confucian canon was the single most important field. Nonetheless, samurai eventually came to form a minority in the classrooms of these private academies, as moneyed commoners sought to acquire for themselves training in all the traditional and previously socially restricted polite arts from knowledge of the esoteric principles of versification, to knowledge of traditional Confucian teachings and their current interpretation.

All this points, of course, to a bedrock of literacy and regard for education that served Japanese society well during the at times tortuous transition to modernity. Though there were many reasons why persons in local communities in Japan endured severe hardship in order to fund the establishment of a public school system at the turn of the twentieth century, the Confucian regard for education was fundamental. Education was both useful and good for its own sake.

The Confucian emphasis on education and the incipient meritocracy it helped to nurture became a full-blown educational meritocracy in Japan during the twentieth century. Starting with a handful of national universities, a network of both public and private colleges and universities grew quickly, proliferating much as the private academies had done in an earlier age. The so-called examination hell (*shiken jigoku* 試験地獄) that one has to survive in order to prevail on this path in today's Japan is, in fact, typical of modern as well as traditional "Confucian" societies, and points too to the value these societies place on human capital. It remains an interesting irony that in order to modernize, Japan embraced an educational meritocracy based on a modern curriculum at roughly the same time that China, in its own modernization efforts, dispensed in 1909 with its six-centuries-old examination system based on a Confucian curriculum.

If educational merit forms one leg of the Confucian legacy to Japanese society, then trust is surely the second leg.[6] Trust (*shin*) is of course one of the traditional Confucian virtues, and is grounded in an understanding of the mutuality of obligations in all relationships. In Confucian vertical relationships, superiors enjoy privileges and can trust their subordinates to provide loyal service, but superiors are also benefactors to their subordinates, ideally caring for them as a loving father cares for his children. Subordinates of course owe allegiance to those in authority over them but can also trust, or at least harbor reasonable expectations, regarding how they will be treated and cared for. Horizontally, one also trusts that one's neighbors and others in one's web of relatively equal associations will not do to us what they would not have us do to them. This element of trust may be the single most distinctive feature of Japanese Confucianism generally as well as its legacy to Japanese society, and in a society with as many stresses and strains as Japan's, with at one point year after year of more than thirty thousand suicides annually, trust becomes a kind of glue holding the society together as well as one of its bedrock values.

Further, though Buddhism can also envision a harmoniously integrated multitiered cosmos as the analog for a feudal society structured on inequalities of every sort, it was under the influence of Confucianism from the seventeenth century onward that one sees the emergence of a societal worldview that imagines society to be like an organism. This organism in theory works to perfection when each of its constituent components, that is, each individual, is fulfilling a personal destiny by attending precisely to individual and collective responsibilities, duties, and obligations, neither exceeding them nor falling deficient in any way. Though this imagines a society built of inequalities of all sorts, the integral role of each individual within the organism provides a powerful leveling influence, since again in theory each individual is equally important to the collective mission's success. This organic way of conceiving of society proposes that all its members share the same ultimate goals and strive collectively toward them, as opposed to a vision of a society in which equilibrium is attained through the successful mediation of competing interests. This worldview survives into the present as the dominant one in Japan and has become fundamental to the present construction of Japanese identity, where it is often conflated with another Confucian virtue: harmony. Thus, even though it is arguable whether there are any Japanese Confucians left in Japan, it is clear that the legacy of Confucianism lives on and will continue to do so for the foreseeable future.

Suggestions for Further Reading

In addition to the works cited in the notes, the second edition of the second volume of Wm. Theodore de Bary, Carol Gluck, and Arthur Tiedemann, eds. (2005), *Sources of Japanese Tradition* has sections on all of the Tokugawa and subsequent era Confucians mentioned herein, including translations of excerpted primary sources. My (1996), *Confucianism and Tokugawa Culture* also has chapters addressing many of the issues in this piece.

On the role of the *Yijing* in Japanese culture generally, see Wai-ming Ng (2000), *The I Ching in Tokugawa Thought and Culture*. Herman Ooms (1985), *Tokugawa Ideology: Early Constructs, 1570–1680* provides an excellent overview of Fujiwara Seika, Hayashi Razan, and Yamazaki Ansai, and their roles in the construction of early Tokugawa ideology. And Richard Rubinger (1982), *Private Academies of Tokugawa Japan* contains excellent portraits of several Confucian academies.

There are several fine studies of individual Confucians and translations of their writings. Among the former, Kate Wildman Nakai (1988), *Shogunal Politics:Arai Hakuseki and the Premises of Tokugawa Rule*; Herman Ooms (1975), *Charismatic Bureaucrat: A Political Biography of Matsudaira Sadanobu*; Olaf Lidin (1973), *The Life of Ogyū Sorai, a Tokugawa Confucian Philosopher*; Mary Evelyn Tucker (1994), *Moral and Spiritual Cultivation in Japanese*

Neo-Confucianism: The Life and Thought of Kaibara Ekken 1630–1714; James McMullen (1999), *Idealism, Protest, and The Tale of Genji: The Confucianism of Kumazawa Banzan (1619–91)*; and Beatrice Bodart Bailey (2006), *The Dog Shogun: The Personalities and Policies of Tokugawa Tsunayoshi* stand out. John Allen Tucker and Samuel Hideo Yamashita have produced exceptionally helpful translations of the writings of Itō Jinsai and Ogyū Sorai.

On the nativist (kokugaku) challenge, see my (1990), *Remembering Paradise: Nativism and Nostalgia in Eighteenth-Century Japan*, and on the later Mito School, see Bob Tadashi Wakabayashi (1986), *Anti-Foreignism and Western Learning: The New Theses of 1825*.

Notes

1. Chinese *li* 理 and *fa* 法. The Confucian terminology in this chapter appears in Japanese.
2. Wm. Theodore de Bary (1959).
3. Chinese *li* 理 and *qi* 氣.
4. Chinese *ren* 仁, *zhong* 忠, and *xin* 信.
5. M. Maruyama (1974).
6. S. N. Eisenstadt (1996).

4

What Is Confucianism?

Roger T. Ames

I want to contest the resistance among many contemporary scholars to thick cultural generalizations by attempting to answer the question: What is Confucianism? I would argue that the canopy of an always emerging cultural vocabulary is itself rooted in and grows out of a deep and relatively stable soil of unannounced assumptions sedimented over generations into the language, customs, and life forms of a living tradition. And further, I would argue that to fail to acknowledge this fundamental character of cultural difference as an erstwhile safeguard against the sins of either "essentialism" or "relativism" is not innocent. Indeed, like the preacher who, come Monday, commits the very sins he railed against the day before, this antagonism to cultural generalizations leads to the uncritical essentializing of one's own contingent cultural assumptions and to the insinuating of them into interpretations of other traditions.[1]

Taking this claim regarding a resilient indigenous impulse—what we might call a cultural common sense—as a starting point, we might define Confucianism as the always changing yet still persistent cultural core or *daotong* 道統 of the Chinese population itself, and then by extension and in different degree, of the sinitic cultures of Korea, Japan, and Vietnam. Interestingly, a porous yet enduring Confucianism thus understood predates the historical figure of Confucius himself. In fact, Confucius allows as much, claiming that he is a cultural transmitter rather than an innovator who has inherited the substance of his philosophy from the legacy of the Zhou dynasty and earlier:

> The Master said, "Following the proper way, I do not forge new paths; with confidence I cherish the ancients—in these respects I would presume to compare myself with Old Peng."[2]

In fact, appreciating his modesty in demurring on the status of innovator, we have the evidence to comfortably assert that Confucius was both a transmitter and an innovator. In broad strokes Confucius does self-consciously continue a tradition that reaches back into the second millennium BCE:

> The Master said: "The Zhou dynasty looked back to the Xia and Shang dynasties. Such a wealth of culture! I follow the Zhou."[3]

But Confucius is also responsible for initiating the transformation of key notions such as *ren* 仁 (consummate person/conduct), *junzi* 君子 (exemplary person), *yi* 義 (optimizing appropriateness), and *li* 禮 (propriety in one's roles and relations) into a defining Confucian philosophical terminology. Again, it is Confucius who grounds Confucian role ethics and the vision of the moral life in family feeling (*xiao* 孝), and who establishes personal cultivation as the basic Confucian project.

David Keightley, in his lifetime study of Shang dynasty divination practices, provides us with retrospective insight into the substance of the cultural legacy that was transmitted by Confucius from earlier times. He claims that "the origins of much that is thought to be characteristically Chinese may be identified in the ethos and world view of its Bronze Age diviners."[4] Indeed,

> [I]t is possible for the modern historian to infer from the archaeological, artistic, and written records of the Shang some of the theoretical strategies and presuppositions by which the Bronze Age elite of the closing centuries of the second millennium BC ordered their existence.[5]

Keightley would insist that certain presuppositions of the Shang culture evolved to become further articulated in what we take to be the formative period of classical Chinese philosophy:

> The glimpse that the oracle-bones inscriptions afford us of metaphysical conceptions in the eleventh and tenth centuries BC suggests that the philosophical tensions that we associate primarily with the Taoism [Daoism] and Confucianism of Eastern Chou [Zhou] had already appeared, in different form, in the intellectual history of China, half a millennium earlier.[6]

Keightley perceives the structure of language itself to be a resource that can be mined to reveal a vein of cultural assumptions and importances:

Without necessarily invoking the Sapir-Whorf hypothesis of linguistic relativity, one can still imagine that the grammar of the Shang inscriptions has much to tell us about Shang conceptions of reality, particularly about the forces of nature.[7]

What, then, specifically are these underlying assumptions that Keightley has identified and recovered in his archaeology of Shang dynasty culture? What is the common sense—the uncommon assumptions, the deep cultural stratum—that persists and is being transmitted as the ancient Chinese worldview? Keightley contrasts a Chinese cosmology of ceaseless process with a classical Greek worldview in which a metaphysical transcendentalism guarantees an idealized reality:

> Put crudely, we find in classical Greece a Platonic metaphysics of certainties, ideal forms, and right answers, accompanied by complex, tragic, and insoluble tensions in the realm of ethics. The metaphysical foundations being firm, the moral problems were intensely real, and as inexplicable as reality itself. To the early Chinese, however, if reality was forever changeable, man could not assume a position of tragic grandeur and maintain his footing for long. The moral heroism of the Confucians of Eastern Chou [Zhou] was not articulated in terms of any tragic flaw in the nature of the world or man. This lack of articulation, I believe, may be related to a significant indifference to the metaphysical foundation of Confucian ethics.[8]

Positively, Keightley ascribes to these divinatory sources what is today being described by many interpreters of classical China as a distinctively Chinese mode of "correlative thinking." According to his reading, oracle-bone divination subscribed to

> a theology and metaphysics that conceived of a world of alternating modes, pessimistic at times, optimistic at others, but with the germs of one mode always inherent in the other. Shang metaphysics, at least as revealed in the complementary forms of the Wu Ting [Ding] inscriptions, was a metaphysics of yin and yang.[9]

Keightley appeals to the *pien-hua* (Pinyin *bianhua* 變化) understanding of this process of change as articulated in the "Great Commentary" to the *Yijing*—a rhythm of "alternation and transformation"—as a later expression of the modality of change already present in Shang dynasty metaphysics. This notion of change is articulated in the language of symbiotic bipolar opposites that entail each other, and together constitute the whole.[10]

The origins of correlative thinking, dating back at least into the Shang dynasty, is a dominant modality of thinking that advances in both complexity and explanatory force through a proliferation and aggregation of productive dyadic associations, novel metaphors, suggestive images, and evocative patterns, all of which are weighed, measured, and tested in ordinary experience. And it is this way of thinking inherited by Confucius and further articulated by him and his protégés, and then continued by the tradition following in their wake, that becomes the core of the vision of the moral life we have come to call "Confucianism."

Confucian is a cultural legacy with ancient roots, but it also branches out across the centuries down to our present day. Tang Junyi (1909–1978) was one of China's great contemporary philosophers, and still decades after his death, has something compelling to say to the question of "What is Confucianism?" To my mind, Tang Junyi's foremost contribution to world philosophy is his synoptic philosophy of culture: his ability to discern and articulate, with truly penetrating acuity, as clear a contrast as can be established between the presuppositions grounding the metaphysical thinking that has had such prominent play in the Western philosophical narrative, and those persistent cosmological assumptions that ground correlative thinking and continue to shape an always changing Chinese worldview. He is able to argue effectively for a range of uncommon assumptions that, giving the lie to the homogenization of Enlightenment universalism, must be taken into account if we are to allow this Confucian cultural narrative its many unique and important contributions.

In this chapter, I will appeal to several propositions that Tang Junyi offers us as a way of recovering and rehearsing an interpretive context within which the Confucian philosophical narrative has evolved. I will then apply the substance of these same propositions in explicating some of the defining Confucian terms of art—that is, the vocabulary of family reverence (*xiao*), consummate person/conduct (*ren*), exemplary person (*junzi*), propriety in ritualized roles and relations (*li*), and optimizing appropriateness (*yi*)—that have been used over the centuries to ground and promote Confucian philosophical thinking. Said another way, I would suggest that this enduring Confucian vocabulary can only be understood within the context of a persisting cultural common sense that Tang Junyi is attempting to make explicit in positing this set of propositions.

In delineating the cosmological background of the Confucian tradition, Tang Junyi takes a holographic, interdependent, and productive relationship between "part" and "whole"—a conception of organismic relationality as *the* distinguishing feature and most crucial contribution of Chinese culture broadly. As the underlying character of Chinese culture, Tang Junyi endorses a philosophical holism that entails

> the spirit of symbiosis and mutuality of particular and whole. From the perspective of understanding this means an unwillingness to isolate the particular from the whole (this is most evident in the cosmology of the Chinese people), and from the perspective of ties of feeling and affection, it means the commitment of the particular to do its best to realize the whole (this is most evident in the attitude of the Chinese people toward daily life).[11]

Tang Junyi uses "particulars" and "whole" here, but such a characterization of the underlying cosmology would be more consistent with his own propositions if he were to use the language of "foci" and "fields," or "ecologically situated events" and their "environments," an alternative vocabulary that entails an assumption about the intrinsic, constitutive nature of relations. We might appeal to the concrete image of this person constituted by these family relations to bring clarity to his abstract description of the relationship between "particular" and "whole." When this idea of optimizing the collaterality and interdependence of what Tang Junyi calls "particulars" and "whole" is translated into the more concrete social and political arena of the human community, it becomes the value of inclusive, consensual, and optimally productive cooperation that emerges from the ground of family feeling.

This wholeness and processual nature of the human experience is captured in several of Tang Junyi's characterizations of Chinese natural cosmology. In framing this philosophical holism, he begins with the Confucian affirmation of the reality and sufficiency of empirical experience and its resistance to any supernaturalism that would seek to go beyond it. In his first proposition—"the notion that there is no fixed substance [無定體觀]"—he rejects outright the relevance of any notion of permanent substratum, and in so doing, acknowledges the fluidity of *qi* 氣 in its ceaseless flux and flow.[12] In *Analects* 9.17 Confucius waxes cosmological:

> The Master was standing on the riverbank, and observed, "Isn't life's passing just like this, never ceasing day or night!"

But this *qi* cosmology is not a reductionistic "one-behind-the-many" monism. Particulars are real. In the absence of any essentializing substratum—"what -it-means-to-be-this-kind of a thing"—and without any "things" that can be parsed as indivisibles into a taxonomy of natural kinds, the human experience is constituted by resolutely unique perturbations of *qi*—what is often referred to as the "myriad of things" (*wanwu* 萬物 or *wanyou* 萬有). Entailed by the uniqueness of each particular as a nexus of specific relations is the absence of any notion of strict identity—no two things are the same. Further, given the intrinsic nature of relatedness, putative "things" that are constituted by their relationships stand in relation to each other as currents in a stream of unique, mutually conditioning "events"—a manifold of events that have ontological parity within the unsummed totality of things. And the web of always shifting relationships that constitutes each "event" is itself a novel and unique construal of the totality—that is, "this" particular focus of "this" particular field of experience.

Using the more traditional Confucian vocabulary, we might say that the manifold or totality of these events is *dao* 道 and the unique "events" themselves are insistently particular foci or *de* 德 that are constitutive of *dao* and that construe the totality from their own perspectives. Importantly, the foci and their unfolding field constitute an always dynamic process. Indeed, the processual flow of experience without initial beginning or end is what Tang Junyi, appealing to language from the *Book of Changes* or *Yijing*, describes as "the notion of ceaseless procreation [生生不已觀]."[13] The human experience is persistent, historicist, and naturalistic in the sense of being autogenerative and emergent without appeal to any metaphysical or supernatural source.

Tang Junyi's corollary to this "notion of ceaseless procreation" is the irrelevance of any kind of hard determinism for Confucian cosmology that would make time stand still—what he terms "the notion of non-fatalism [非定命觀]."[14] Experience is the bottomless unfolding of an emergent, contingent world according to the rhythm of its own internal creative processes without any fixed pattern or guiding hand. Tang Junyi, aware that a teleologically predetermined universe would preclude the possibility of any meaningful notion of temporality, sees time itself as inseparable from the emerging world of unique "things." Indeed, genuine change—that is, life as the spontaneous emergence of novelty in the unique relations that are constitutive of things—is just another way of saying genuine time.

The penumbra of indeterminacy that honeycombs an always provisional cosmic order means that erstwhile forms and functions entail each other in their continuous process of forming and functioning, where all form is constantly undergoing adjustment to maintain functional equilibrium, and is ultimately vulnerable to and outrun by the process itself. There is nothing that does not give way ultimately to trans-*form*-ation.

This transformative character of the Chinese cosmology undergirding Confucianism is described by Tang Junyi with two additional propositions: "the notion that nothing advances but to return [無往不復觀]," and the "the notion that there is a continuity that obtains between determinacy and indeterminacy, motion and equilibrium [合有無動靜觀]."[15] Tang Junyi in describing Chinese cosmology references "the world as such"—a unique and boundless world within which the observer is always reflexively embedded. In his language:

> When Chinese philosophers speak of the world, they are thinking of the world that we are living in. There is no world beyond or outside of the one we are experiencing. . . . They are not referencing "*a* world" or "*the* world," but are simply saying "world as such" without putting any indefinite or definite article in front of it.[16]

Without an external standpoint for asserting objective truths about the world, subjects are always reflexively implicated in the way in which they organize the world. As a consequence, saying something about the world is always a matter of selected interest that says something about one's own self-understanding. The absence of a basis for making objective statements makes fact and value interdependent and mutually entailing, and makes objective definition and simple description problematic. The values of the always interested observer are implicated in the observation. The line, then, that divides science from art, chemistry from alchemy, astronomy from astrology, geology from geomancy, and psychology from physiognomy, is always tenuous. Indeed, the distance between description and prescription becomes a matter of the degree of one's own self-consciousness.

The related proposition that underscores the contingent nature of emerging order is its underdeterminacy. That is, there is an indeterminate aspect (*ji* 幾) entailed by the uniqueness of each participant that qualifies order, making any pattern of order novel and site-specific, irreversible, reflexive, and in degree, unpredictable. All human beings might be similar enough to justify certain generalizations, yet each person is at the same time a unique, *one* of a kind. It is this uniqueness of each person that precludes the possibility of any logarithmic understanding of human conduct, and that keeps the definition of humanity an open-ended and ongoing proposition.

As we can see from this set of propositions, Tang Junyi's characterization of the cosmology that grounds Confucianism is resolutely hierarchical, historicist, particularist, and emergent. Tang Junyi takes as a generic feature of the Chinese processual cosmology: "the inseparability of the one and the many, of uniqueness and multivalence, of continuity and multiplicity, of integrity and integration [一多不分觀]."[17] Importantly, this notion of intrinsic relationality is an aspect of Chinese natural cosmology that is organically related to the other propositions described above. In procreativity, such a characterization is only another way of affirming the inseparability of *paisheng* 派生 and *huasheng* 化生—of the derivation of the unique particular and of its transformation into something else in an ongoing process.

Cosmologically, this proposition asserts that any phenomenon in our field of experience can be focused in many different ways. On the one hand it is a unique and persistent particular, and on the other, it has the entire cosmos and all that is happening implicated within its own intensive and extensive patterns of relationships. For example, persons begin their careers as inchoately both one and many. That is, persons at their inception as human beings have little to distinguish themselves, and usually passively defer to the care of a small circle of family intimates. Over time, they have the opportunity to become increasingly distinctive as personalities, and to develop a widening and deepening field of constitutive relations. They are "one" both in the unbroken continuity they have in their relations with their environing others, and in their subsequent unique, emerging individuality, and yet at the same time they are a divided and sometimes conflicted "multiplicity" in the field of selves through which their many personas are manifested: someone's parent and someone else's child, someone's colleague and someone's else's adversary, someone's teacher and someone else's lover, someone's benefactor and someone else's judge. Using a Confucian vocabulary, we might describe the emergence of a distinguished member of the community from being a mere person (*ren* 人) to becoming a person of real distinction (*daren* 大人) through a consummate relational virtuosity (*ren* 仁).

Given that order is an always negotiated, emergent, and provisional harmony contingent upon those elements that constitute it, it is neither linear nor disciplined toward some given end. Hence, Confucian harmony (*he* 和) is not expressible in the language of completion, perfection, or closure. Rather, harmonious order is an aesthetic achievement made possible through *ars contextualis*, "the art of contextualizing," and hence is most appropriately expressible in an aesthetic language of elegance, complexity, intensity, balance, disclosure, efficacy, and so on. As we read in the *Analects* 1.12:

> Achieving harmony (*he* 和) is the most valuable function of observing propriety in one's roles and relations (*li* 禮). In the ways of the Former Kings, this achievement of harmony through observing propriety made them elegant, and was a guiding standard in all things large and small. But when things are not going well, to realize harmony just for its own sake without regulating the situation through observing propriety will not work.

Without appeal to some originative principle and the linear teleology that comes with it, the world has no governing purpose, no pre-assigned design. And the alternative to some given and governing purpose is localized and temporalized self-sufficiency—getting the most out of each situation. This then is the meaning of harmony.

Perhaps the most fundamental consideration in Confucian philosophy is a reflection on the nature and the possibilities of the human experience itself as an achieved harmony. Tang Junyi invokes yet another feature of Chinese cosmology that underscores the vectoral yet contingent nature of the human experience that is fundamental to the Confucian project of personal consummation. For Tang Junyi, "human nature" is a function of the ongoing propensity of circumstances—a provisional disposition that is both persistent and always under revision in its interactions with other things. In Tang Junyi's own words, Chinese cosmology entails the notion that "human nature is nothing but the natural and cultural processes themselves [性即天道觀]." He clarifies what he sees as a continuing dynamic process:

> Within Chinese natural cosmology what is held in general is not some first principle. The root pattern or coherence [根本之理] of anything is its "life force [生理]," and this life force is its "natural tendencies [性]." Anything's natural tendencies are expressed in the quality of its interactions with other things. Natural tendencies and life force then being principles of freedom and transformation have nothing to do with necessity. . . . What is held in general is the product of experience. . . . The emergence of any particular phenomenon is a function of the interaction between its prior conditions and other things . . . and is not determined by the thing itself. . . . Thus the basic "nature" of anything includes this transformability and malleability.[18]

To illustrate this notion of contingent, relational emergence, Tang Junyi provides a gloss on the familiar *Zhongyong* passage—"what *tian* [conventionally translated 'Heaven'] commands is called natural tendencies [天命之謂性]." In providing a context for the easily misinterpreted claims of this passage, he cites the *Zuozhuan*: "It is people being born into the conditions of the world that is meant by *ming*—the propensity of circumstances [民受天地之中以生乃所謂命也]." Tang Junyi states explicitly:

> What is meant by this claim is not that *tian* according to a certain fixed fate determines the conduct and progress of human beings. Indeed it endows human beings with a natural disposition that, being more or less free of the mechanical control of one's previous habits and of external intervening forces, within its context undergoes a creative advance that is expressive of this freedom.[19]

All teleological and genetic assumptions have to be qualified by the spontaneous emergence of novelty within any specific context, and by a creative advance in the situation's continuing present. "Human nature" for Tang Junyi then, is the aggregating yet open-ended disposition of human beings over time, and is an expression of the ongoing attainment of relational virtuosity, or *ren* 仁, within our inherited natural and cultural legacy, *tiandao* 天道.

The Confucian conception of consummate conduct (*ren* 仁) is the determining source of what it means to become human. In Tang Junyi's extensive work on "human nature" (*renxing* 人性), he demonstrates a great sensitivity to the existential coloring of the classical Confucian conception of the human being. For Tang Junyi, "in speaking of a thing's *xing*, what is important is not to say what the *xing* of this entity is, but to say what the vectoral direction of its existence is. It is only in that it has growth that it has *xing*."[20] And among things, the human being is a special case.

The *xing* 性 of human beings cannot be approached in the same way as the *xing* of other phenomena because humans have an internal perspective on their own constitution that is not available to them in the investigation of other things. In reflecting on the relationships between experience and conceptualization, Tang Junyi asserts that:

> Coming to know the human possibility is not like seeking to know the possibilities of other things that can, on the basis of inference and hypothesis, be known objectively. Rather it comes from the way in which persons realize their internal aspirations and how they come to know them. Once we have an understanding of this human *xing*, we will of our own accord surely have the linguistic concepts through which to express it. Such linguistic conceptualization follows upon what is known of it, and is formed continuously as the opportunity presents itself. It is not the case that we first have conceptualizations to which we then add conjectures, anticipations, or presumptions.[21]

Tang Junyi thus emphasizes the primacy of the realization of the human aspirations over the conceptualization and articulation of them, giving full notice to the personal locus of that realization. He disassociates the conversation among classical Confucian philosophers over the meaning of *xing* from the contemporary science of psychology by asserting that, in the latter case, there is a desire to treat the human being descriptively as an objective phenomenon. For Tang Junyi, it is the existential project that is the fundamental distinguishing characteristic of the classical Confucian conception of *xing*, and whence we derive our understanding of it. In fact, it is precisely the indeterminate possibility for creative change that Tang Junyi identifies as the most salient feature of the human *xing*. He says that where *xing* in reference to some "thing" might refer to stable characteristics, properties, or propensities, from the perspective of the embodied idea that we have of human beings in relationship to their world, there is a real question as to whether or not human beings have any fixed nature. This is because the world and the idea that human beings face both entail limitless change. . . . The discussion of the human *xing* in Chinese thought has had as its one common feature the reference to this locus for boundless change in which it locates the special *xing* of the human being. This then is the human's spiritual *xing* [靈性] that differs from the fixity and lack of spirituality in the *xing* of other things.[22]

What is understood as the generalized initial condition in the *xing* of persons is most importantly the propensity for growth, cultivation, and refinement.[23] *Xing*, then, denotes the human capacity for radical changeability that is qualitatively productive.

In Tang Junyi's general discussion of *xing*, he notices that *xing* often has two referents: it refers to the continuing existence of a particular thing itself, and also refers that which in a thing continues the life of other things.[24] He cites an example from the *Zuozhuan* in which the *xing* of the soil lies not only in its own conditions, but also in its propensity to grow things conducive to *human* life.[25] It is thus that throughout Tang Junyi's analysis, especially in reference to the human being, he underscores the fundamental relationality of *xing*:

> It is my opinion that in looking at the beginnings of a theory of *xing* in China's early philosophers, the basic point was not to take the human being or its *xing* as some objective thing that can be looked at and discussed in terms of its universal nature or its special nature or its possibilities. As humans perceived the myriad things and heaven and earth, and as they perceived their inner thoughts about the human being that they embodied, what was important for them was to reflect on what the *xing* of this human being is, and what the *xing* of heaven and earth and the myriad things is. The way the human being was perceived within the mainstream of Chinese thought was as a kind of thing amidst and among the myriad things, and not just as one kind of the myriad things.[26]

Tang Junyi's definition of the *xing* of human beings in terms of their ongoing relations within their several environments exemplifies his proposition that "the one and the many are inseparable" and at the same time challenges the common interpretation of *xing* as a "given" essence or *telos*—some innate endowment present in us from birth.

Tang Junyi's processual understanding of "human nature" takes seriously both components of this graph *xing* 性: both "heart-mind" (*xin* 心) and "growth" (*sheng* 生). In other words, "human nature" (性) as an achievement is "the birth, growth, and life" (生) of the personal and communal "heart-mind" (心). In this Confucian tradition, we might say that *becoming* human is made explicit when *xin* is taken as the generalized initial conditions (what we are conventionally inclined to consider inherent "nature") and *xing* is construed as the ongoing cultivation and articulation of these initial conditions through effective social living (what we would generally consider as "second nature").[27] The important point here is that Confucianism would place an emphasis upon an aggregating "second nature" as the primary locus of culture and the resource for the enculturation of succeeding generations. When we ask the question, "Who comes first, parent or child, teacher or student?" the answer must be that as correlatives these dyads are isomorphic, emerging simultaneously as the context for each other. This is also the case with "first" and "second" nature. After all, there can be no "first nature" that is not embedded within "second nature" as its initial conditions, and there is no "second nature" that is not grounded in and ultimately the product of a cultivated "first nature."

Tang Junyi makes much of how Confucian culture is rooted in the everyday lives of the people and the natural deference that pervades family living.[28] For Tang Junyi, the meaning and value of family relations is not simply the primary ground of social order—it has cosmological and religious implications as well. Family bonds properly observed are the point of departure for understanding that we each have moral responsibility for an expanding web of relations that reach far beyond our own localized selves.[29] The family is the center of cosmic order, and as we see in the *Great Learning*, all order ripples out in concentric circles from and returns to nourish this primary source. In the *Zhongyong* 20 we are told explicitly that family feeling is the source of the civility fostered by our ritualized roles and institutions:

> Consummate conduct [*ren* 仁] means conducting oneself like a human being [*ren* 人], wherein devotion to one's kin is most important. Optimal appropriateness [*yi* 義] means doing what is most fitting [*yi* 宜], wherein esteeming those of superior character is most important. The degree of devotion due different kin and the degree of esteem accorded those who are different in character is what gives rise to propriety in one's roles and relations (*li* 禮).[30]

In the Confucian worldview, family is *the* governing metaphor. In fact *all* relationships are familial. The signature of Confucianism is that human morality is an expression of immediate family feeling—what Tang Junyi calls the natural life-force (*shengli* 生理). At the very beginning of the *Analects* we read:

> It is a rare thing for someone who has a sense of family reverence and fraternal deference (*xiaoti* 孝弟) to have a taste for defying authority. And it is unheard of for those who have no taste for defying authority to be keen on initiating rebellion. Exemplary persons concentrate their efforts on the root, for the root having taken hold, the way will grow therefrom. As for family reverence and fraternal deference, it is, I suspect, the root of consummate conduct (*ren* 仁).

The underlying wisdom in this Confucian tradition is that family is the single human institution to which persons are most likely to give themselves utterly, and without remainder. To transform the world into a family, according to the Confucian sensibility, is to promote the model that will best accomplish the goal of getting the most out of your constitutive relations by applying the logic that when your sibling does better, you do better, and by extension, when your neighbor does better, you do better.

For Tang Junyi, as we have seen, Confucianism is not rooted in some exclusionary idealism or privileged revelation. Instead, it appeals to an inclusive particularism available to everyone that is expressed rather simply in the *Analects* passage: "Studying what is near at hand, I aspire to what is most lofty [下學而上達]."[31] Given the relational focus-field nature of person, this is a formula for everyone-in-community aspiring to become their own best thoughts. Tang Junyi's Confucianism—his vision of the flourishing communal life made possible by the contributions of the uniquely distinguished persons that constitute it—is a pragmatic naturalism directed at achieving the highest integrated cultural, moral, and spiritual growth for the individual-in-community.

As an expression of the highest form of this achievement, the familiar Confucian claim that "everyone can become a sage"[32] is often read essentialistically as an assertion that the sage is some universally given potential in human nature that if actualized provides every person with those extraordinary talents through which to affect the world in some incomparable way—the assertion that "every human being is like that." We have seen that Tang Junyi's processual understanding of "human nature" precludes this possibility. Indeed, for him this same claim that "everyone can become a sage" is an assertion that the spontaneous emergence of real significance in the ordinary business of the day is itself the meaning and content of sagely virtuosity, and that "only if you achieve this virtuosity can you be considered a sage."[33] It is not individuated and discrete human beings that have the innate potential for sagehood; rather, it is through optimizing the potential that resides within the transactional human experience that sages emerge as distinguished persons. Indeed, those ordinary persons who in their own lives achieve *real* significance are sages. What these Confucian texts claim is that all of us have the opportunity to live such significant lives.

In Confucianism, optimal relationality is expressed in the notion of "propriety in observing ritualized roles and relationships" (*li* 禮) that has its origins specifically in "family reverence" (*xiao* 孝).[34] Tang Junyi describes the function of *li* in the following terms:

> When the "Ritualizing Experience" [禮運] chapter of the *Book of Rites* discusses the ideal of the era of Great Harmony [大同], what is intended is simply that everyone should get what they deserve.... Persons in the process of realizing this purpose must participate fully in their symbiotic ritualized roles and relations before each person can get what they should out of these relationships.[35]

After all, Confucian "harmony" is fundamentally participatory and inclusive, and must be distinguished from indiscriminately enforcing social order. The ultimate goal is to produce a self-regulating community in which everyone develops a sense of belonging and takes responsibility for everyone else:

> Lead the people with excellence (*de* 德) and promote social order through the observance of ritual propriety (*li* 禮) and they will develop a sense of shame, and moreover, will order themselves.[36]

On the informal and uniquely personal side, full participation in a ritually constituted community requires the personalization and reauthorization of prevailing customs, institutions, and values. What makes ritual profoundly different from law or rule is this process of making the tradition one's own. The Latin *proprius*, "making something one's own" as in "appropriate" or "property," gives us a series of cognate expressions that are useful in translating key Confucian philosophical terms to capture this sense of participation and personalization: *yi* 義 is not "righteousness" as compliance with some external divine directive, but rather is "appropriateness" as "a sense of what is most fitting" for me and everyone else in this particular communal context. *Zheng* 正 is not "rectification" or "correct conduct"—again, an appeal to some external standard—but "proper conduct" as determined by this person within this context. *Zheng* 政 is not simply "government" but "governing properly," and *li* ("ritual propriety") is not just "what is ritually appropriate," but "*personally doing* what is ritually appropriate."[37]

A careful reading of the classical Confucian literature uncovers a way of life carefully choreographed down to appropriate facial expressions and physical gestures, a world in which a life is a performance requiring enormous attention to detail. Importantly, this *li*-constituted performance begins from the insight that personal refinement is only possible through the discipline provided by formalized roles and behaviors. Form without creative personalization is coercive and dehumanizing law; creative personal expression without form is randomness at best, and license at worst. It is only with the appropriate combination of form and functional personalization that family and community can be self-regulating and refined.

Of course, the Confucian appeal to family as the organizing metaphor for the human experience is not altogether benign. Indeed, the preponderant emphasis upon family feeling as the source of the Confucian vision of the moral life has led many to worry that so much personal investment in what is immediately at hand leaves little human resources for the civil society. As Bertrand Russell opines:

> Filial piety, and the strength of the family generally, are perhaps the weakest point in Confucian ethics, the only point where the system departs seriously from common sense. Family feeling has militated against public spirit, and the authority of the old has increased the tyranny of ancient custom.[38]

Although a community modeled on family might sound liberating, at the same time, it can also be a disintegrative source of nepotism, cronyism, parochialism, and corruption. Russell's assumption here is that the intimacy of family feeling is a universal stage in civilization, but one that, in the fullness of time, is properly superseded:

> Filial piety is, of course, in no way peculiar to China, but has been universal at a certain stage of culture. In this respect, as in certain others, what is peculiar to China is the preservation of the old custom after a very high level of civilization had been attained. The early Greeks and Romans did not differ from the Chinese in this respect, but as their civilization advanced the family became less and less important. In China, this did not begin to happen until our own day.[39]

This problem alluded to here by Russell—that is, the fact that there are many important dimensions of the human experience that require transparency, impartiality, and regulative ideals—has not been entirely lost on the Confucian tradition. Beginning with the distinction between "optimal appropriateness (*yi* 義)" and "personal advantage (*li* 利)" that we find as early as the *Analects* and the *Mencius*, Confucianism has struggled with the seemingly necessary relationship between ethical conduct and impartiality.[40] But rather than invoking some transcendental moral standard or the functioning of impersonal reason as a strategy for claiming such impartiality—a strategy that is hobbled by the contingencies of circumstances—the Confucian tradition remains true to the family metaphor. Impartiality is served practically by extending one's range of concern from "the master's-eye view" (*zhuguan* 主觀) that is self-serving personal advantage (*li* 利) to "the guest's-eye view" (*keguan* 客觀) that seeks what is most appropriate for all concerned (*yi* 義). The Confucian formula of "putting oneself in the other's place" (*shu* 恕) and then "doing one's best" (*zhong* 忠) is another variation on this deferential attempt to keep one's range of concern open in determining what is moral.

In summary, in our contemporary era, perhaps the most profound insight Confucianism has to offer the world today lies in prompting us to rethink the role of family as the ground and primary site of the moral life and by extension, of a truly robust democracy. Ironically, we might argue that at the same time, inopportune intimacy in relations is also China's primary obstacle on its own road to democratization. With so much investment in intimate and informal familial relationships, the Confucian tradition has been slow to produce the formal, more "objective" institutions necessary to sustain a Confucian version of democracy, and when it has produced them, these same institutions are often compromised and eroded by the excessive intervention of personal relationships.

While the familiar appeal to universals might suffer from the ambiguity of practical applications, the Confucian attempt to extend consideration to all involved is handicapped by the need for more abstract regulative ideals such as fairness and justice that provide direction for what is a legitimate claim for consideration and inclusion. Indeed, as democracy emerges in China, the cure for the ills of a decidedly Confucian democracy might well be an appeal to rule of law and the formal institutions of democracy to contain the excesses of family feeling.

Suggestions for Further Reading

In addition to the works cited in the notes, a broad overview of Confucianism is available in John Berthrong's (1998) *Transformations of the Confucian Way*. For a conceptual overview, see Antonio S. Cua, ed. (2002), *Encyclopedia of Chinese Philosophy*, and for an interpretive philosophical exploration of the ideas of Confucius, see David L. Hall and Roger T. Ames (1987), *Thinking*

Through Confucius, and the sequels to it, *Anticipating China* (1995) and *Thinking From the Han* (1998). For gender issues, there is Li-hsiang Lisa Rosenlee's (2007) *Confucianism and Women: A Philosophical Interpretation*. On Confucian attitudes toward the environment, see Mary Evelyn Tucker and John Berthrong, eds. (1998), *Confucianism and Ecology: The Interrelation of Heaven, Earth, and Humans*. On the religious dimension of Confucianism, see Tu Wei-ming and Mary Evelyn Tucker, eds. (2004), *Confucian Spirituality*.

Notes

1. One might argue that the bugbear of "essentialism" is itself a culturally specific worry. Essentialism arises from familiar classical Greek assumptions about ontology as "the science of being," and from the application of strict identity (or "essences") as the principle of individuation that follows from such an ontology. The well-intended and hugely erudite scholar Zhang Longxi is concerned that the assertion of radical difference he quite properly ascribes to my interpretation of Chinese language and culture leads to "relativism" and thus incommensurability. In promoting his alternative version of cultural translation, he insists that: "Against such an overemphasis on difference and cultural uniqueness, however, I would like to argue for the basic translatability of languages and cultures. . . . Only when we acknowledge different peoples and nations as equal in their ability to think, to express, to communicate, and to create values, we may then rid ourselves of ethnocentric biases" (Zhang Longxi 1999, 46). The claim about being "equal" in the ability to think might sound inclusive and liberating, but it is anything but innocent. Why would we assume the possibility that other traditions have culturally specific modalities of thinking is claiming that they do not know how to think unless we believe that our way of thinking is in fact the only way? Further, the uncritical assumption that other cultures must think the same way that I do is for me the very definition of ethnocentrism. I would argue that it is precisely the recognition and appreciation of the degree of difference obtaining among cultures that properly motivates cultural translation in the first place, and that ultimately rewards the effort. Indeed, arguing that there are culturally contingent modalities of thinking can be pluralistic rather than relativistic, and accommodating rather than condescending. At the very least, we must strive with imagination to take other cultures on their own terms if comparative studies is to provide us with the mutual enrichment that it promises.

2. Translating *shu* 述 as "to follow the proper way" enables us to maintain the "path" (*dao* 道) metaphor that it suggests. Throughout the early corpus, the term "to initiate" *zuo* 作 is frequently associated with "sageliness" *sheng* 聖. Hence Confucius's description of himself here is an expression of modesty. "Old Peng" is Peng Zu 彭祖, a minister during the Shang dynasty who legend has it lived to be some eight hundred years old. With the name "Peng Zu"—literally "Peng Ancestor"—and with his remarkable longevity, he is emblematic of historical continuity. See *Mozi* 63/39/19 and 81/46/50 where Confucius is taken at his word as being wholly a transmitter, and is criticized for offering the world a lifeless conservatism. This Mohist criticism of Confucianism

is alive and well in contemporary scholarship. Ted Slingerland in interpreting this passage is not alone in suggesting that Confucianism is fundamentally retrospective, harkening back to a Zhou dynasty Golden Age. As he observes: "It is more likely that transmission is all that Confucius countenanced for people in his age, since the sagely Zhou kings established the ideal set of institutions that perfectly accord with human needs"; see Slingerland (2003), 64. Hsiao Kung-chuan (1979), 79–142 describes this same Confucian conservatism at length as "emulating the past" 法古.

    3. *Analects* 3.14. See also *Analects* 8.20. All translations from the *Analects* are mine; chapter and passage numbers refer to all standard editions.

    4. David N. Keightley (1988), 389. Keightley here is positing a position shared by several of our most distinguished interpreters of the Shang dynasty, including Kwang-chih Chang (1964) and Marcel Granet (1977).

    5. Keightley (1988), 367.

    6. Ibid., 388.

    7. Ibid., 389 n1.

    8. Ibid., 376.

    9. Ibid., 377.

    10. Ibid., 374–75.

    11. Tang Junyi (1988b), 11:8. Quotes from Tang Junyi are my translations. This passage restated positively is an expression of the *yinyang* 陰陽 correlativity ubiquitous in Chinese cosmology that, in one of its most abstract iterations appearing first in the Wang Bi commentary on the *Daodejing*, entails the "continuity between reforming and functioning" (*tiyong heyi* 體用合一).

    12. Tang Junyi (1988b), 11:9–11.

    13. Ibid., 20–22.

    14. Ibid., 17–19.

    15. Ibid., 11–16.

    16. Tang Junyi (1988a), 101–103.

    17. Tang Junyi (1988b), 11:16–17.

    18. Tang Junyi (1988b), 4:98–100.

    19. Ibid., 100.

    20. Tang Junyi (1988b), 13:28.

    21. Ibid., 22.

    22. Ibid., 24.

    23. I avoid the word *innate* because it can be read as a reference to some nonempirical, essential condition that is of or produced by the mind rather than by experience. It is better to think of *xing* as those generalizable initial conditions we experience at birth within the family context.

    24. Tang Junyi (1988b), 13:28–29.

    25. Tang Junyi (1988b), 13:29 cites this passage from *Zuozhuan* Duke Zhao 25. He also cites the example of medicine that is most often defined in terms of its effects on the human subject.

    26. Tang Junyi, (1988b), 11:3.

    27. See Tang Junyi (1988b), 13:27–32. Perhaps the most persistent feature of scholars who offer an essentialistic understanding of the Mencian notion of *renxing*

人性 is their failure to distinguish clearly between heart-mind 心 as initial conditions and natural tendencies 性 as the vectoral growth of these conditions.

28. Tang Junyi (1988b), 4:219–302.

29. Ibid., 210–15.

30. My translation. Note the paronomastic definitions for *ren* and *yi*: that is, definition by semantic and phonetic association.

31. *Analects* 14.35.

32. See *Mencius* 2A2 and 6A7, or *Xunzi* 88/23/29 in Knoblock (1994), 3:154.

33. I owe this language distinguishing an essential theory of human nature from an achievement theory to Carine Defoort.

34. I translate *xiao* 孝 as "familial reverence" rather than "filial piety." "Family reverence" disassociates 孝 from the duty to God implied by "piety" and the top-down obedience that is assumed in *pater familias*. Also, "familial reverence" preserves the sacred connotations of 孝 that might have originally referred to a specific ancestral sacrifice.

35. Tang Junyi (1988b), 15:99.

36. *Analects* 2.3.

37. *Analects* 3.12: "The expression 'sacrifice as though present' is taken to mean 'sacrifice to the spirits as though the spirits are present.' But the Master said: 'If I myself do not participate in the sacrifice, it is as though I have not sacrificed at all.' "

38. Bertrand Russell (1922), 40.

39. Ibid., 41.

40. See for example *Analects* 4.16, 14.12, 14.13, 16.10, and 19.1, and *Mencius* 1A1, 2A2, 7A33, 7A34, 7B31.

5

Confucian Person in the Making

Wonsuk Chang

What does it mean to be human? As an explicit topic for philosophers in all time periods, understanding what it means to be a person has been the focus of philosophical controversies in the histories of both Western and Asian philosophy. The pervasiveness and persistence of this shows that implicitly, philosophical anthropology is at the bottom of many philosophical discussions: the relationship between individuals and communities, the place of humans in the world, the claims of ethics, and the meaning of happiness.

Answers to perennial philosophical questions about personhood vary according to cultures, epochs, and philosophical stances. "Know thyself," the maxim inscribed at the Delphic oracle and also identified with sayings of Socrates, is a recurring theme in the history of philosophy but at the same time expresses a uniquely Western philosophical way of framing this question.

When Socrates asks what it means to "know yourself" he uses the reflexive pronoun to point to the essence by which humans are universally defined. Greek minds, including Socrates, Plato, and Aristotle, share the assumption that there is a substantial essence or transcendental first principle giving order and meaning to temporal, contingent appearance. In the history of Western philosophy, there have been various views as to what constitutes this essence. The substance of the self has been conceived of as rationality by Greek philosophers, as the immortal soul in the Judeo-Christian tradition, as the Cartesian *res cogitans*, and as Kantian transcendental pure reason. In spite of their differences, these traditions share the assumption that there is a universal characteristic, quality, or property by which all humans can be defined. A major belief in the Western tradition since Greek times is this: it is self-evident that there is something called human nature, something that constitutes the universality of humanity. There are various views about what constitutes this nature, but there is agreement that such an essence exists. Furthermore, it follows that ethical conduct can be deduced from this essence. According to the Western philosophical project, if we can only recognize our essential nature, then we can act in accordance with it.

How does Confucianism frame the big questions of humanity? While the Western philosophical tradition poses the question, "What is essence of the humanity?" Confucius poses the more pragmatic question, "How does a person achieve meaning in a given situation?" While Western minds search for pure essences and transcendental reasons, Confucius begins his research within the matrix of the qualitatively permeated world of *qi* 氣. One of the distinctive features of the Confucian view of humans is a lack of interest in the universality of human nature. As we shall see in the following section, *xing* 性—one of the most important terms for the Confucian concept of the self—does not indicate a transcendental essence that all human beings share in common but a naturally arising disposition.

In the Confucian classics, we do not find definitions of the general qualities of human beings. Instead, we see an emphasis on different varieties of people and how they are interrelated with and distinguished from each other at their peculiar levels of self-cultivation in the concrete situations, roles, and relationships that constitute them. The *Book of Changes* (or *Yijing*) is populated by great persons, exemplary persons, sages, wise persons, retarded persons, village people, a one-eyed man, and other lame persons, as well as warriors, fathers, mothers, sons, daughters, husbands, wives, families, masses of people, bosses, dead men, lucky men, men in fellowships, flocks of merchants, and old ladies. Here, humans are not explicable by some single given design that underlies natural and moral order in the cosmos. Humans are concrete individuals participating in specific situations. Persons are not obliged to comply with objective and universal standards; instead they re-create themselves by maximizing their own potentials in response to changing environments.

To further explore the becoming of the person in Confucianism, we need to understand the use of important terms such as *tian* 天, *ming* 命, and *xing* 性 in the Confucian classics.

What Is the Proper Relationship Between Heaven and Humans?

One characteristic of Confucian anthropology is the idea that humans, *ren* 人, are defined, situated, and understood with respect to their context, *tian*, a term conventionally rendered as "heaven." Anyone expecting to find clear-cut definitions of humans and heaven, *ren* and *tian*, in the Confucian classics—such as the definitions sought in the Platonic dialogues—will be disappointed. In the *Analects*, terms related to the Confucian notion of the self include *tian*, *wu* 吾 (I, my, or me), *wo* 我 (I, my, or me), *ji* 己 (self), *gong* 躬 (body or person), *shen* 身 (body or person), *ren* 仁 (benevolence), *yi* 義 (appropriateness), and *li* 禮 (ritual propriety). These terms derive their meaning from the specific contexts in which Confucius employs them, although he rarely articulates in detail how he intends a given term to be understood. The Confucian tradition often formulates questions about the self in light of the relationship between *tian* and *ren* (天人關係), rather than giving clear, separate definitions of the two ideas. This way of thinking and philosophizing stems from the processual worldview on which Confucianism is based. The interrelatedness of things and events, not some external agent or prime mover, constitutes ultimate reality. Neither heaven nor humans can be properly perceived independently of each other. We will now look at the two notions and how they are interrelated in contemporary Confucianism.

Tian

Many expressions used to designate heaven in the Confucian classics are not discrete terms but paired compounds such as *tiandi* 天地 and *qiankun* 乾坤, both used to mean "heaven and earth" or "the universe." The implication is that a single term would not constitute a self-sufficient entity. Nevertheless, some interpreters have tried to relate *tian* with God or heaven in the Judeo-Christian tradition. For example, James Legge, the first professor of sinology at Oxford University and a Scottish Congregationalist, translated *tian* into "heaven" with a capital "H," which is enough to evoke the notion of God in Western readers' minds. However, it is questionable whether the heaven of Confucian texts can be equated with the atemporal, transcendental heaven of the Christian Bible. Confucian notions of heaven are irreducibly process-oriented and temporal. *Tian* endows the ten thousand things (*wanwu* 萬物) attaining self-realization with creativity (*sheng* 生) and sincerity (*cheng* 誠). Whereas Heaven or God in the West is a transcendental reality independent of space and time, *tian* is not transcendental in this sense. It generates the ten thousand things and transmits its creativity to the self-realizing of the ten thousand things, but there is no significant chasm between *tian* and *wanwu*. All events and all things including *tian* and *wanwu* are processual. This is not a dualistic world but a unified world in the sense that each unique being and event directly constitutes the world without mediating categories. That is, there are no imposing prototypes according to which a unique being could be considered merely a representative member of a larger genus. The creator and the created, the one and the many, mutually entail each other; this may be one reason why the Confucian tradition commonly uses compound terms such as *tiandi* and *qiankun*, which emphasize interdependence and correlativity.

If *tian* is not God as the Creator of the universe or the prime mover who determines the movement of things, then what is *tian* responsible for? In the Confucian tradition *tian* as immanent force expresses the ineluctability of situations. The different configurations of *tian* provide a context for the actualization of the ten thousand things and events, including the self-realization of humans. In the *Book of Changes*, the configuration of the initial pairs, heaven high and earth low, is the key to the movements of *dao* 道 and the fulfillment of the natural tendencies of things and events: "With heaven and earth having their dispositions determined, the changes ensue within them. *Dao* fulfills and sustains the natural tendencies of things and events. This is the gate whereby the appropriateness of *dao* operates."[1]

To be sure, *tian* is an indispensable factor for human life in Confucianism. Precisely speaking, an unchanging Confucian premise is that all things are changing such that *tian* and humans mutually benefit each other. *Tian* provides the natural and cultural context for human growth; and in turn, it is altered and augmented through human flourishing. Devoid of the bifurcation of fact and value, or nature and nurture, Confucian *tian* is not simply a natural phenomenon exhibiting a certain potential but is comprised of consummate persons embodying the potency of heaven and serving as examples for others. Etymologically, *tian* is an ideograph of a person writ large, suggesting a great person. Throughout the Confucian corpus, Confucius himself and other exemplary persons are equated with the sun, moon, and celestial objects.

> The superior character of other people is like the mound of a hill which can be scaled, but Confucius is the sun and moon, which no one can climb beyond. When people cut themselves off from the sun and moon, what damage does this do to the sun and moon? It would only demonstrate that such people do not know their limits.[2]

A corollary to the absence of universal principles in Confucian philosophy is the emphasis on concrete exemplary models such as sage-kings, Yao, Shun, the Duke of Zhou, and Confucius. These models function in place of transcendental structures to provide people with an understanding of what it means to be human. By acting in ways analogous to these models, people who aspire to become consummate persons learn to embody *tian*. This person-making is possible through "modeling after" (*fa* 法), "following the example of" (*xiao* 效), and "taking the example of" (*ze* 則). These activities of emulation should be seen as creativity rather than as mere replication. *Tian* is productive because it is vague, indirect, and open, which inspires people to optimize the most appropriate resolution in a given situation. By doing this, the human is capable of creating cultural meaning in an inherited cultural context and attaining a level comparable to heaven: "The Master said, 'It is the person who is able to broaden the way, not the way that broadens the person.' "[3]

This is the way in which Confucian cultural heroes such as the Three Sovereigns and the Five Emperors—as well as philosophers such as Confucius, Mencius, Xunzi, Zhu Xi, Chong Yagyong, and Ogyu Sorai—develop and finally become part of civilized traditions. Confucius is referred to not as a successful politician but as a man of culture who inherits a tradition and reformulates it as his time demands. He is not only an authentic follower of Zhou Culture but also a cardinal reformer of inherited classical documents. Confucius is more than a transmitter of insight but also an editor and interpreter who sheds new light on the past and reveals novel significance to his contemporaries, as well as to his descendants in the present.

Ming

Now we proceed to the notion of *ming*, variously translated as command, decree, fate, or destiny, which will further clarify the aforementioned idea of *tian* as context or situation. A statement in the *Yucong* 1, a bamboo text excavated in Guodian and arguably belonging to the Confucian school, may serve as a starting point for exploring the notion of *ming* in Confucianism: "Where there is *tian* there is *ming*; where there are events (物) there are names (名); where there is earth (地), there is shape (形)."[4] Here, we need to broaden our horizon to look at other ancient Chinese philosophical schools that share certain similarities with Confucianism, though they may differ on strategies for self-consummation or the purposes of philosophy. There is a correspondence between the shape of the earth, the names of events, and the *ming* of *tian*. The notion of *xing* 形, translated as shape, configuration, or situation, is an important concept in military theory, referring to terrains on which a good general can easily gain victory. *Xing* is the inherent force in a situation, often illustrated as the cascading of pent-up waters thundering throughout a steep gorge, or a crossbow drawn back and ready to discharge its arrow. Having figured out the terrain, the good military commander will be able to get the most out of the situation. Exploiting the situation, the commander gains victory where victory is easily gained. Thus, a victorious army only enters the battle after first having won the victory in the mind of the commander.

By analogy, we can refer to *ming* as the immanent propensity of heaven available for the self-realization of persons. However, the difference between the shape of the earth and *ming* of heaven is that the latter largely concerns communicative activities in the human world rather than geographical factors. Etymologically, the etymological dictionary *Shuowen* regards *ming* as composed of two parts: 口 "mouth" and 令 "to command." In addition, it defines *ming* as *shi* 使, "to make something happen" or "to cause." Other important terms that contain the "mouth" component in Confucianism are *jun* 君 (exemplary), *sheng* 聖 (sage), and *zhi* 知 (wisdom). Like *ming,* these terms show that Confucianism prizes verbal and communicative activities as tools for person-making. *Ming* in Confucianism is concerned with images, words, and meanings—the communicative activities that create and coordinate the behavior of the members of a community.

Much controversy centers on whether *ming* as a force efficacious in person-making has deterministic implications. Compare *ming* to the ancient Greek forces of *ananke* or *moirae,* the unalterable fates, often personified as a mother and her child. As Aristotle tells us, Sophocles' Greek tragedy shows us the ruthlessness of fate in the life of the tragic hero, who becomes a prototype of Western heroism. In the *Oedipus the King,* the oracle persists in prophesying that inevitably Oedipus will kill his father and marry his mother. Laius, Oedipus's father, tries to avoid his fate by killing the infant Oedipus. Although Laius has the infant's ankles pierced and feet punctured, Oedipus survives and is raised in the court of King Polybus of Corinth. Eventually, Oedipus hears the same prophecy that Laius heard and, believing that Polybus is his real father, tries to escape his fate by leaving Corinth. Nevertheless, on his way he unknowingly happens to meet and kill his real father, Laius. Later, for solving Sphinx's riddle, he is welcomed into the city where Laius's wife—and Oedipus's true mother—Jocasta is queen. In ignorance he marries the widowed Jocasta. Finally, when he realizes that the oracle has been fulfilled, he stabs out his own eyes in despair and lives as a cursed wanderer in his empire. Aristotle names the tragic hero's sudden recognition of his fate *anagonorisis* in the *Poetics.* Heroic confrontation with the ruthless and deterministic order of the cosmos is an archetypical theme in Western history. The tragic hero is a man isolated, fierce, and creative, who challenges the unchallengeable. Tragic death is a fate he must bear for his *hubris.* Examples of the tragic hero are seen in Prometheus, Goethe's *Faust,* Nietzsche's *Ubermensch,* and even Jim Morrison.

What is the attitude of Confucius, a cultural hero of East Asian civilization, toward *ming*? He confesses that he was already fifty years old before he recognized the command of heaven. However, contrary to any tragic heroism, Confucius reports progress during the subsequent decades, in which he becomes attuned to his surroundings and able to freely resolve conflicts between his inner desires and the circumstances of the outer world: "From fifty I realize the command of heaven; from sixty my ear was attuned; from seventy I could give my heart-and-mind free rein without overstepping the boundaries."[5]

It is also true that Confucius could not resolve every force at play (*ming*) in his life in a favorable manner. When his favorite disciple Yen Yuan died, he felt that heaven had abandoned him. Furthermore, his lifelong aspiration to find a wise sovereign who could practice the way according to Confucius's counsel was never fulfilled. Notwithstanding, his harmony with the propensity of heaven may come partly from his consummate level of cultivation and partly from the immanent nature of *ming*.[6]

In the Confucian philosophy of process, there is no counterpart to *moirae* as inexorable and inalterable destiny. A common phrase in Chinese, "movement of propensity," implies that *ming* is subject to change and requires that people's aesthetic sensibilities respond to its propensity for achieving productive harmony. This is why Confucianism cherishes the collaboration of heaven and humans over human obedience to transcendental law. The Oedipus tragedy is the product of a culture where transcendental agency predetermines the irresistible course of life for its creatures. However, Confucius, though he fluctuated between confidence in his own heavenly mission and despair over being abandoned, could attain reconciliation and greater levels of artistry in life.

We should take situations and situated persons into account when asking to what extent *ming* is a determinant force. While in some passages *ming* is a force beyond human control, in others *ming* seems to be a weak causal force that humans are able to exploit. Zigong, one of Confucius's disciples, discontented with his conditions (*ming*), takes steps to enrich himself. The consummate person is advised that on seeing danger, one should be ready to lay down one's life. Yet at other times the *Yijing* advises that one should not yield to *ming*.

The degree of determination may be closely related with the degree of consummation one achieves in cultivation. The more one understands the propensity of heaven and brings relevant fields into focus in oneself, the greater is one's influence over the environment. Becoming a holographic entry point in whole fields, one comes to be unaware of a dichotomy between self and *ming* as environing forces. Therefore, just as Confucius does not feel any conflict between what he desires and what the environing forces limit, so too will a man who understands the propensity of heaven not go on standing under a precarious wall.[7] The Confucian consummate person in this sense has the capacity to carry out a course of action requiring other people and other environing ingredients. Because some critics, such as Mozi (473–390 BCE) or Lu Xun (1881–1936) accuse Confucianism of fatalism, we need to elaborate this point.

Here, it is useful to remind ourselves that heaven is a field that can be variously focused according to relationships with particular perspectives. When people need an exemplar for emulation, heaven seems to be a moral paragon. However, from the perspective of immanent force, it becomes the complement of human co-creativity. Thus, it is productively vague, roundabout, amorphous, and, does not speak. We can understand the indirect presence of heaven only through various situations and configurations: climates, political and historical events, people's minds, cracks on tortoise shells and buffalo bones, and records of exemplars' deeds and behaviors. All these require exemplary persons or sages who are entrusted to hear, speak, and present on behalf of heaven. The consummate person in Confucianism is the one who can focus the accumulated tradition to give it meaningful wholeness and novel significance. He or she is the person who determines the indeterminate. From the standpoint of heaven, the human relationship with *ming* can be receptive. Thus, expressions such as "to receive *ming*" and "to follow *ming*" are permissible. But from the standpoint of the human, this relationship is not just receptive but is also a conscious response to the context of heaven. It is the effectual production of novel harmony. In this case, expressions such as "responding to *ming*" or "changing the *ming*" are adequate.

The cognate *ming* 名, which refers to the act of naming, connotes a concerted effort to optimize one's resources for creating adequate sociopolitical order. It is used interchangeably with *ming* 命 in the sense of "commanding propensity." The *Showen* explains *ming* 名 as depicting self-expression in the unidentifiable darkness. The act of naming is to focus an image out of vague fields. The naming of events corresponds with the commands of heaven in the aforementioned passage. By naming an event, we become able to identify the event. Understanding the terrain, we can negotiate the earth. Realizing the propensity of heaven, we can be consummate in our responses to forces of the environment. When responding to Sima Niu's compliant about lacking brothers, Confucius's disciple Zi Xia inspires Sima Niu with hope by redefining the meaning of brother—that is, altering the *ming*—such that brotherhood could be thought of as an ethical and religious relationship, rather than a biological one.[8] When calling tyrants not sovereigns but outcasts, he altered the conventional name according to his political and historical judgment.[9]

Xing

Xing 性, which has traditionally been rendered as "nature" or "human nature," is an important notion in the Confucian vocabulary of person-making. I know of no better way to begin the discussion than by referring to sinologist Angus Graham's question of whether the Chinese *xing* is equivalent to the English "nature" in his book *Disputers of Tao*. His careful reading of classical Chinese texts leads him to suspect the conventional rendering of *xing* as nature. According to him, Arthur Waley's mistaken construal of *xing* as nature is a result of the assumption that *xing* is a "quality that a thing had to start with." Such an assumption comes from the meaning of the English term *nature*, which originates in the Latin *nascor*, meaning "to be born."

There seems to be agreement among scholars that the character *xing* 性 is derived from *sheng* 生 (to grow, to generate, to be fresh) with the addition of *xin* 心 (heart-mind). In the *Shuowen* lexicon, *sheng* depicts a sprout putting forth shoots from the earth. *Xing* refers initially to productive forces (*sheng*), as expressed distinctively in humans (*xin*). In the "Great Treatise" of the *Book of Changes*, *xing* is illustrated as a process of consummation in the continuous alternation of the way: "That which consummate is *xing*."[10] What we can learn from this is that *xing* is not a thing at all but a process or force. While the term *nature* implies something a priori or transcendental in origin, Graham's alternative reading sees *xing* as an emerging process. In his view, *xing* is "a course on which life completes its development if sufficiently nourished." Now we see two different understandings of *xing* as either transcendental nature or immanent process.

We must consider the history of the ontological tradition in Western philosophy in which the English term *nature* is embedded, in order to get a comparative picture of the understanding of personhood as captured by terms such as nature and *xing*, in both the East and the West. Since the Greek philosophers, the Western tradition has often taken it as self-evident that there is something called "human nature"—a universal, transcendental, determining substance beyond spatiotemporal instantiations.

For Plato, for example, humans share a common property, "humanness," and this universal property is not limited by specific instantiations in time and space. It is immaterial and transcends any particular human. Plato conceives of an immortal soul in which the universal Ideas are implicit but forgotten. The immortal soul experiences direct contact with the eternal Ideas, prior to birth, but the postnatal human condition of bodily imprisonment causes the soul to forget the Ideas. Particular humans are temporal, transient beings, finite imitations of true reality, for whom the eternal is veiled. The philosopher's task is to recollect the transcendental Ideas. The Socratic dictum "Know thyself" must be understood in the following sense: "Grasp your transcendental principle in your soul and permit yourself to conform to it." The transcendental self is the essential "humanness" that determines the selfhood of particular people, in terms of both ontology and axiology.

Rene Descartes also subscribes to the idea that some essence or human nature links particular humans to the universal. He relies on skepticism and mathematics to create his definition of human nature. In the process of methodically doubting everything, Descartes concludes that there is one fact that cannot be doubted—the fact of his doubting. At least the "I" that is conscious of doubting exists, as a thinking subject. At least this much is certain: "*Cogito, ergo sum*"; or "I think, therefore I am." All else can be questioned, but not the irreducible fact of the thinker's self-awareness. In addition, in recognizing this one certain truth, the mind is capable of perceiving that which characterizes certainty itself. For Descartes, the *cogito*, the thinking subject, is an immutable substance serving as the first principle for all other knowledge, providing both the basis for subsequent deductions and the model for all human thought. His use of the term *res* (thing, substance) exemplifies his substantive approach to the self. The *res cogitans* (thinking substance) is understood as fundamentally different and separate from *res extensa* (extended substance). The senses are prone to flux and error, the imagination is prey to fantastic distortions, and the emotions are irrelevant to rational comprehension; but the mind is capable of comprehending clear and distinct knowledge. Descartes' invariable universal principle, the thinking self, gives authority to the procedural clarity of mathematical reasoning. He declares: "I rightly conclude that my essence consists solely in the fact that I am a thinking thing (or substance whose sole nature or essence is to think)."[11]

More recently, the substantive view of human nature has begun to be questioned in Western philosophy. One reason for this doubting is the increasing emphasis placed on the immanent, processual, experiential approach to the idea of being human. The crack in the monolithic substance tradition can be traced to the emergence of new thinkers such as Friedrich Nietzsche (1844–1900), Maurice Merleau-Ponty (1908–1961), William James (1842–1910), John Dewey (1859–1952), and Alfred North Whitehead (1861–1947). These new philosophers, defying the substance notion of human nature, tend to see the self as neither atemporal nor absolute, but as immanent and processual. Instead of being characterized by an underlying essential substance, a person is characterized by his or her actions and experiences, such as talents, skills, capabilities, dispositions, habits, inclinations, and tendencies. For example, John Dewey disapproves of the rights-based liberalist notion of the original and isolated constitution of human nature. Dewey creatively employs the notion of habit in discussing human nature. Being aware that the term *habit* is usually used to refer to the repetitious routines of daily life, he discloses new dimensions of the meaning of habit in the understanding of the self. He suggests not that we have habits but that *we are habits*. Habit is a mode of "predilection and aversion" that readily responds to a set of stimuli, and is deliberately modified and refined by conscious efforts. It is an enduring, yet amenable, pattern of the self through which the hylozoistic energies of the person, such as passion and emotion, find their channel for expression.

His view reminds me of the Korean Confucian Dasan Chong Yagyong 茶山丁若鏞 (1762–1836) and his argument for interpreting *xing* (Korean *seong*) as predilection (嗜好). He thinks of *xing* as an inchoate predilection that is consummated by responding properly to the natural, personal, and social environment. For him, *xing* is captured well by comparison to the growing force of living organisms. His perception of *xing* as predilection leads him to insist that a person is responsible for accomplishing his or her good life. Accordingly, he sees personhood as an indeterminate tendency between the incorporeal predilections of the human mind and the spiritual predilection of *dao* mind. Human *xing* is construed as a process of ethical cultivation, using methods of self-accusation throughout one's entire life. He is adamant in criticizing any determinant notion of *xing*. He is concerned that deterministic views of human nature may thwart human efforts to become consummate. He accuses the Chinese scholar Han Yu (768–824) of adhering to a deterministic view in Yu's commentary on the *Analects*, in which Yu argues for three grades of human nature. For Dasan, *xing* is immanent and processual, continuing to grow throughout an entire human lifetime, coming to full blossom only through social, collaborative relationships, and requiring attentiveness toward the environment.

For Dewey, experience comes to be construed through the cumulative meaning arising from the encounter of an experiencing subject with things and events in the world. Thus, experience becomes relevant to the formation of habit, enabling a person to learn to properly respond to situations encountered. Dewey argues that personhood should be understood in light of habit and predilection, and in terms of responsiveness to the environment.[12]

The processual notion of natural tendency and the idea of self-consummation for whoever succeeds in flourishing are quintessential themes in Confucian philosophy. Mencius says that humans have a natural tendency to be efficacious (*xingshan* 性善) but they may be corrupted into developing bad habits by their circumstances unless they strive to nurture and cultivate their tendencies to the fullest. One of points at issue between Mencius and Gaozi was whether natural tendency has a vector or not. Gaozi claims that as a whirlpool flows through a channel, our natural tendency itself does not have any inherent direction. To the contrary, for Mencius, all people have four limbs in the body, four "emergent shoots" from which benevolence, rightness, ritual propriety, and wisdom arise. The process of growth is never effortless but requires strenuous endeavors. However, once the inherent natural tendency is adequately nurtured, it gains momentum and becomes irresistible and spontaneous. The joy of self-consummation happens of its own accord, like dancing with one's feet and waving one's arms without knowledge. Full-fledged human *xing* extinguishes malignity as water subdues fire. Mencius, invoking the notion of *qi* as the hylozoistic energy of the cosmos, says that one cultivates oneself by nurturing oneself in step with changes in environing forces, just as farmers expect plants to grow from within in cooperation with seasons and climates. This growth must not only be the spontaneous generation of natural tendency but also a collaboration with environing forces. Finally, Mencius presents the consummate level of human cultivation, the convergence of the person and cosmic moral forces, as flood-like *qi*:

> It is the sort of *qi* that is utmost in vastness, utmost in firmness.
> If by upbringing you nourish it and do not interfere with it, it
> stuffs the space between heaven and earth. It is sort of *qi* that

matches the right with *dao*; without this it starves. It is generated by accumulation of rightdoing; it is not that by sporadic rightdoing one makes a grab at it. If anything in conduct is dissatisfying to the heart, it starves.[13]

Continuity of Heaven and Humans: The Productive Relationship between Humans and Environing Forces

In this chapter, the strategy I have adopted has been to expound upon notions relevant to personhood by tracing patterns of thinking embedded in Confucianism and not exclusively limited to the human sphere. In the Confucian formulation of the question of the proper relationship between heaven and humans, the person is not a discrete entity but is constituted by complex roles and relationships. Thus, in the Confucian world of process and essential relatedness, seeing how patterns of *tian*, *ming*, *xing*, and *ren* relate and mutually form meaning among one another is more viable than identifying some irreducible element at the base of discrete objects.

The Confucian tradition answers the question of how we achieve the most productive harmony between heaven and humans with the phrase "the continuity of heaven and humans." Although this is a phrase coined by later Confucians, it aptly expresses Confucius's reconciliation to the situations of his time and Mencius's attainment of flood-like *qi*. *Tian,* which provides persons with a context for their growth, accrues with the achievements of persons. In what we discussed earlier, *tian* is not only the natural, cultural, and social context available to persons, because whoever attains excellence in self-cultivation becomes an integral part of *tian* by focusing the whole field of *tian*. In the above chapter, Mencius, who professes that the ten thousand things and event are in him, is simply an intensely focused and highly integrated person within the whole field of *qi*.

In the human-centered Confucian tradition the act of determining the field of *tian* is related to the act of naming (*ming*), through which new cultural meaning is defined and enacted. Confucius's concern about the ordering of names—"the ruler must rule, the minister minister, the father father, the son son"—expresses his creative reshuffling of the cultural nexuses that coordinate roles and relationships in the community. The confluence of the way of *tian* and the way of humans is possible with effective communication, that is, with the act of continuous re-naming by intensely focused and highly integrated persons. The verbal articulations of the consummate person are conduits whereby humans and *tian* converge, as expressed in the *Mencius*: "To express fully thoughts and feelings of one's heart-and-mind is to realize one's *xing*, and if one realizes one's *xing*, one is realizing *tian*."[14]

In the Judeo-Christian tradition, humans are naturally disposed to perversity and require justification through the sacraments and other consecrated rituals. In turn, religious authorities demands that people conform to their ethical standards. The Judeo-Christian God alone has the power to save humans; their own effort is comparatively inconsequential. While God is sole origin of the good, humans play a weak and inferior role. In contrast, humans in the Confucian classics have the capacity to create meaning in collaboration with their fellow humans and environmental forces. So, the realization of a person's power of consecration—his or her capacity to coordinate cultural meaning in collaboration with *tian*—is properly named as a counterpart of *tian* in the thirty-first chapter of the *Zhongyong*:

> Only those who possess utmost sagacity in the world have the acuity and quick wittedness needed to oversee the empire.... So broad, expansive, and profoundly deep, they exhibit these several qualities whenever needed. So broad and expansive like the heavens themselves, so profoundly deep like a bottomless abyss, they appear and all defer to them; they speak and all have confidence in what they say; they act and all find pleasure what they do.... Thus it is said that they are the complement of *tian*.

To be "the complement of *tian*" does not simply mean to be ruled by the will of heaven. The experience of the consummate person, in whom the distinction between the self and environing forces (*tian*) collapses, cannot be adequately described in terms of the dichotomy between freedom and determinism. Consummate persons are compelled to act, not because they are ruled by external forces, but because they are integrated with and responsible for whole fields of actions while remaining the unique and unrestricted foci of those fields.

Suggestions for Further Reading

For a survey of interpretations of the Confucian self and related issues, see the articles by Kwong-loi Shun, Irene Bloom, and Chung-ying Cheng (1997) in *Philosophy East and West* 47, no. 1. A New Confucian interpretation of the Confucian self may be found in Tu Wei-ming (1985), *Confucian Thought: Selfhood as Creative Transformation*. The second chapter, "Focus-Field Self in Classical Confucianism," in David L. Hall and Roger T. Ames (1998), *Thinking from the Han* provides comparative philosophical inquiry into this theme, showing adequacy of idea of focus and field. Francois Jullien (2000), *The Impossible Nude* discusses different understandings of the human body

in Western and Chinese arts and philosophy. For recent work on process
thinking and human nature in Confucianism, see James Behuniak Jr. (2004),
Mencius on Becoming Human.

Notes

1. *Yijing*, Xici Zhuan 1–7. My translation; passage numbers refer to all
standardized editions.
2. *Analects* 19.24. My translation; passage numbers refer to all standardized
editions.
3. Ibid. 15.29.
4. *Yucong* 1. My translation.
5. *Analects* 2.4.
6. Interestingly enough, Xiang Wu, a tragic hero in the Chinese tradition,
receives more criticisms than compliments. When Xiang Wu was trapped at the battle
of Gaixia, he sang his famous songs to Yuji, his beloved concubine, lamenting that an
opportune time was missing: "My strength could pull mountains, my spirit pales the
world. Yet, opportune time is missing and my horse just refuses to gallop! What can
I do if my horse denies me even a trot? Oh my dear Yu Ji, what would you have me
do?" Later historians' opinions of him are generally low—he may have bravery but lacks
wisdom. He is unable to listen to the criticism and wise counsel of his subordinates.
Even at the last minute, he blames missing opportunities for his failures. But destiny
is not an excuse for an individual's wrongdoings in Confucianism.
7. *Mencius* 7/1/2. My translation; passage numbers refer to all standardized
editions.
8. *Analects* 12.5: "Sima Niu lamented, 'Everyone has brothers except for me.' Zi
Xia said to him, 'I have heard it said: Life and death are a matter of one's lot; wealth
and honor lie with *tian*. Since exemplary persons are respectful and impeccable in their
conduct, are deferential to others and observe ritual propriety, everyone in the world
is their brother. Why would an exemplary person worry over having no brother?' "
9. *Mencius* 1B8; my translation. For English translations see D. C. Lau (1970),
Mencius; and James Legge (1985), *The Chinese Classics*. "King Hsun of Chi asked, 'Is it
true that Tang banished Jie and King Wu marched against Zhou? 'It is so recorded' said
Mencius. 'Is regicide permissible?' 'A man who mutilates benevolence is a mutilator,
while one who cripples rightness is a crippler. He who is both a mutilator and a
crippler is an outcast. I have indeed heard of the punishment of the 'outcast Zhou,'
but I have never heard of regicide.' "
10. *Yijing*, Xici Zhuan 1/5.
11. Rene Descartes (1970), 190.
12. I have recently seen emerging dialogues between these Western philosophies
and the Confucian philosophical tradition. I believe these dialogues can contribute to
providing us with rich vocabularies for understanding the Confucian tradition. Joseph
Needham compares the neo-Confucian tradition with Whitehead's philosophy of
organism. See his (1956), *Science and Civilization in China,* Vol.2. Roger T. Ames and

David Hall observe: "If contemporary comparative philosophic activity is any indication, it might be the pragmatic philosophies associated with Peirce, James, Dewey, and Mead, and extended toward a process philosophy such as A.N. Whitehead, that can serve as the best resource for philosophic concepts and doctrines permitting responsible access to Confucius' thought." See Ames and Hall (1987), 15. They, placing great emphasis on the pragmatic tradition in America, combine philology and philosophy to find innovative translations for philosophical terms in Confucianism. See their (2001), *Focusing the Familiar: A Translation and Philosophical Interpretation of the* Zhongyong. See also Ames and Henry Rosemont Jr., (1998), *The Analects of Confucius: a Philosophical Translation*. John Berthrong relates process philosophy with the neo-Confucianism that culminates in Zhu Xi. See Berthrong (1998), *Concerning Creativity: A Comparison of Chu Hsi, Whitehead, and Neville*. In Korea, process philosophy is widely seen as a suitable partner in the dialogue with Korean philosophy, but this has not yet received proper attention in the West.

   13. Mencius 2A2.
   14. Ibid. 7A1.

6

Confucianism and Democracy

Sor-hoon Tan

Is Confucianism democratic or antidemocratic? Could Confucianism and democracy at least coexist in a society? Could there be more than coexistence: positive mutual transformation that brings the two closer or even effects a fruitful merger? These are questions of importance beyond the ivory tower. They have consequences for the future of many societies in East Asia, and the relationship between East Asian societies and other societies in a globalizing era. This chapter will begin with a brief introduction to the wide and growing range of literature on the relationship between Confucianism and democracy by highlighting and comparing some major positions. It then advocates a Confucian democracy by reconstructing, in the sense of a transformative understanding that renders past meanings relevant to the future, some key aspects of Confucianism.

Confucianism and Democracy Are Incompatible

Chen Duxiu, one of the standard bearers of the New Culture movement in Republican China, argued in 1916 that Confucian thought and teachings belonged to the feudal age: its "objectives, ethics, social norms, mode of living, and political institutions did not go beyond the privilege and prestige of a few rulers and aristocrats and had nothing to do with the happiness of the great masses."[1] Many Chinese intellectuals of the time believed that China's Confucian heritage was holding back China's modernization, especially its pursuit of democracy. From the early twentieth century, liberal-minded Korean intellectuals also saw Confucianism as conservative and backward, and attacked it for obstructing modernization, and *minjung* scholars opposing the authoritarian regimes of Park Chung Hee and Chun Doo Hwan also regarded Confucianism as an obstacle to the realization of democracy and social justice in South Korea.[2]

Lucian Pye argued that Confucian political culture was authoritarian and an obstacle to democratization in Asia, while Samuel Huntington saw Confucianism and democracy as a "contradiction in terms."[3] Huntington predicted a "clash of civilization" between the illiberal antidemocratic Islam and Confucianism on the one side and Western liberal democracy on the other. Likewise, some Asians have argued that the values of liberal democracy are incompatible with the Confucian culture of their societies, and they have brought forth Asian values to challenge Western models in the international discourse on human rights.

We need to separate what are merely politically opportunistic positions from serious reflection on the issues. Asian societies have a right to choose or find their own paths, and their specific historical and cultural circumstances may allow and even require them to shape their futures differently from other societies. Even if the price is a loss of democracy, societies with a long historical legacy of Confucian influence may not be better off if that influence is completely destroyed, assuming that it is possible to do so. Even Western scholars are not unanimous in their praise of liberal democratic values. Those who maintain that the values of Confucianism and liberal democracy are inherently incompatible may still believe that they can coexist as "independent value systems" in the same society. Chenyang Li, for example, argues for coexistence of both sets of values, despite their inherent incompatibility, in China's future.[4]

Confucianism and Democracy Are Compatible

Asians are also divided about the desirability and validity of liberal democratic values. Among those in favor of liberal democracy, not all believe that it must come at the expense of their Confucian legacy. One could argue that the two most Confucian societies in Asia, Taiwan and South Korea, rank among the most democratic. Kwon Tai-Hwan and Cho Hein's study of the historical basis of Korean democratization concluded that the Confucian residuals played a dual role in the recent democratization process, and predicted that "in the long run, the Confucian legacy may play an increasingly positive role in the democratization of Korea" through mutual adjustments in the interface between Confucian and western ideals.[5] Japan, which had its share of Confucian influence, is one of the oldest and most stable Asian democracies. However, skeptics might respond that these countries have democratized *despite* Confucianism—in becoming democratic, they become less Confucian.

A strong argument for Confucian democracy would require showing that Confucian values, institutions, and practices are or can be democratic, or at least need not be contradictory to democracy.

The national confidence brought by economic successes of East Asian societies from the 1970s has led to renewed positive interest in their cultural heritage. Confucianism has been credited with the economic boom of the Asian tigers and featured prominently in discussions about the Asian model of development. Even in the People's Republic of China, Deng Xiaoping's reforms allowed a reevaluation of Confucianism, which turned to democratic reconstruction by the mid-eighties. Earlier, Chinese scholars such as Carsun Chang, Tang Junyi, Xu Fuguan, and Mou Zongsan advocated "a reconstruction of Chinese culture" that would include reconciling its Confucian heritage with modern democratic aspirations.[6] Prominent Confucian scholars such as Wm. Theodore de Bary and Tu Wei-ming, have devoted their careers to showing that Confucian philosophy is humanistic and liberal, even though political institutions and practices in Confucian societies historically may have been authoritarian. The less optimistic, Liu Shu-hsien among them, see the compatibility of Confucianism and democracy as requiring significant sacrifices on the part of Confucianism, but without destroying it altogether.

Denying Essentialism and Democratizing Confucianism

Those who maintain that Confucianism and democracy are inherently incompatible usually adopt the liberal conception of democracy and interpret Confucianism as essentially collectivistic, patriarchal, and authoritarian. However, democracy is a contested concept in Western philosophical discourses, just as Confucianism is not a homogeneous tradition. Those who believe that Confucianism has no place for liberal individual autonomy may nevertheless see Confucianism as compatible with a democracy that adopts a social conception of the individual, such as that found in John Dewey's philosophy. Roger Ames and David Hall have argued that Dewey's "communitarian" conception of democracy is the best bridge between China's Confucian civilization and a democratic future. My earlier work includes an attempt at a Deweyan reconstruction of both Confucianism and democracy for a Confucian democracy.

The position I shall advocate adopts an antiessentialist hermeneutical stance. In my view, Confucianism does not have an unchanging essence; it lies in the meaningful continuity of a tradition of scholarship and social practice, wherein discourses about ideals and norms relate to actual practice in dynamic tension. Even if we grant that Confucianism might not be recognizable without values such as emphasis on the family, filial morality, loyalty, and respecting tradition, what these values *mean* and how they are actualized could change over time and space. In any case, not everyone agrees that these values represent what is most valuable to Confucianism; they could be seen as variously derived from the primary notions of *ren* 仁, *yi* 義, *li* 禮, and *zhi* 知 in contingent social contexts. The Confucian tradition is not homogeneous in content; instead, it is constituted by the continuity of interpretive practice focusing on certain core texts (the inclusion and exclusion of which is also contested). The reconciliation of Confucianism and democracy I shall attempt in this chapter will focus on what I consider the most important of these texts, the *Analects*.[7]

Deweyan Conception of Democracy

There are many different conceptions of democracy. Democracy could be seen as nothing more than a political system wherein governments are elected for limited terms by universal suffrage. Some argue that popularly elected governments will become mob rule without the rule of law and universal rights limiting government and protecting individual autonomy. Some emphasize the values of liberty and equality, with different weightings between them. Others insist on the need for more comprehensive citizen participation at various levels of the polity, shared values nurturing community life, and civic virtues. The limited space of this chapter does not allow an extensive exploration of the pros and cons of various conceptions. I shall merely set out the basic outline of John Dewey's conception, which will be adopted for my purpose here.

In Dewey's view, democracy is not just a political system of selecting and regulating government; it is an ethical and social ideal. Democracy represents the complete and perfect community. This idea (also ideal) of community is conceived by extracting the desirable characteristics or forms of community life that has actually existed, and using them to criticize undesirable features and suggest improvement; the ideal is the final limit of all desirable traits and tendencies of community life. Dewey came up with two criteria for existing community life: (1) How numerous and varied are the interests that are consciously shared? (2) How full and free is the interplay with other forms of association? Democracy optimizes both criteria.[8] For Dewey, democracy is the only method by which human beings can succeed in "the greatest experiment of humanity—that of living together in ways in which the life of each of us is profitable in the deepest sense of the word, profitable both to a single person and helpful in the building up of the individuality of others."[9]

Rearranging the battle cry of the French Revolution, Dewey placed fraternity before liberty and equality, and insists that all three are meaningless outside communal life. Liberty as a democratic ideal is understood as "the power to secure release and fulfillment of personal potentialities which take place only in rich and manifold association with others," and equality is "the unhampered share which individual member of the community has in the consequences of associated action."[10] Freedom and equality thus understood are important in communication, which is critical to creating and sustaining community. In a community, individual members "hold things in common." For Dewey, this does not mean that they are clones with homogeneous beliefs and interests, nor does it mean that some "shared values" with mysterious sources should be imposed on them. Rather, what is held in common is achieved over time through communication among those who come together to form a community.

As an idea of community, democracy does not deny importance to the individual. Dewey considers democracy "a personal, an individual, way of life." "The cause of democracy is the moral cause of the dignity and worth of the individual." The "idea of democracy as opposed to any conception of aristocracy is that every individual must be consulted in such a way, actively not passively, that he himself becomes a part of the process of authority, of the process of social control; that his needs and wants have a chance to be registered in a way where they count in determining social policy."[11] Democracy is participative. Democratic politics is constituted by the organization of publics, which are comprised of individuals who are affected by transactions that they are not part of, and who therefore share an interest in controlling those transactions. A democratic public does not organize itself by electing officials through a simple majority vote and leaving them to speak for those they represent, nor is democratic government a matter of following "public opinion" in the sense of an aggregate of the arbitrarily formed views of the majority (or worse, views manipulated by special interests). A public organizes itself democratically through social inquiry, where efficacious communication allows every member the opportunity to change his or her mind after thinking through the issue with other participants in the inquiry. A member of a democracy not only has a right, but a duty to participate in social inquiry.[12]

Ren: Confucian Personal Cultivation and the Making of Community

The list of Confucian virtues begins with *ren* 仁, translated variously as benevolence (Lau), humanity (Wing-tsit Chan), authoritative person or conduct (Ames and Rosemont), or goodness (Watson). The centrality of this concept is clear from the frequency of its appearance in the *Analects*. Confucian scholars through the ages have reaffirmed its importance in individual treatises as well as the commentaries on the classics. In recent times, Wing-tsit Chan singled out *ren* as the general virtue that encompasses all other Confucian virtues.[13] For Confucius, a person who is not *ren* could not have anything to do with *li* 禮 (ritual) and music, which he values very highly (*Analects* 3.3). *Ren* unites Confucian personal cultivation and community making. It will provide us with an understanding of the Confucian idea of community. By examining this idea, we may ask if Confucian community is antidemocratic in the sense that its members are denied self-government either over their respective lives individually or over the collective.

Confucius taught his students to become exemplary persons (*junzi* 君子). One who abandons *ren* does not deserve the name of *junzi* (*Analects* 4.5). *Ren* is more valuable than life (*Analects* 15.9) because it constitutes true humanity. To be human is to be related to others. As in Dewey's philosophy, the Confucian conception of the self is social. Peter Boodberg suggests that *ren* is best translated as "co-humanity." Tu Wei-ming elaborates the script as "man in society."[14] Personal cultivation, as a process of realizing one's humanity, achieves *ren* through extending and improving one's relationship with significant others. It begins in the family, where one learns to be a filial son and to be brotherly (*Analects* 1.2), extends to the friendships one enters into with others outside the family, leads to one's contribution to sociopolitical order, and ultimately enables a spiritual unity with the cosmos.

The process of personal cultivation is at the same time a process of creating community. The "method of *ren*" is to "establish others in seeking to establish themselves and to promote others in seeking to get there themselves."[15] This is remarkably close to Dewey's idea of democracy as the method for "living together in ways in which the life of each of us is . . . profitable to himself and helpful in the building up of the individuality of others." The answers Confucius gave to the question, "What is *ren*?" include "Do not impose upon others what you yourself do not want" and "loving others."[16] Thus, Confucian community is sustained by members consciously sharing numerous and varied interests. Constituted by members' ever-expanding relational network, the boundaries of Confucian communities are fluid enough to allow each community full and free interplay with other communities. The Confucian idea of community is compatible with Dewey's conception of democracy as it also optimizes Dewey's two criteria of community life.

When Confucius's favorite student Yan Hui, whom Confucius praised for being more accomplished in *ren* than any other students (*Analects* 6.7), asked about *ren*, Confucius replied, "Through self-discipline and observing ritual propriety one becomes *ren*" (*keji fuli weiren* 克己复禮为仁).[17] D. C. Lau translates *keji fuli* 克己复禮 as "return to the observance of the rites through overcoming the self."[18] Does this imply a subordination of the individual to the collective? Without assuming a self that is an ego existing prior and separate from relation with others (a conception contrary to Confucian conception of self), we need to answer this question by considering the self-transformation that takes place in the process: is it one of growth or one of oppressed individuality?

The Chinese language uses two terms for "self," *zi* 自 and *ji* 己. *Zi* is used to express reflexivity. When an act in some other contexts may involve more than one person, *zi* indicates that the speaker is both the source (a related meaning of *zi* is "from") and the object of the act.[19] *Ji* indicates not only reflexivity, although that is certainly involved, but also emphasizes a contrast with others—I/me *rather than* others. This is not necessarily reprehensible, as Confucius himself says that learning should be for oneself (*ji*) rather than others (*Analects* 14.24). In the *Xunzi*, Confucius is said to grade "self-love" (*ziai* 自爱) above "causing others to love oneself" (*shiren aiji* 使人爱己) and "loving others" (*airen* 爱人) as the answer to the question, "What is *ren*?"[20] In contrasting oneself (*ji*) with another, one is drawing a boundary, however transitory.[21] The superiority of *ziai* lies in achieving a situation where self and others are not divided and opposed, so that loving oneself is at the same time loving others. It is the self-love of one who has attained the greater self constituted by *ren*. In the context of personal cultivation and achieving *ren*, *ji* is the less developed self with more rigid boundaries. Boundaries need to become fluid for growth to take place, for one's relational network to expand, for one to share others' concern.

In other words, one overcomes the self or exercises self-discipline (*keji* 克己) when one de-emphasizes the boundaries between oneself and others, and gives one's own and others' concerns as much weight as is appropriate to the situation. The explication of *ren* as "overcoming the self" does not imply oppression of individuality; it offers a reconciliation of community with individuality so that individual growth enhances the growth of community and vice versa. "Overcoming the self" or "self-discipline" could also be understood as self-government. At the same time, *ren* is associated with government of others; although everyone should aim to be *ren*, it is especially valued in rulers. Mencius specifically advocated *ren* government. As the virtue of other-directed government, it encompasses compassion and care for others. Such compassion and care require self-discipline so that one does not give one's own selfish interests greater weight than others' interests. Only sageliness exceeds *ren* in its "broad generosity towards the people and its ability to help the multitude."[22]

Confucian *Li* and Communicative Community

How participatory is Confucian community? While *ren* may accommodate self-government and government over the collective, does it restrict the latter to a select few? Some may argue that, far from advocating democracy, Confucius advocated an aristocratic community, albeit he favors rule by an aristocracy of virtue instead of any de facto aristocracy. It would be anachronistic to attribute the idea of democracy to Confucius. However, even if the concept did not exist within the actual Confucius's intellectual horizons, it does not mean that modern readers today cannot understand *The Analects* in ways that are compatible with democratic thinking. I shall argue that this could be done by understanding Confucian *li*—variously translated as "rites," "rituals," "ritual action," "ceremony," "propriety," "decorum," "manners," "courtesy," and "civility"—as a system of symbolic action facilitating what could be democratic communication, rather than rigid rules of behavior entrenching an authoritarian social structure. A community's *li* would then constitute a form of communication that enables its members to hold and value things in common without oppressing individuality.

The early script of *li*, depicting a sacrificial vessel, first signifies religious sacrifices. Later, the term extended to the modes of conducting religious ceremonies, and further to all modes of conduct that were deemed to be proper. *Li* came to be understood as traditional or conventional "rules of conduct." A. S. Cua, who characterizes *li* as rules of conduct, paraphrases Wittgenstein to elucidate such rules: "[R]itual rules, like all rules, stand there like signposts for the guidance of our will and action."[23] It is one's sense of what is appropriate for a particular stage of one's journey that provides guidance as to whether, and how, to follow a particular ritual signpost. Although *li*, as David Nivison points out, "are rules that are flexible and humane," in actual practice, they could degenerate into rigid and oppressive social shackles.[24] Treating *li* as universal and immutable rules is contrary to Confucius's own example of refusing to be inflexible or to insist on certainty (*Analects* 9.4).

Understood as ritual, *li* belongs to a generic kind of social action, similar to greetings, promises, commitments, excuses, pleas, compliments, and pacts, that uses symbolic forms to communicate the actors' intentions and expectations, to elicit certain behavior, and generally to make it possible for human beings to predict one another's actions and coordinate them. Rituals are embodiments of shared meanings. They guide actions so that better coordination can be achieved with less effort than would be possible if one had to search anew for appropriate ways of interacting in every situation. Ritual forms organize social life, enhance efficiency of interaction and provide continuity and stability. Participants in ritual practice communicate with one another, acknowledging their interdependence and reaffirming their mutual trust and commitment to their shared goal.

The communicative capacity of *li* is the source of social harmony. According to Master You, who was said to resemble Confucius, "Achieving harmony is the most valuable function of *li*."[25] Harmony involves diversity rather than homogeneity. According to the *Guo Yu*, "There is no music with one note, no culture with one object, no satisfactory results with one flavor."[26] The *Zuo Zhuan* records an important discourse in which *he* 和, as harmony in the sense of a minister's views complementing the views of his ruler, is distinguished from *tong* 通, the minister and ruler having identical views. It explicates harmony with the metaphor of making broth from various ingredients, which is described in the *Lüshi chunqiu*: "[T]he business of mixing and blending must use the sour, the sweet, the bitter, the spicy and the salty. Bringing the ingredients together is a very subtle art, each has its own expression."[27] A harmonious community does not suppress the individuality of its members; instead, it flourishes only when individuality and harmony enhance each other.

A Confucian community is participatory because successful *li* requires every participant's personal investment of meaning in the performance, in other words, *li* must be accompanied by *yi* 義, or appropriateness.[28] *Li* fulfils its function only when each and every participant is able to appropriate the ritual forms and render them meaningful for himself or herself, and thereby to communicate efficaciously and act in harmony with fellow participants. *Li* represents the cultural legacy that transmits meanings created by one generation to future generations; *yi* is each individual's personal appropriation of this legacy and her contribution of novel meaning to it, based on her interaction with her particular environment in each specific situation. *Yi* is developed and transmitted in *li* (*Analects* 15.18). Participants in *li* come to share meanings and norms of appropriateness (*yi*), which constitute the community's moral values. Therefore, it is through *li* that one cultivates oneself: one develops a sense of *yi*, which is the basic disposition of the exemplary person (*junzi*), through *li*. The mutual enhancement of *li* and *yi* contributes to *ren* in both personal and communal cultivation.

Although *li* is not coercive, it is critical to self-discipline, that is, self-government. *Li* provides the forms through which one governs one's own emotions, thoughts, and actions. The sense of *yi* developed in ritual participation transforms our ways of feeling and thinking, especially in relation to others. Acting contrary to those ways of feeling and thinking engenders a sense of shame, which discourages us from transgressing.[29] This is why Confucius believed *li* to be crucial to sociopolitical order.

> The Master said, "Lead the people with administrative injunctions (*zheng*) and keep them orderly with penal law (*xing*), and they will avoid punishments but will be without a sense of shame. Lead them with excellence (*de*) and keep them orderly through observing ritual propriety (*li*) and they will develop a sense of shame, and moreover will order themselves."[30]

Unfortunately, the governments that have appropriated Confucianism through the ages have ignored this important distinction between government by *li* and government by penal law (*xing* 刑) in coercively imposing a ritual order enforced by indoctrination and punishments. Participative self-transformation is replaced by coerced compliance. Dynamic and creative order that emerges from participative performance is replaced by stagnant passivity. Critics of Confucianism have been justifiably hostile to dogmatic Confucian ritual teachings and practice (*lijiao* 禮教), which Lu Xun famously condemned as "cannibalistic" in his *Diary of a Mad Man*. However, these pernicious practices that destroy individuality in the name of community should be seen as perversions resulting from a loss of the flexibility and appropriateness that should be part of ideal ritual practice.

Equality and Confucian Differentiated Order

If governments should lead with excellence, then those with excellence should rule. Does this mean that Confucianism advocates an elitist government, a hierarchical social order, contrary to the democratic value of equality? Equality, however, does not translate into a "one-size-fits-all" kind of extreme egalitarianism; even if such a society is possible, its desirability is doubtful. Western democratic theory is mainly concerned that only *relevant* differences should be allowed to affect social distribution and rewards. For example, race, gender, age, or lineage should not be allowed to undermine equality before the law and equality of opportunity, which are usually considered part of democratic society. However, unequal wages are justifiable if the jobs require different effort and qualifications; it would not be undemocratic to give limited places in a university to those who perform better in entrance exams appropriate to the course of study.

The fact that people are treated differently need not be contrary to democracy. Equality is an essentially contested value in Western thought. Dewey's understanding of equality as "unhampered share in the consequences of associations" does not require absolute equality in terms of identical quantities. Instead, it allows for functional differentiation and quantitatively different distribution of resources, and different levels and kinds of participation based on different needs and capacities relevant to specific situations. I shall try to show that Confucian social order is differentiated without necessarily being hierarchical and that its justification for inequalities is not undemocratic but compatible with Dewey's conception of equality as distribution based on needs and capacities contributing to personal-communal growth.

Distinction between superior and inferior, between better and worse, different social statuses and unequal power is part of the differentiation required in a Confucian community. However, inequality need not be so totalistic that if one is superior, one is superior always and in all things; it need not be so inflexible that one is born into a fixed place in a rigid social order and must live one's life as prescribed by one's position with no possibility of change. Inequality and equality in the differentiated order of a Confucian community are relative rather than absolute. Such a community distributes respect, power, goods, and services *proportional* to the degree each individual meets the criteria ethically relevant to what is to be distributed. In a Confucian differentiated order, there is no permanent elite who enjoys more of everything at the expense of the rest of the people.

In Confucius's view, a good ruler of a state or head of a household "does not worry that his people are poor, but that wealth is inequitably distributed (*bujun*)."[31] Other translations of *bujun* 不均 include "inequality," "ill-apportioned," and "uneven distribution." It is highly unlikely that Confucius would recommend the same quantity for all, more likely that the shares should be proportional to some ethically acceptable criteria. One such criterion is need since, "Exemplary persons help out the needy; they do not make the rich richer."[32] The responsibility of a government is to satisfy its people's material and educational needs (*Analects* 12.7). Confucius disapproves of the extravagance of the powerful at the expense of others (*Analects* 12.9). He went so far as to disown his student Ranyou for adding to the coffers of the House of Ji, which was already richer than the Duke of Zhou (*Analects* 11.17).

In Confucianism, political participation is justified by abilities. Regarding the question, "Who should govern?" Confucius is seen as replacing an aristocracy of birth with a meritocracy of ethical achievement. Only one with the abilities to discharge the responsibilities of a position should be allowed to occupy it (*Analects* 4.14, 13.2, 15.14). Democratizing Confucianism will require recognizing that participation itself is educational. Meritocracy is compatible with equality if everyone has a chance of rising to the highest office. If a society historically has been rigidly stratified, the language of meritocracy fosters elitist tendencies that, more often than not, underestimate both the needs and the abilities of those in the lower social strata. In contrast, the language of democracy, by nurturing a public ethos that explicitly rejects historical social stratifications and by requiring that any inequalities be justified rather than taking them for granted, is more favorable to participation by those from lower social strata. To compensate for its pernicious historical associations, Confucian democracy would have to be more self-consciously critical of existing inequalities to ensure that only those fulfilling its philosophical ethical standards are permitted; it must also avoid going to the opposite extreme of adopting a hostile attitude toward all inequalities, even deference to excellence.

For a social order to be differentiated rather than hierarchical there should be no entrenched social inequalities. Not only must distribution and participation be based on needs and abilities, but as needs and abilities change so must the distribution and participation. Any judgment of superior and inferior must be specific to a situation. It is meaningless to ask if a person is superior or inferior without specifying superior and inferior in *what*? A superior business executive may be an inferior parent. Someone superior to you in calligraphy now may become inferior later if you improve your skill more rapidly than she. Empirically, superiority in one area is sometimes related to superiority in other areas. But this should be determined through empirical investigation, not asserted as some kind of a priori truth. Moreover, such relations are always contingent and subject to change. A person's superiority in a specific area justifies her having more of some resources or goods only if such distribution contributes to growth, such as talent in sports and admission to a sports college. There is no superiority that justifies a higher entitlement to all resources and goods.

In a Confucian differentiated order, the distribution of political power and social prestige, though based on merit, is not a reward for abilities. The more capable does not therefore deserve more. One's position only entitles one to what is required to discharge one's responsibilities. Ritual forms of deference toward those in superior positions, for example, are not simply for the superior's personal gratification, but have the communicative function of recognizing the authority of those positions and thereby subjecting the occupants to evaluation by making them more visible to others. One would be less concerned about how much better one's boss is if one were not expected to show deference. The greater the deference shown to an individual, the higher the standard she is expected to meet. In terms of material goods, those in higher positions are not automatically entitled to more by virtue of their position. What is sufficient for the people should be sufficient for the ruler (*Analects* 12.9).

"From Seventy, I Could Give my Heart-and-Mind Free Rein . . . "

Besides equality, freedom is also important to a democratic community. Isaiah Berlin distinguishes between two concepts of liberty.[33] Negative liberty answers the question, "What is the area within which the subject—a person or group of persons—is or should be left to do or be what he is able to do or be, without interference from other persons?" Positive liberty is concerned with "What, or who, is the source of control or interference that can determine someone to do, or be, this rather than that?"[34] Although Dewey (who died before Berlin published that essay) would not have rejected negative liberty, he would have considered it inadequate; his understanding of freedom leans toward positive liberty. Dewey understands freedom as "the power to be an individualized self making a distinctive contribution and enjoying in its own way the fruits of association."[35] Freedom must be reconciled with the promotion of the common good in a democracy. At the same time, it is closely related to a person's growth and intelligence because "[w]hat men actually cherish under the name of freedom is that power of varied and flexible growth, of change of disposition and character, that springs from intelligent choice."[36]

Scholars have also argued that if there is any concept of liberty in Confucian thought, it would be closer to positive liberty. I shall try to show what kind of freedom may be found in the teachings of *The Analects*, and defend it against Berlin's criticism of positive liberty. In *The Analects*, we do not find any single term that could be translated as "freedom." However, is Confucius not claiming a kind of freedom when he tells us that "from seventy, I could give my heart-and-mind [*xin* 心] free rein without overstepping the boundaries?"[37] This freedom is achieved only after a long and arduous process of cultivating the person, in which the person or self, far from being fixed and given, changes for the better over time. There is also freedom in "setting his heart-and-mind on learning" when he chose and committed himself to the path, but relatively less in scope and quality than the freedom he achieved from seventy. Freedom is a relative concept for Confucius. As a person successfully cultivates himself and grows ethically, his freedom increases.

In his criticism of positive freedom, Berlin identifies a strand of it as "self-abnegation in order to attain independence."[38] To avoid being crushed by external constraints, be they laws or accidents of nature, deliberate malice of others or unintentional effect of their acts and human institutions, one liberates oneself from desires that one cannot realize. This is the freedom of Epictetus who claims that he, a slave, is freer than his master. This conception of freedom aids authoritarianism by relocating the problem from others imposing constraints—whether they are justified—to the agent herself. It is only the agent, not the world, who must change if she is to be free. Is Confucius's freedom such a case of "internalizing" external constraints—is he a man who grew to love his chains?

Although some later Confucians adopted a repressive attitude toward human desires, Confucius does not reject desire totally; rather, he speaks of "desiring authoritative conduct" (*Analects* 7.30). However, he praised one Meng Gongchuo for "not desiring." (*Analects* 14.12). In the absence of an absolute opposition between desires and ethical conduct, what matters is the distinction between ethical desires and unethical ones. One should liberate oneself from greed, from any kind of *excesses* in gratifying one's own physical appetites, which is unethical. Avoiding such unethical desires would re-channel one's energy into ethical desires. A closer look at the use of *buyu* 不欲 or "not desiring" in *The Analects* itself substantiates this. Confucius considered Meng Gongchuo qualified to be household steward to the Zhao or Wei families (*Analects* 14.11). A greedy man in such a position would easily succumb to corruption or misappropriation. Meng Gongchuo was eminently qualified for that post because he was "free from [excessive] desires," in other words, he was not greedy. Another instance where *buyu* is understood as the lack of greed is in the case of Master Jikang, whose family was "richer than the Duke of Zhou," worrying about thieves. Confucius said to him, "If you yourself were not so greedy (*buyu*), the people could not be paid to steal."[39] Master Jikang's greed was at the expense of the people, making them so poor and desperate that they resorted to theft.

Confucius's freedom is not self-abnegation in the sense of getting rid of all desires. Contrary to the self-abnegation Berlin criticizes, a Confucian liberates herself from some desires not because she *cannot* realize them, but because she *should not* realize them. In the former, "internalization" takes place regardless of the ethical nature of the external constraints. In the latter, the ethical or unethical nature of the constraints is of paramount importance to one's action. While it involves evaluating desires and avoiding some in favor of others, Confucius's freedom is not a case of "reducing the area of one's vulnerability" to external factors. The "pruning" of desires, instead of stultifying oneself, would help one grow better. It is an open question whether that reduces or increases one's vulnerability to the world. Confucius does not see the world as completely within one's control, even if one is a sage. It is quite possible to find more of one's desires frustrated with greater positive freedom; being able to follow one's desires without overstepping the boundaries is no guarantee that those desires will be fulfilled. In a degenerate world, when the way does not prevail, it might be easier to gratify unethical desires than fulfill ethical ones (consider the frustration of Confucius's desire to bring good government to the world).

The boundaries that Confucius from seventy no longer overstepped are those between ethical and unethical desires. They are the boundaries of the Confucian way of ethical living (*dao* 道). The way is not a fixed standard of conduct, a perfectionist ideal. It is something that emerges from one's personal experience, albeit an experience which always involves others with whom we interact; it cannot bring ethical success if imposed from without. "Becoming authoritative in one's conduct [that is, personal cultivation] is self-originating, how could it originate with others?"[40] "It is the person who is able to broaden the way, not the way that broadens the person."[41] Such "emergence" of the *dao* requires an organic integration of one's actions with the rest of one's experience, which precludes coercion as a means. Coercion results only in external compliance. One may force another to follow a way, but such compliance does not guarantee understanding; the other person cannot be coerced into "realizing it" (*Analects* 8.9). An argument can be made that *zhi* 知 is not merely knowing intellectually, but requires knowing in practice, or implies *knowing how*. It is "to realize" in both senses of "coming to know" and "making real." Realizing a Confucian way requires integrating it with one's experience through learning and reflecting. Confucian freedom lies in realizing a way, not in merely following one—it cannot be forced.

Democratic Participation and "Realizing the Way"

The distinction between "realizing the way" and merely following it is crucial in steering Confucianism away from an elitist meritocracy toward democracy. It opens up the possibility of asserting the educational nature of participation. To realize the way, to know what to do in various situations, one must learn. Learning is a social activity, so that the capacity to contribute to political order is best developed in political participation. One could reconstruct Confucian learning as participation in social inquiry.

The *Analects* is a collection of conversations, questions, and answers between Confucius, his students, and others. They are records of social inquiries in which everybody participates according to their abilities rather than one-directional transmission of knowledge, as witnessed in the reciprocity between learning and teaching. Learning is social in the way it is carried out, as a cooperative activity involving a group rather than as a solitary endeavor. For Confucius, knowledge and wisdom are best gained in community, among people who are *ren* (*Analects* 4.1). Learning is also social in its consequences. Confucian inquiry would aim at the cultivation of persons in community; when effective, it changes a community through changing its members and their relations with one another. The wise devote themselves to what is appropriate for the people; they contribute to people's personal cultivation by promoting those upright in their conduct to serve as examples to others (*Analects* 6.22, 12.22).

Social inquiry arises when people encounter problems. Contrary to the common belief that Confucian education is book learning by rote, Confucius teaches his students the importance of learning from the problems encountered and not repeating one's mistakes (*Analects* 1.8, 9.25, 15.30, 16.9). Puzzling over practical problems is what drives learning. As a teacher, Confucius admits that there is nothing he could do for someone who is not constantly asking herself, "What to do? What to do?" (*Analects* 15.16). Confucius advocates "learning much, selecting out of it what works well, and then following it" (*Analects* 7.28). Even his interest in ancient texts is pragmatic: Both the *Book of Songs* and the *Books of Rites* should be studied because they enable people to interact better, and to contribute to the community in various ways (*Analects* 13.5, 16.3, 17.9). In learning, as social inquiry, we seek the answers to "What to do?" in problematic situations. Finding those answers means knowing our way, or realizing the way (*zhidao* 知道). Just as becoming *ren* begins with oneself, learning and realizing the way requires personal participation in solving the common problems of the community. To realize the way rather than merely follow it, there must be democratic participation in social inquiry to solve the shared problems of the community.

I have attempted to re-create Confucius's learning and teaching in democratic ways by showing how individuality and community can be reconciled, how Confucian *li*, far from being rigid rules of behavior entrenching social hierarchy, enables people to hold things in common and achieve harmony through communication, how Confucian meritocracy is compatible with a Deweyan conception of equality, how the Confucian way of life is positively free through and in its ethical quest, and how realizing the Confucian way requires participatory learning. This attempt describes what is possible and desirable rather than any actual Confucian community. It offers an idea of Confucian democracy that would hopefully guide the actions of those who would like to be both Confucian and democratic; the greater achievement would be to persuade others that a democratic Confucianism is the best option for Confucians in the modern world, and that a Confucian democracy is more satisfactory than other kinds of democracy in some ways, at least for societies that value their Confucian legacy. This is a project for another day.

Suggestions for Further Reading

Sor-hoon Tan (2004), *Confucian Democracy: A Deweyan Reconstruction* has more extensive discussions of a Deweyan reconstruction of Confucian Democracy; Roger Ames and David Hall's (1999), *Democracy of the Dead* also discusses John Dewey's concept of democracy and Confucianism in the context of China's future. An interesting proposal for "democracy with Confucian characteristics" is presented in Daniel A. Bell (2006), *Beyond Liberal Democracy*. A special issue of the *Journal of Chinese Philosophy* (vol. 34, no. 2, June 2007) is devoted to the theme of "Democracy and Chinese Philosophy" with heavy emphasis on Confucianism. Many people interested in the compatibility of democracy and Confucianism are concerned about the issues surrounding human rights. Good discussions on this could be found in Joanne R. Bauer and Daniel Bell, eds. (1999), *East Asian Challenge for Human Rights*; Wm. Theodore de Bary (1998), *Asian Values and Human Rights*: de Bary and Tu Weiming, eds. (1998), *Confucianism and Human Rights*. Other examples dealing with the relevance of Confucianism to the modern world, including its compatibility with various aspects of democratic life include Daniel Bell and Hahm Chaibong, eds. (2003), *Confucianism for the Modern World*.

Notes

1. Chen Duxiu (1960), 2:153–56.

2. John Duncan (2002), 37–38.

3. Lucian Pye (1985), 55–89; Samuel Huntington (1996), 21.

4. Chenyang Li (1999), 172–89.

5. Kwon Tai-Hwan and Cho Hein (1997), 321–338. See also, Duncan (2002), 40.

6. Carsun Chang et al. (1958), 455–83.

7. Quotations from the *Analects* will be cited in the notes. References to ideas and themes in the *Analects* will be cited in the text, for the readers' convenience.

8. On constructing social ideals, see John Dewey (1916), 89 and Dewey (1927), 286–87, 328.

9. Dewey (1938), 303.

10. Dewey (1927), 329.

11. Dewey (1939), 226; Dewey (1938), 295, 303.

12. Dewey (1927), 345–50.

13. Wing-tsit Chan (1955), 4:295–319.

14. Peter Boodberg (1953), 2:317–32; Tu Weiming (1979):18.

15. *Analects* 6.30. Unless otherwise stated, all translations from *The Analects* are from Roger T. Ames and Henry Rosemont Jr. (1998).

16. *Analects* 12.2 and 12.22.

17. *Analects* 12.1.

18. D. C. Lau (1979),112.

19. The graph for *zi* begins as a pictogram showing a human nose; pointing to one's nose is a way of self-reference. Edoardo Fazzioli (1986), 29; Leon Wieger (1965), 325. It is also used as an emphatic pronoun: "I myself did it" in contrast with the reflexive use, "I did it to myself."

20. *Xunzi* 29/143/8. See the translation in John Knoblock (1994), Vol. 3.

21. This implied sense of drawing boundaries is supported by the gloss of *ji* in the *Shuowen jiezi* as "having definite shape or form" and "the warp and weft of a loom" indicating an organized structure. Xu Shen (1966), *Shuowen jiezi zhu*, 748/14b:21A.

22. *Analects* 6.30.

23. A. S. Cua (1983), 13; Cua (1985), 98.

24. David S. Nivison (1966), 47, 67.

25. *Analects* 1.12.

26. *A Concordance to the Kuo-yu* (1973), 11679–82.

27. Author's translation. For alternate translations see *The Chinese Classics* (1970), 5:679, 684; and Lau (1994) 14.2/71/19.

28. For an interpretation of *yi* as the personal investment of meaning in action, based on the interaction between a person's individuality and her environment in specific situations, see Ames and David Hall (1987), 89–110.

29. Mencius (2A6) saw the "heart of shame" as the "sprout of *yi*," although he used a different term, *xiuwu*, instead of *chi*, they are close enough in meaning for both to be translated as "shame."

30. Analects 2.3.
31. *Analects* 16.1.
32. *Analects* 6.4.
33. Isaiah Berlin (1969), 135–41.
34. Ibid., 121–22.
35. Dewey (1927), 329; Dewey (1928), 111.
36. Ibid.
37. *Analects* 2.4.
38. Berlin (1969): 121–22.
39. *Analects* 12.18.
40. *Analects* 12.1.
41. *Analects* 15.29.

7

Confucianism and Human Rights

Sangjin Han

The relationship between Confucianism and human rights has been explored by many authors from various perspectives. Some have attempted a liberal interpretation of Confucianism to argue for the compatibility between Confucian thought and certain aspects of civil and political rights as enunciated by the Universal Declaration of Human Rights.[1] Others have paid attention to the question of how Confucian traditions could be more fruitfully utilized to support economic and social rights, such as the right to subsistence, rather than the individual entitlements of liberal rights.[2] Still others have attempted to show the precise conceptual relationships—similarities and differences— between the Confucian ideas of rites, norms, virtues, harmony, and so on, and human rights as a modern achievement.[3] Taking one step further, we can also find Chinese scholars digging deeply to lay a new basis for a universal framework of human rights, which is neither a copy of Western hegemonic individualism nor a parochial confrontation with it.[4]

In this chapter I wish to explore the idea of a people-centered, participatory, communitarian human rights based on certain Confucian traditions and examine the Kwangju democratic self-rule of 1980 from that standpoint. I am referring to the historical event initiated on May 18, 1980, when citizens of Kwangju in South Korea rose up in protest against the country's military dictatorship and took control of their city. To be sure, my argument is selective and normative. In other words, the paper is concerned more with communitarian than liberal approaches to human rights, but with a specific focus and orientation.[5] The term *communitarian* in this chapter differs from other conventional usages of this term, which have been accused of justifying authoritarian power structures in one way or another. In contrast, my use of the term advocates a participatory and discursive approach to consensus formation as the basis of the common good or collective interest. I argue that the Confucian heritage of *minben* 民本 philosophy—which, loosely, means "the people are the root of the country"—can be normatively reconstructed so as to yield such a participatory communitarian concept of human rights.[6] As such, it neither excludes nor is identical with individual (subjective) liberal rights, but includes these in its own way.

To be more precise, this chapter attempts to reinterpret the experience of the Kwangju democratic self-rule of 1980 from the perspective of people-centered participatory communitarian human rights.[7] As we will see, the Kwangju popular uprising in May 1980 was unique in its rich, practical consequences. The citizens, when threatened by extraordinarily repressive military forces dispatched by the central authoritarian government, not only protested against it vigorously but also shared a collective experience of peaceful self-rule from May 22 to 26 after the collapse of the local state apparatus and with the military forces pushed back to the outskirts of Kwangju city. I would like, therefore, to examine to what extent, if any, this experience of self-rule can be considered as a realization of a people-centered participatory communitarian human rights, however imperfect and short-lived it might have been.

Three Puzzles of the Kwangju Uprising and the Struggle for Recognition

There are three puzzles we encounter when we try to understand the significance of the Kwangju popular uprising in May 1980. First, why was a specially trained army unit, paratroopers, dispatched to the city of Kwangju despite there being no particular unrest, crisis, or urgent situation up to May 18, when the students and citizens had a peaceful night street march with torches? This puzzle or anomaly arises because it deviates from the conventional assumption that paratroopers are professionally trained to be sent to enemy territory on special missions.

Second, given the extremely savage attacks and suppression by paratroopers, how was it possible for the citizens of Kwangju to engage the army and push them back to the outskirts of the city so that the citizens became liberated, so to speak? This puzzle arises because according to the conventional assumptions of social science, in a setting of confrontation, protesters tend to lose vigor and energy when faced with far more aggressive forces than foreseen. They are shocked and scattered and remain silent with fear. Contrary to this, however, the citizens of Kwangju rose, armed themselves, and made successful offensive attacks.

Lastly, according to the conventional assumptions of social science, society will come close to anarchy, full of violent crimes such as murder, arson, and looting, if law enforcement breaks down. Yet the experience in Kwangju was exactly the opposite. Despite a state of "anarchy" as officially defined by the military regime—that is, in a situation where law enforcement agencies were absent—the citizens of Kwangju shared genuine cooperation and solidarity. An ethic of care and comradeship spread among the citizens to overcome fear and anxiety in the midst of an intense crisis. The Kwangju uprising demonstrated that the absence of law enforcement agencies does not necessarily bring chaos and social threats. On the contrary, communal solidarity blossomed, replacing the egocentric pursuit of interests and hostility. So, the third puzzle arises.

Of fundamental significance for our discussion of a people-centered participatory communitarian approach to human rights is the Kwangju citizens' unique experience of self-rule touched upon by the third puzzle. But let me mention some salient issues related to each of these three puzzles.

The first puzzle has been a source of various conspiracy theories. According to the statement issued by the United States State Department, the paratroopers dispatched to Kwangju were under the jurisdiction of the Korean Army. For this reason, it was said that neither prior approval of, nor subsequent consultation with, the U.S. Army in Korea was made when this unit was dispatched. Thus, it might be the case that the then military regime dispatched this special unit with the expectation that they would immediately crack down on the protest movements and maintain order. In fact, this is exactly what they had done when dispatched to the areas of Pusan and Masan some months earlier. However, the resistance was unexpectedly intense in the case of Kwangju, since the army's cruelty invited the extreme moral outrage of the citizens. When the crisis consequently emerged, however, this was, in turn, used as a pretext for establishing another military regime in Korea as we can confirm from what followed thereafter.

As for the second puzzle, the Kwangju citizens' experience of inhuman treatment by the paratroopers seemed to create unbearable pain and anger, to the effect that they became firmly united in the struggle for human dignity. One may say that the gap between the experienced world of brutality and human dignity as a norm became dangerously widened as a consequence of the paratroopers' "barbaric and atrocious treatment of the Kwangju citizens."[8] Indeed, the citizens were shocked when they saw the troops "shoot and kill unarmed students and put their corpses on trucks to throw them away."[9] It was beyond their imagination that soldiers who were paid by their taxes could assail innocent citizens in such a cruel way. Thus, they painfully questioned how these soldiers were "any different from communists." This means that core values in the moral community were severely violated. The question of human dignity became a burning issue "when they saw the paratroopers kick their fellow citizens 'like dogs' and [they] found themselves agonizing over the fact that they were not risking their lives in the struggle to put a stop to the violence."[10]

In addition, the denunciation by the military regime of the Kwangju citizens' democratic protest as a "violent mob" or "unlawful rioting led by communists" created anger. Against these sorts of misrecognitions, biases, and distortions, the citizens desperately fought to reconstitute their own identity as defenders of democracy and human rights. The following two statements demonstrate how important the struggle for recognition was for the citizens of Kwangju, and how deeply they felt humiliated:

> From now on, we cannot walk on two feet. We are animals and should crawl like animals on four limbs because we were treated like animals. They dragged us into corners, shot us as if we were animals being hunted down. How was this possible and who will be responsible for this atrocity? Furthermore, we are degraded as "mob" and we will continue to be categorized as such in years to come. Everyone from our province, our sons and daughters in the future, will be called "mobs."[11]

> The Kwangju incident was not a communist riot but a righteous movement against the oppression of democracy and freedom. Thus, the main force behind this noble movement was neither mobs nor communists. It was we, the democracy-loving Chonnam people, who rose to protect our rights in the name of democracy.[12]

So, the key to the second puzzle can be found in the concept of struggle for recognition. The citizens of Kwangju, as individuals, made their decision to risk their lives and join the popular uprising in order to recover their dignity as humans. It is very likely that this decision was tightly interwoven with moral and emotional concerns. Yet it is clear that individual self-determination by the citizens of Kwangju gave rise to the "absolute community" that Jungwoon Choi describes, and this made it possible for them to liberate the city from the army.[13]

The recovery of human dignity sought by the citizens was realized not only through the self-affirmation resulting from the brave struggle of the individual, but also by means of the recognition one received from one's fellow citizens, from the newly formed absolute community. At the heart of the absolute community was love—the human response to an existence more elevated than one's own. Following the emergence of the absolute community, those citizens who had hesitated to join the struggle flocked to it to receive its blessing and were liberated from their fear. It was as if they were "reborn" in the absolute community, and from that moment forward, participating in the movement became a joyous self-affirmation.[14]

Communitarian Self-Rule as Human Rights

As for the third puzzle, it should be noted that something like consensual will or ethos was operating in the minds of the Kwangju citizens, such that strong cohesion and unity emerged. It not only regulated but also constituted social intercourse in the direction of mutual care and cooperation. Why did cooperation and solidarity blossom instead of chaos and unrest despite the breakdown of legal order? What does this experience of self-rule mean for human rights? Here we need to pay attention to the communitarian aspect of human rights as exercised by the citizens of Kwangju, though they had no clear recognition of it. The citizens went beyond individual concerns in order to reconstitute the well-being, dignity, and respect of the community. In a desperate crisis, they voluntarily cooperated and sustained a respectable community as a condition of their own individual dignity. This is what I mean by the communitarian aspect of human rights. In other words, we, as members of a community, are entitled to seek a good community as a condition of our well-being. Being preoccupied with egocentric interests and having little consideration for collective well-being was not the case in Kwangju. On the contrary, the individual struggle for recognition was in harmony with the realization of collective well-being and dignity. As such, one may argue that one of the essential characteristics of the absolute community lies in a symbiotic relationship between the human dignity of individuals and the well-being of the community.

Citizens risked their lives in the struggle in order to confer human dignity upon themselves. Human dignity, of course, is less important to the individual than life itself. One could, however, obtain human dignity only by risking one's life in the struggle. The essence of human dignity, then, is not to be found in the pursuit of personal rewards or social standing, but in the acknowledgment of an entity more valuable than one's own life and in the act of risking one's life for the sake of this entity. For many, this entity can be the nation, or God. In the case of Kwangju's citizens, it was community, the life of one's fellow citizens, their dignity.[15]

Needless to say, the experience of self-rule in Kwangju was not only short but also highly unstable. The absolute community was a kind of utopia, "a place to which one could never return."[16] Despite these intrinsic shortcomings, however, we need to pay careful attention to this experience to explore its significance for human rights today. For instance, as a kind of collective self-determination, the Kwangju experience of self-rule differs significantly from an institutionalized form of self-determination such as representative democracy. Choi correctly points out that "[t]he human dignity sought by the citizens of Kwangju during the uprising differed from the legal concept of human rights found in the modern Western nation-state."[17]

For the citizens of Kwangju, the absolute community contained implicitly the ideals of human rights, freedom, equality, democracy, the state. We encounter difficulties, however, when we attempt to understand the uprising by separating, one by one, these terms from each other, treating them, as is done in Western thought, as concepts that represent discrete phenomena. The moment we engage in such an analysis, we find that these concepts betray the spirit of the uprising, particularly the spirit of the absolute community. In the absolute community, all of these ideals were intertwined as a unity, existing as an unnamed feeling.[18]

We see here a primordial capacity that arises when ordinary people, not through such institutions as election, directly participate in and lead the dynamic process of collective decision making. I am interested in pursuing this possibility from the vantage point of the Confucian *minben* philosophy.[19] Before I do so, however, I would like to sketch how I want to resolve the relationship between the Kwangju uprising in 1980 and human rights.

Insofar as we agree that the Kwangju citizens struggled for human dignity, it seems obvious that human rights were built into the Kwangju uprising. The moral outrage was constitutive of a struggle for recognition.[20] As the main energizing force, it helped the citizens to join the popular uprising. Thanks to its temporary success, the uprising produced a peculiar community in which communitarian solidarity, fraternity, and cooperation were created and maintained over egocentric interests. This was socially constructed neither by any decision of an authoritarian government nor by a revolutionary organization, but through the processes of negotiation and cooperation in which the citizens took part in public assemblies, volunteer services, and many other activities. This experience is provocative and challenging in that it reveals how popular sovereignty might take place before, or even without, the representative institutions of democracy. This is why we need to pay careful attention to this experience despite its short-lived and unstable status.

The Human Rights Debate and Confucianism

The above discussion is intended to bring to the fore a concrete historical reference to which I would like the following discussion on Confucianism and human rights to address itself. The self-rule in Kwangju in May 1980, as a rare example of primordial popular sovereignty, was realized through neither state apparatuses nor representative institutions but instead by way of public assemblies and discussions as well as armed struggles by citizens. It is from this experience that we ask about the possibility of people-centered participatory communitarian human rights. With this objective in mind, let me first briefly reiterate the debate between liberalism and communitarianism over human rights.

For the sake of convenience, we can deal with human rights in both its subjective and public dimensions. The first refers to individual sovereignty. We are all equally entitled to pursue our interests freely unless our expressions or actions harm others. The public dimension of human rights, in contrast, is meant to be about collective self-determination. There may arise problems if one sticks strictly only to one of these dimensions without proper consideration of the other. The liberalists who are preoccupied with individual choices are likely to object or at least raise doubts when they hear somebody claiming the right to define collective interests. Liberalists fear that collective claims are likely to lead to an authoritarian leadership that prioritizes order and stability.[21] In contrast, those who are more concerned with the well-being of a community tend to argue that the liberal version of human rights, when pursued one-sidedly, destroys community insofar as it fosters the egocentric pursuit of individual interests. Each side has its own point, of course. The question is how to reconcile these two dimensions of human rights in a balanced way.

The liberalist position is all too well known. It insists that "each is equal as a moral being and should enjoy substantial personal independence immune from coercion by the will of others."[22] As far as the concept of sovereignty is concerned, the same logic is applied to the state and individuals: "Just as a sovereign state rules over its territory, onto which no other state can trespass, a sovereign individual rules his or her own life and action so long as the actions do not harm others."[23] Individual sovereignty is as effective as state sovereignty in that "one is entitled to absolute control of whatever is within one's domain however trivial it may be."[24] Thus, individuals are entitled to enjoy pornography, for example. No state power can be legitimately used to control this individual freedom.

Communitarians would find it difficult to accept this sort of liberal idea of individual sovereignty, since they are deeply concerned about the moral fabric of a community and the social consequences of individual-centered human rights. They do not deny human rights as such but argue that it is necessary to keep under control those excessive views and lifestyles, including pornography, which "are considered morally corrupt or debased, even if they do not harm others."[25] They justify this in the name of the well-being of the community. More precisely, they welcome and encourage human rights insofar as these rights are instrumental for promoting a moral and ethical life, but would become doubtful if these were used to promote the bad instead of the good. Simply put, "Individuals do not have the moral right to moral wrongdoing."[26]

This argument may sound compelling in non-Western countries where the liberal tradition is lacking and some kinds of communitarian traditions remain strong. Excessive individualism may be viewed as a cause of moral decay in the community, along with the materialist values associated with the "cronyism" of capitalistic development. In this view, human rights, particularly liberal rights, are seen not only as too Western but as being likely to destroy the community. Westernization, for some, becomes "a convenient label for all the evils that eroded the foundation of a sound, non-corrupt Asian society."[27]

One may argue, as Lee Kwan Yew does, that the American failure to deal with the problems of drugs and guns effectively has something to do with the Western tradition of individual-centered human rights. Certainly, it would make no sense to reject individual sovereignty as such. Nevertheless, there do arise problems when individuals remain overwhelmingly preoccupied with their private affairs in the name of human rights and have little consideration for the possible negative consequences of their actions on the community. Communitarians may respond that to prevent this kind of moral decay we must nurture a good community as the condition for individual development.

However, we should ask if it is sufficient for communitarians simply to voice such complaints. We must raise seriously the question of how we can best conceptualize communitarian concerns within the language of human rights. In other words, we must address the charge that the communitarian critique of individual rights tends to support authoritarian power structures, one way or another.

It is against this backdrop that prominent scholars of Confucianism such as Theodore de Bary have launched an impressive project investigating the liberal aspects of the Confucian heritage. It is no less wrong, they argue, to deny Confucianism in the name of human rights than to deny human rights in the name of a conservative interpretation of Confucianism.

> It is obvious enough that Confucianism itself did not generate human rights concepts and practices equivalent to those now embodied in the Universal Declaration; it is not obvious that Confucianism was headed in an altogether different authoritarian or "communitarian" direction, incompatible with the rights affirmed in the Declaration. Thus our aim is not to find twentieth century human rights in Confucianism, but to recognize therein certain central human values—historically embedded in, but at the same time at odds with, repressive institutions in China—that in the emerging modern world could be supportive of those rights.[28]

Confucian scholars of human rights generally do not accept the rigid Western dichotomy between individual and community and, hence, between liberal and communitarian traditions. They argue it is a fundamental shortcoming to assume "the radical autonomy of persons abstracted from communal bonds, social roles and historical and cultural traditions," as the starting point of human rights discourses.[29] Such a liberal understanding of human rights is "implicitly imperialistic," since it imposes once and for all the "truncated conceptions of persons and communities," such as "isolated individual monads and market societies of unrelated strangers," upon all cultures and societies in the globe.[30] Consider that, in a liberal discourse, the primary function of rights is to protect individuals against the community. Community is here presupposed to be antithetical to individual liberties. The question of how to nurture a good community is rarely seen as relevant to advancing the quality of individual rights. This has given rise to a dubious presupposition widely held in Western societies that genuine human rights are exclusively civil-political liberties. Against these approaches, dichotomies, and presuppositions, Confucian scholars argue that "[r]igid dichotomies as well as static understanding of the historical sources of human rights may be quite misleading with regard to the conceptual flexibility and development of international human rights."[31]

In badly characterizing civil-political human rights as the "negative liberties" advanced by liberal individualism (that is, "freedom from" oppressive political authority), one risks deflecting attention away from the fact that these liberties are also means of "enablement" or "empowerment" for persons to function as flourishing members of a polity or community—where they may indeed debate with others about the best way to live together in their society. That is to say, civil-political liberties are not simply the negative "freedoms from" associated with a caricatured liberal individualism concerned with protecting the privacy of radically autonomous, isolated, self-interested, ahistorical and acultural selves, but rather they positively empower a person's involvement in a flourishing community and are thus compatible with, for example, communitarian traditions of moral and political thought.[32]

A fruitful way of understanding the reciprocity referred to above is to bring to light individuality and sociality as two indispensable and equally fundamental conditions of human existence.[33] A person exists as an individual, but leads his or her life as a member of a group and a society. Individuals become members of a society through the process of socialization. Correspondingly, there may be two different modes of raising the claim to rights, that is, individual and communitarian.[34] In the former, I am thinking, speaking, and acting in my capacity as an independent person, and I pursue what I consider to be worthy and important for realizing the dignity of my own individuality. In the latter, however, I am acting in my capacity as a member of the community where I belong, and I pursue what I take to be worthy and important for realizing the common good of the community or public interests. What is at stake here is not only my own individuality, but also the question of how to keep the community healthy and flourishing, since my individual life is sustainable only when grounded in a flourishing community.

Rigorously speaking, the correct conceptualization of human rights can be neither need-based nor supplier-based, but should be rights-based. In this sense, it is considerably ambiguous whether Confucian traditions can provide a clear-cut conception of human rights. However, as Confucian scholars such as de Bary insist, the simple dichotomy of individual versus communitarian rights is misleading. To learn from the experience of Confucianism "need not mean surrendering any individual rights to the community or state, but only gaining a deeper awareness of human independence and social sensibility."[35] The ideas put forward by neo-Confucian thinkers—such as anti-torture laws and penal reforms, the idea of individual perfectibility, the inherent worth of the individual, the autonomy of the moral mind and individual conscience, the reformed conception of law as a check on political abuse, and the role of public education in enhancing people's participation—are significant enough to make it plausible to argue for a compatibility between Confucianism and civil-political liberties.[36]

Simultaneously, the affinity between Confucianism and economic and social rights, particularly the right to subsistence, calls for careful attention.[37] The Confucian tradition is well known for stressing benevolent government, fairness in taxation, and charitable granaries, with particular emphasis on "the responsibility of the rulers to ensure the subsistence, livelihood, and education of the people as a qualification of political legitimacy."[38] Given this tradition, it may be easier to see the positive relationship between Confucianism and human rights. According to an old saying, in the world there is nothing more important than the right to subsistence; it is so fundamental that, without it, it is impossible to enjoy civil-political rights in practice even if one is entitled in principle. The right to subsistence entails an appeal to humaneness: it is not merely about existing or being alive. "It is about living in a fuller sense having food, shelter, clothing, access to healthcare, and even, in some formulations, some considerable political and cultural opportunities."[39] This humane concern over people's subsistence long predates the emergence of an explicit concept of the right to subsistence in nineteenth-century China, when, for example, Gao Yihan (1884–1968) coined the phrase *shengcumquan* 生存權 or "the right to subsistence."

For Gao, the abstract ideas of freedom are meaningless if not well supported by concrete institutions and social arrangements. He ridiculed how absurd it was to ask the poor "who cannot even find work pulling rickshaws to choose freely an occupation. Before they can begin to put self-sovereignty into practice, they need a modicum of material well-being on the basis of which they can seek training or other forms of education."[40] Because of the "rich and strong connection" between the right to subsistence and Confucianism and Marxist traditions, as well, this idea has enjoyed wide support and sympathy in China.[41]

De Bary's liberal approach to neo-Confucianism is sensible, but I would say not strong, in that he tacitly presupposes global standards of human rights and seeks the availability of Confucian equivalents in support of these. Not only the Western tradition of individualism but the Chinese tradition also can provide those human values that could be supportive of human rights. One may even say that, by taking up a liberal approach, he seeks the Confucian conditions for the universality of human rights as established by the United Nations. What is missing is a rigorous reconstruction of a communitarian approach to human rights.

Although the Confucian communitarian tradition has been overshadowed by state power and bureaucratism, it did continue to propose, albeit in adverse circumstances, consensual alternatives for promoting a more balanced relationship among the individual, the community, and the state. It is to such Confucian advocates, and not spokesmen for state power, that one should look for a genuine Chinese communitarianism as the basis for the advancement of human rights.[42]

The communitarianism de Bary defends differs from any traditional collectivism that would tend to favor collective interests over those of individuals. But he does not go farther to reconstruct a needed communitarian approach in its own right. Thus, it still remains ambiguous how the common good of the community is be defined, who is in the position to define it, and why we should understand these questions in terms of human rights.

Communitarian Approaches with Authoritarian Consequences

We have started from the premise that as human beings we are entitled to both individual and collective self-determination. The latter is no less important than the former since individual sovereignty can be best sustained in a flourishing community. The relationships between individual and communitarian human rights are complex.[43] However, I shall focus here only on the dimension of collective decision making. As regards individual self-determination, there seems to be no ambiguity involved since it is clear that individuals can make their decisions through their own choices, wills, and preferences. They have a full control over their thoughts, beliefs, tastes, and so on. No one can arbitrarily intervene in their sovereignty, so to speak. However, there seem to be left a number of ambiguities with respect to collective self-determination. Who is in the position to define collective interests? What are the rights-based procedures for arriving at the common good of a community? How can we exercise these allegedly communitarian rights?

After all, communitarian traditions are supposed to offer a better answer to these questions than liberalism, according to which the sum of individuals' choices constitutes collectivity. More often than not, however, the claim to the well-being of the community has been raised by authoritarian figures. Thus, we must ask whether there can be an alternative approach within communitarian traditions that overcomes the shortcomings of the state-centered approach to collective interests.

With this in mind, I would like to differentiate two approaches within Confucianism. One is oriented toward legitimizing the state as the source of public authority. In this approach the government has the right to define collective interests de jure as well as de facto. This mainstream solution, however, leans unavoidably toward authoritarianism. Contrasted to this is the approach that focuses more on the consensual processes of communication and consultation. Community compacts formulated and implemented in sixteenth-century Korea may serve as a case in point.[44] Of course, in reality, this model was far from being perfect. However, if we want to extrapolate an idealized communitarian model from this, it would certainly not be the state but the discursive formation of public opinion that defines the common good of a community.[45]

We can then conceive of two different modes of the communitarian approach. One is an institutional solution in which the role of the state or political leadership is decisive in defining collective interests. Beng-Huat Chua's point is penetrating in this respect:

> Central to communitarianism is the idea that collective interests are placed above individual ones. Logically, what constitute the collective interests should be based on "consensus." However, as suggested earlier, the technical difficulties of soliciting opinions from every interested and affected party tends to be resolved, in practice, by a conflation of state/society, in which the elected political leadership assumes the position of defining both the consensus and the national interests by fiat.[46]

To be sure, a communitarian approach presupposes a consensual culture. In practice, however, it tends to endorse authoritarianism and paternalism of various kinds by enabling "the rationalization and preservation of an entrenched centralized power."[47] Ultimately, the state is supposed to define community needs in an efficient and authoritative manner.

Probably, the best case in point can be found in Singapore where the influence of Confucianism is still pervasive. In his keynote address at the Create 21 Asahi Forum on November 20, 1992, for instance, Lee Kwan Yew pointed out three pathologies of American society which include: (1) law and order out of control, with riots, drugs, guns, muggings, rape, and other crimes; (2) poverty in the midst of great wealth; and (3) excessive rights of the individual at the expense of the community as a whole.[48] Explaining why the United States has been unable to deal effectively with a particularly sensitive problem, namely drugs, he proudly declared that Singapore had been able to contain its drug problems owing much to "Asian values." "To protect the community," said Lee, "we have passed laws which entitle police, drug enforcement, or immigration officers to have the urine of any person who behaves in a suspicious way tested for drugs. If the result is positive, treatment is compulsory."[49] He continued:

> Such a law will be unconstitutional [in the United States], because it will be an invasion of privacy of the individual. Any urine test would lead to a suit for damage for battery and assault and invasion of privacy. . . . So in the US the community's interests have been sacrificed because of the human rights of drug traffickers and drug consumers. Drug-related crimes flourish. Schools are infected. There is high delinquency and violence amongst students, a high dropout rate, poor discipline and teaching, producing students who make poor workers. So a vicious cycle has set in.[50]

Indeed, Singapore is an interesting example of Confucian communitarian ideology and practice. Certain Confucian ethics have been selectively used to establish a corruption-free, clean government as well as a clean society that protects the interests of the community.[51] Beginning with the premise that what people want is good government, Lee argues that good government depends on the values of a people, which means that Asian values are different from American or Western values. Lee's identity is well expressed when he states: "As an Asian of Chinese cultural background, my values are for a government which is honest, effective, and efficient in protecting its people, and allowing opportunities for all to advance themselves in a stable and orderly society where they can live a good life and raise their children to do better than themselves."[52] He then listed seven requirements for good government as follows: (1) the people are well cared for regarding their food, housing, employment, and health; (2) there is order and justice under the rule of law, and not the capricious arbitrariness of individual rulers; (3) there is as much personal freedom as possible without infringing on the freedom of others; (4) there is growth in the economy and progress in society; (5) education is good and ever-improving; (6) both the rulers and the people have high moral standards; and (7) there is good physical infrastructure supporting facilities for recreation, music, culture, and arts, as well as spiritual and religious freedoms, and a full intellectual life.

Here we find a Confucian path of development toward the expanded role of the state. Benevolent leadership is called for to protect and nurture the collective interests of the community. Human rights are not flatly rejected. Rather, a step-by-step incremental approach is recommended, with heavy emphasis on community and state interests. In addition, there is consultation among diverse interest groups to secure and preserve social consensus. Nonetheless, it remains the case that this path of communitarian development is more likely to lead to paternalistic authoritarianism than to democracy.[53]

Normative Reconstruction of a People-Centered Participatory Approach

Another mode of communitarian approach is more participatory. It is here that we should try to make clear what has remained only implicit in the liberal interpretation of Confucian traditions represented by de Bary and his followers. We search for a model of consensual determination of the common good of a community based on participation. What is central is the capacity of the people—not the state or political leaders—to be the ultimate source of popular sovereignty. We are here concerned with the question of how to preserve and maintain the common good of a society within the framework of the right to collective self-determination. The Confucian teachings of Zhu Xi, Cheng Yi, and Wang Yangming, among others, deserve our attention for their emphasis on the essential voluntarism of the political and social order of a self-governing community.

The methodological problem of a normative reconstruction is a delicate issue, however. To begin with, much in a given tradition is open to interpretation. In this respect, I am interested in an approach aimed at deconstructing mainstream Confucianism associated with the status quo, while reconstructing "those traces within Confucianism which, though marginal to the mainstream, are still valid and allow the exploration of the possibility of a more humane society based on these."[54] We may then move "from deconstruction to reconstruction via the reshaping of the foci of tradition."[55] This might break down the dominant tendency in Confucianism to legitimatize the relationship of power, while releasing its hidden but normatively valid "earlier meanings lodged within the same tradition."[56]

In a nutshell, then, our normative reconstruction depends on what we take to be the relevant meaning of the tradition in question. Though expressed only in an implicit, often hidden, and marginal form, this meaning may still have strong normative force. Reconstruction aims at making explicit this implicit meaning while breaking down the hegemonic uses of Confucianism.

Perhaps, the potentially universal significance of Confucianism lies in its emphasis on the profound role of language and consensual communication rather than in any of its relatively fixed hierarchical relationships, such as that between father and son, husband and wife, ruler and ruled, and so on.[57] A conception of language as the performative practice by which reality is created and shaped is implicit in the Confucian worldview.[58] As Chad Hansen puts it:

> Language is a social practice. Its basic function is guiding action. The smallest units of guiding discourse are *ming* (names). We string *ming* together in progressively larger units. The salient compositional structure is a *dao* [guiding discourse]. . . . In learning a conventional name, you learn the socially shared way of making discriminations in guiding your action according to *dao*.[59]

A pragmatic, nonmetaphysical view of language and communication seems to be deeply built into Confucianism.[60] The discursive nature of learning and knowledge formation is assumed in Confucian traditions, and its political significance becomes discernable in the *Zhongyong*, one of the four Confucian classics.[61] "The process of decision-making is depicted here as the process of deliberative communication: it is open to include 'two extremes,' nothing should be arbitrarily excluded, while, at the same time, it must be deliberative enough so that the best choices can be made and applied to the people."[62]

The normative orientation underlying the liberal interpretation of Confucianism can be made explicit by highlighting Confucianism's emphasis on the discursive nature of human interaction and knowledge formation. This normative layer of Confucianism can be reconstructed as the basis of a communitarian approach to human rights, which may differ significantly from the authoritarian tracks mentioned above. In this way, I believe that we can conserve the essential aspects of Confucianism while methodologically keeping our distance from its conventional preoccupation with hierarchical relationships. At the same time, we will make the Confucian traditions more relevant to contemporary issues.

We take up this perspective when we deal with the Confucian question of rites. Confucians advocate learning by education, not by punishment. "Lead them with edicts, keep them in line with punishment, and the common people will stay out of trouble, but have no sense of shame. Lead them by virtue, keep them in line with the rites, and they will not only have a sense of shame but order themselves."[63] Confucianism is emphatically communicative. Human subjectivity as well as social relationships are understood as shaped through discourse and communication. The observance of rites is nothing but the discursive process of learning to emulate moral exemplars. Comparative evaluations, persuasion, and consensual agreement are pursued and take place. No direct coercion, no violence, no economic incentives are presupposed for this learning.

In reality, however, the Confucian rites were hierarchical. They followed hierarchically differentiated social relationships, albeit with no violence. "Rites support a hierarchy in which moral elites determine what is right and people defer to the judgment of the elites."[64] One may complain that there are no significant differences between the Confucian emphasis on the rites, the paternalistic attempts to provide moral education, and the socialist propaganda campaigns aimed at developing socialist ethics in today's China, since these all serve the interests of the elite and those in power.[65]

I have no dispute with the claim that the paradigm of rights differs from that of rites. Yet I would consider it not only possible but desirable to view Confucian rites as discursively oriented instead of hierarchically prescribed. What is important in the rites are the discursive procedures open to all, not any moral substance privileged by Confucian traditions. In other words, whether the validity of Confucian moral relationships can be accepted today cannot be determined by any privileged authority but must be decided by discursive processes through which individuals and groups put the validity of such relations to the test. This is possible because Confucianism is capable of providing such a framework of discursive learning, as an open-ended process whereby individuals jointly pursue the common good of a community.

In a similar way we can reexamine the conception of *minben* as a normative layer in Confucianism. A typical expression of *minben* thought in ancient Confucianism says that the people are the only basis of the world, and the world enjoys well-being only when the basis is solid (*minweibangben, bengubangning* 民惟邦本, 本固邦寧). This raises a new a set of questions significant for a normative reconstruction of Confucianism. For instance, when we see the people as the basis, what do we mean by the basis? Who are the people? How do they act as the basis of the world, as the root (*genji* 根基), as the origin or the internal essence (*neihe* 内核) of the order, as the subject (*zhu ti* 主體) of action? Certainly, the ruler can be neither the subject of *minben* nor the basis of the people. *Minweibangben* is radically opposed to *junweibangben* 君惟邦本 in which the ruler is treated as the basis of the world. In Confucian political philosophy, the people are assumed to be, collectively, an independent agent, the subject of politics, capable of even communicating with, and representing, the authority of the heaven (*tianming* 天命).

Ancient Confucianism is well known for its remarkable upgrading of the status of the people by advocating a symbiotic relationship between the people and heaven (*tianminguanxilun* 天民關係論). There is the semantic homology among such concepts as *tianfa* 天法 (heaven's model), *tianxia* 天下 (the world under the heavens), *tianmin* 天民 (heaven's people), and *tiande* 天德 (heaven's excellence). It is through the authority of heaven that the people become the collective owners of the world, exercising their inborn natural rights.

Care must be taken, however, not to confuse the normative question with the institutional one. Insofar as normative orientation is concerned, as Xia Yong demonstrates, ancient Confucianism offers profound imaginings and sensibilities. It regarded the people as the ultimate origin of the legitimacy of power and saw the interests of the people (such as welfare) as the supreme value to pursue. Xia Yong refers to "the law of value" and "the law of right rule."[66] The former means the primacy of the people as the basis of the world, and the latter comes close to meaning popular sovereignty, in that the people's consent is the criteria of political legitimacy. According to him, however, because the political reality was despotism, all these normative orientations associated with *minben* thought could be expressed only implicitly via the symbolic metaphors of heaven's order (*tianming*).

In reality, consequently, the normative idea of *minben* politics has been largely appropriated by the ruling elites in an instrumental way—as a governing technology. The people are regarded as an important resource of political leadership. This is quite evident in an expression such as "one gains the world with the people, but loses the world without them." This is also why Liang Qichao concluded, in his comparison between Mencius's idea of *minben* and the modern concept of democracy, that the former expresses "of people" and "for people," but not "by people." We may say that Confucianism could have embraced a normative idea of popular sovereignty but fell short of the institutional procedures by which this idea could be implemented.

Despite this shortcoming, however, it is an open question as to how to reconstruct the normative potential of *minben* thought as the basis of a participatory communitarian approach to human rights. Such a concept as *yiminweibenti* 以民爲本體, or "making the people fundamental," is an explicit negation of despotic politics, but the extent to which the people can empower themselves remains to be seen. The concept of *minben* supports the notion of righteous rebellion by the people, as Mencius explicitly discusses. The people are morally entitled to repel those rulers who treat them inhumanely and fail to serve their fundamental interests. We can easily imagine *minben* philosophy, combined with Western liberal ideas, naturally embracing ideas such as *minquan* 民權 (people's rights) and *minzu* 民主 (democracy). Yet of course, the ideas of *minquan* and *minzu* could have been realized within the constitutional framework of representative democracy.

The question of whether people can empower themselves as the subjects of a direct democracy in modern society is an interesting question and hard to answer convincingly. Of course, people can make initiatives, as can be easily seen in many citizens' movements today. But no agreement is available concerning the extent to which we can trust popular empowerment, that is, the capability of the people to generate and sustain the common good of a community on the basis of voluntary participation. It is not clear whether we can assume that ordinary people have the ability to create collective order through joint efforts. Yet the Confucian *minben* traditions recognize this possibility. As the basis of the world, as the root and origin of order, and as the subject of politics, the people are assumed to be capable not only of constructing consensual order but also of performing actions in terms of virtues. As inborn moral assets, virtues are said to be evenly distributed to all human beings regardless of wealth, power, and status. Mencius thus referred to virtues as *tianjue* 天爵, or predispositions bestowed by heaven.

There are at least two aspects under which a people-centered participatory communitarian approach to human rights, as derived from the Confucian tradition of *minben* thought, can be applied to the Kwangu citizens' experience of self-rule in May 1980. First, seen from the normative idea of the *minben* tradition, the maltreatment by the military of innocent citizens was beyond imagination and unbearable, giving rise to a righteous rebellion by the people. The paratroopers dangerously violated the most primordial Confucian norm of regarding the people as the basis of the world and, consequently, the citizens of Kwangju as a whole were united in their struggle for human dignity. They wanted to be treated as human beings, not as animals. They were against the misrecognitions, systematic biases, and prejudices greatly reinforced by the military regime and the mass media subjugated to it. The struggle for recognition bears rich implications for human rights, since the pursuit of human dignity was the major motivating factor of the Kwangju Uprising.[67]

Second, of more significance for human rights is the fact the citizens not only made a righteous rebellion against a nakedly savage military dictatorship but were also capable of cooperating with each other to create and sustain peaceful order on the basis of voluntary participation. Here we see a rare example of collective self-determination outside the institutionalized framework of representative democracy. Peace and order were achieved by such means as public assemblies, discussions, mutual care, voluntary services, and so on. In this way, the collective will of the citizens was formed spontaneously, capable of regulating affairs in a surprisingly peaceful and orderly way. This experience is highly suggestive in that it points to the possibility of autonomous self-rule independent of top-down regulation by the state.

Conditions for Feasibility

In the foregoing discussion I have attempted to examine salient aspects in the relationship between Confucianism and human rights. Within Confucian traditions, I can say that there are two mutually interrelated modes of approaching human rights. Simply put, I am entitled to my subjective sovereignty as much as I am to a good, flourishing community. The Kwangju experience as I have discussed refers to an extreme case in which the dignity of a community was completely shaken and torn apart to the extent that the citizens rose up to protest against it and recover their communal dignity and well-being. I have paid attention to Confucianism in order to open up a new space of human rights, that is, a participatory and communitarian mode of self-determination. This mode differs significantly from the conventional authoritarian mode of collective decision making as well as an institutional framework of indirect, representative democracy.

I argue that the normative potential of the Confucian *minben* traditions, when adapted to contemporary democratic environments, aspires to not only representative constitutional democracy but also direct, participatory democracy. The full implications of regarding the people as the basis of the world can be better explored in depth through participatory democracy. The claims that I have raised may be more feasible in South Korea than elsewhere. Therefore, I would like to close discussion by suggesting why I think so.

First, the historical conditions are unique. The way in which Korea received Confucianism from China was distinctive in that enormous emphasis was placed on the normative idea of *minben* politics and the role of the public sphere. From the beginning of the lengthy Chosŏn dynasty (1392–1910), this normative idea was used to legitimize a new kingdom. The Confucian idea of the public sphere was visible in the censor's role of public and critical debate within government as well as public discourse in the community. By and large, it was the Confucian literati that actually joined this discourse. However, owing much to this tradition, the normative expectations of an unbiased public sphere and the critical role of intellectual discourse remain higher in Korea than elsewhere in East Asia. This helps facilitate a pro-participatory revitalization of Confucianism.[68] The well-being of a community no longer has to be defined by the state, but needs to be worked out via the discursive formation of consensus and compromise, in which individuals and groups are entitled to join with no exception.

Second, we need to take into account sociological conditions, by which I mean the formation of a distinctive social force with people-centered orientation.[69] The best example is those groups who were born in the 1960s and attended college during the 1980s, where they acquired a people-oriented identity. Interestingly enough, many of them have kept this identity even after becoming members of a full-fledged middle class. They are not only critical of the authoritarian heritages in politics and society but are also more capable of understanding the situations of minorities. They are eager to foster participatory democracy, while strongly supporting the Confucian normative idea of *minben* development.[70]

Third, a participatory communitarian development may be more feasible in a country where civil society functions well independently and autonomously. In this regard, there is no doubt that the civil society sector has gained a more prominent role in South Korea than in any other Confucian society. Politics is no longer a monopoly of parties and politicians but has become subject to the ever-increasing influence of civil society.

Last, but not least, communications technology is important. In order for the people to act as the ultimate origin of public order, it is necessary that they be able to express what they want, aggregate, articulate their demands, and pursue alliances with others with whom they share common interests. The more effectively the state controls the means of communication, the more difficult it is for people to communicate freely. However, recent revolutions in Internet technology have made it increasingly difficult to keep the Internet, and its format for public discourse, under control. Here again, we can see that an Internet-based public sphere has been most intensively developed in South Korea today.

When we discuss the relationships between Confucianism and human rights with a forward-looking perspective, we see that it is feasible to test the possibilities for Confucian innovations against historical developments in South Korea.[71] When speaking of China, we may easily fall into the trap of confusing the shortcomings of the Chinese authoritarian regime with those of Confucianism. This mistake can be avoided when we situate our discourse in South Korea where such factors as the steady advance of democratization, the increase of the middle class, the expanded role of civil society, and a vibrant online community, seem to support the possibility of a people-centered participatory communitarian approach to human rights. Revitalizing Confucian traditions will be greatly affected by these sociological changes.[72]

Suggestions for Further Reading

Jeong Dojeon (1342–1398) was an early advocate of *minben* politics, arguing passionately that people are not a simply objects of rule but are indispensable subjects of politics together with the king and public servants. He helped to legitimize the overthrow of the Koryŏ dynasty, arguing that the rulers had given up their right to rule. See his work in the (1961), *Sambongjip* (*Collected papers of Sambong*). For a discussion of discursive politics in the Chosŏn dyansty, see Lee Sang-Hee (1993), *Chosenjo sahoe communication hyunsang yeongu* (*A Study of Communication Phenomena in Chosŏn Society*). The author demonstrates how important the idea of *eunro* 言路 or "discursive roads" was in shaping and justifying politics during the Chosŏn dynasty, and how the Confucian idea of *minben* led to the widely held belief that the health a nation depends upon the extent to which communicative channels remain open such that all citizens have access to public sphere.

For an English language overview of the history and relevance of Confucian *minben* thought, see Enbao Wang and Regini F. Titunik (2000), "Democracy in China: The Theory and Practice of *Minben*," in *China and Democracy: Reconsidering the Prospects for a Democratic China*, ed. Suisheng Zhao. For a discussion of *minben* politics during the Chosŏn dynasty from the perspective of *sonbi* culture, see Han Young-Woo (2008), "The Historical Development of Sonbi Culture and its Future," in *The Flow of Ideas and Institutions: Korea in the World and the World in Korea*, proceedings from Seoul National University.

Notes

1. Wm. Theodore de Bary (1983), (1998b).

2. Stephen C. Angle (2002).

3. Wejen Chang (1998); Chung-ying Cheng (1998); Randal Peerenboom (1998).

4. Tinyang Zhao (2005a), (2005b).

5. By "communitarian" here I mean more of a discursively formed voluntary consensus than an authoritarian definition of collective interests by the state; see Charles Taylor (1992). I think it possible to work out this approach based on certain Confucian traditions strong in Korea; Sangjin Han (1999c). It should be noted that this communitarian approach with discursive orientation is not identical with the brand of communitarianism advocated by authoritarian figures in East Asia; Han (1999b).

6. In the actual political histories of China and Korea, this idea has been examined and appropriated in many different ways depending on historical contexts. As intensively discussed in late Qing, for instance, the differences in conceptual implications among *minben, minquan* (human rights) and *minzu* (democracy) are undisputable; see Joan Judge (1998).

7. Much research is needed to make clear the relationship between the experience of the Kwangju uprising in 1980 and human rights. This paper owes much to *Korea Journal* 39, no. 2, where we find papers drawing careful attention to the processes and consequences of how participants in the uprising came to understand the meaning of the event.

8. Han (1999a), 191.

9. KHMC (1997), 22.

10. Jungwoon Choi (1999), 275.

11. IMKH (1990), 106.

12. KHMC (1997), 218.

13. Choi (1999), 273–74.

14. Ibid.

15. Ibid., 275.

16. Ibid., 279.

17. Ibid., 276.

18. Ibid., 276–77.

19. This requires the radicalization of the Confucian idea of people-centered development. Apart from this, such historical factors salient today as political democratization, the overall advancement of the level of education, the revolution of information technology, and Internet communication not only foster a more active role of the citizens but also make participatory democracy more plausible than ever.

20. Axel Honneth (1995).

21. Jack Donnelly (1999).

22. Thomas Nagel (1995), 94.

23. Joseph Chan (1999), 231.

24. Joel Feinberg (1986), 55.

25. Chan (1999), 230.

26. Ibid., 232.

27. Eddie C. Y. Kuo (1996), 297.

28. de Bary and Tu Weiming (1998), 5–6.

29. Summer Twiss (1998), 44.

30. Ibid., 29.

31. Ibid., 34.

32. Ibid., 33.

33. Han (2007).

34. The private and public domains can also be distinguished. The private autonomy of citizens has been legally institutionalized in the form of privacy and civil rights. At the collective level, human rights means that citizens, as members of a political community, are equally entitled to take part in the formation of legitimate government This public autonomy of citizens has been institutionalized in the form of the right to political participation, national self-determination, territorial sovereignty, and so on.

35. de Bary (1998b), 156.

36. Twiss (1998), 40–42.

37. Angle (2002).

38. Twiss (1998), 41.

39. Angle (2002), 244.

40. Ibid., 190.

41. Ibid., 244–45.

42. de Bary (1998b), 157.

43. Han (2007).

44. Peter H. Lee (1996); de Bary (1998b).

45. The idea of discursive formation is important to the work of Jürgen Habermas. See Habermas (1996).

46. Beng-Huat Chua (1995), 191.

47. Ibid.

48. Han Fook Kwang, Warren Fernandez, and Sumiko Tan, eds. (1997), 380.

49. Ibid.

50. Ibid., 381.

51. Tu Weiming (1984); Kuo (1996).

52. In Kwang, Fernandez, and Tan, eds. (1997), 380.

53. Chua (1995).

54. Han (1999b), 35.

55. Ibid.

56. David Gross (1992), 119.

57. The importance of language and communication for the Confucian way of life is evident. Good relationships depend on how one employs appropriate language. Scholarly dispute, for example, requires a commitment to mutual accommodation, not just contentiousness but an active cultivation of the art of accommodation. Normatively speaking, dispute is "a cooperative exercise among responsible participants that proceeds beyond obstinacy to search for an alternative on which all can agree"; see the preface in Ames (1994). This discursive paradigm is also present in ritual, and understood as a "scheme of mutual accommodation of differences in attitudes, beliefs, and values in social intercourse."

58. Peerenboon (1998), 246.

59. Chad Hansen (1992), 3–4.

60. Roger T. Ames and David Hall (1987), 268.

61. Han (1999), 38–39.

62. Ibid., 39.

63. *Analects* 2.3.

64. Peerenboom (1998), 251.

65. Ibid., 246.

66. Xia Yong (2004).

67. Han (1999a); Choi (1999).

68. The participatory tradition can be seen in the channels of direct appeal available to ordinary people during the Chosŏn dynasty. Apart from the channels of participation for the Confucian literati, the bottom-up channels of direct communication began to significantly expand after the seventeenth century. Examples were *sangeon* 上言 and *kyŏkchaeng* 擊錚 as two ways of direct appeal by the ordinary people to the king. The total of these appeals during the reign of the King Cheongjo were as many as 4,427 cases; Sang-Kwon Han (1996). This participatory tradition was greatly reinforced in the late nineteenth century when, as a popular response to the heightened perception of national crisis, a number of voluntary associations competed with each other to draw public attention and opened up a wide space for public discourse and mobilization; Lee (1996).

69. I have called these people *jungmin* 中民 or "the middling grassroots" as a distinctive segment of the middle class in Korea. As a combined fruit of the university-centered popular movements and industrial modernization, they were inspired by the *minjung* 民衆 culture spread all over the colleges and universities during the 1980s. See see Han (1997b).

70. According to the analysis of a survey on this group in 2000, as many as 97.6 percent of the respondents considered the idea of *minben* to be most amenable to providing the means for the revival of Korea in the twenty-first century.

71. For this reason, I would like to advance a thesis that the Confucian future in Korea will differ significantly not only from the Chinese or Singaporean paths but also from Korea's own past as well. In the future, more emphasis will be placed on humanity-enriching traditions within Confucianism that are, by nature, participatory and deliberative.

72. When I suggest this possibility, I do not intend to offer a clear-cut causal relationship between Confucian traditions and a particular pursuit of human rights (such as participation in the Kwangju uprising) in terms of either a cognitive belief system or membership in a Confucian community on the part of the participants. I only wish to suggest that a participatory communitarian approach to human rights seems to be plausible in Korea today and in the future as well, and that this possibility can be better understood within the Confucian *minben* traditions, which this chapter has attempted to reactivate and radicalize.

8

The Short Happy Life
of Boston Confucianism

Robert Neville

There are Confucians and Daoists who are not East Asians, just as there are Platonists who are not Greek or even Western. But the idea of a Western Confucian seems more problematic to some than the idea of a non-Greek Platonist. Confucianism, of course, is not limited to China, having spread to Korea, Japan, Vietnam, and elsewhere in East Asia, and to diaspora communities of these nationals outside of East Asia. But it carries with it, according to the common belief, a rich East Asian primary culture of family life and authority structures distinctive to Confucianism and yet alien or irrelevant to the primary cultures outside of East Asia. Confucianism is thought by many not to be able to flourish outside of an East Asian family culture. This chapter examines, by means of an extended anecdote, the conditions under which Confucianism might be transported to cultures wholly outside the East Asian type.

At the Second Confucian-Christian Dialogue Conference, held in Berkeley, California, in 1991, three participants—John H. Berthrong, Chung Chai-sik, and I—attended from Boston. At the First Confucian-Christian Dialogue Conference, in Hong Kong in 1988, we three also were in attendance, but then only I was from Boston; Tu Weiming from Boston attended the first conference and helped plan the second. So as the conference opened in Berkeley, many joking remarks were made about the growing school of "Boston Confucianism." Part of the joke had to do with people moving from Korea (Chung) and Canada (Berthrong) to Boston. But the larger part was that the phrase "Boston Confucianism" is oxymoronic: Bostonians might be brahmins but only East Asians can be Confucians. Tu Weiming might be acknowledged to be a Confucian in Boston but the next topic is always how the Chinese are in diaspora.[1]

As the conference progressed, a major theme dividing the participants was whether Confucianism indeed is so intimately related to and expressive of Chinese ethnic culture that it can be transplanted to other lands only through the massive infusion of Chinese influence. Is Confucianism rooted and rootable only East Asian culture? To those who argue that one cannot understand Confucianism without being born into or adopting an East Asian culture pre-formed by Confucianism, I answered that these conditions do not obtain even within parallels in Western traditions of philosophy. Very few American philosophers have a Greek ethnic heritage, and few have a working knowledge of the classical Greek language. Yet nearly every American philosopher identifies herself or himself as a Platonist or an Aristotelian. And every American philosopher without exception who holds a Ph.D in the field can discuss ideas attributed to Plato and Aristotle. Plato and Aristotle are world philosophers to Westerners who are not Greek; they are also world philosophers in the curricula of most contemporary philosophical academies in East Asia and India. Now the Chinese philosophies also should be world philosophies in all philosophic academies.[2]

Of course, East Asian Confucian philosophers have been responding to Western philosophies for well over a century.[3] They have asked how Chinese traditions can learn from and also criticize Western thought. The wholesale adoption in this century of Marxist philosophy by at least one large segment of Chinese scholar-officials is an extraordinary chapter in the world history of cross-cultural borrowings. But there is a difference between relating Western philosophy to the East Asian situation and what I am talking about. My point concerns living as a Confucian outside the East Asian situation. My own Confucianism grows not by responding to Western influences but by being used for living philosophically in the Western situation, or rather in a world situation with mixed cultural heritages.

Is Confucianism, then, a philosophic way of life that in its heart takes a dialectical and critical reformist attitude toward culture so that, although it developed historically in East Asia, in principle it could be re-indigenized in Boston? Some of us at the conference argued that Confucianism and Daoism from the beginning have been critical philosophies that have existed in serious dialectical tensions with their indigenous cultures. Confucius, Mencius, and Xunzi complained that the ancient practices that constitute harmonious civilization had been corrupted so that people no longer by habit were filial, capable of true friendship, or socially responsible. Laozi and Zhuangzi complained that the human assertion of artificial forms obscured the natural connections with the *dao*. The ancient Moists and Legalists too were reformers. Over the centuries East Asian cultures became deeply influenced and shaped by these philosophies. At various times one or another of these philosophies, and others, had official sanction at court. Although both Confucianism and Daoism sometimes argued by appealing to lost virtues of the past, and therefore presented themselves as appearing conservative (see *Analects* 7.1, 19), in fact they called for change, often for radical change.[4] Because of the centuries of dialectical interaction, it is impossible to understand East Asian culture except as reflecting changes wrought by Confucianism and Daoism.

Nevertheless, it may be possible also to translate the ancient Chinese traditions of philosophy into the context of non–East Asian cultures and learn from their critical and speculative perspectives. Thus, although I *read about* Confucianism in the context of East Asian culture in order to understand its critical and speculative perspectives, philosophically I *think with* Confucianism in relation to my own mainly Western culture and in relation to the various problems of world cultures. Confucianism today faces problems of multicultural embodiments and indigenization analogous to those faced by Christianity, Islam, and Buddhism. "Boston Confucianism" became identified with this view at the Berkeley conference because those of us from Boston defended it, and the oxymoronic sound of the name emphasized the point.

Then an extraordinary thing happened. Partway through the conference, two feminist participants attacked Confucianism for its patriarchal oppression of women in East Asia, and there were several interesting responses to the attack. One was to admit its validity and reject Confucianism, an unpopular response at a conference of Confucian scholars. Another was to admit the validity of the claim but say that Confucianism was right to subordinate women; this position was argued meekly and only during coffee breaks out of earshot of women. A third response was to say that the claims about patriarchal oppression are exaggerated; no women responded this way.

The fourth and most interesting response was to draw a sharp distinction between primary or "primal" East Asian culture, which is admittedly patriarchal, and the Confucian movement that offers a critical lever in favor of harmony and against any oppression that fails to honor "principle" in each person. "Principle" (*li* 理) is the neo-Confucian category for the ground of definiteness and the drive toward harmonization in process. Identified with the Boston Confucians, the fourth response can admit that, although Confucianism often became male-oriented and forced women into servile roles, this is not the fault of Confucianism as a living philosophy but of the primal culture over which Confucianism never fully prevailed. Like Daoism, Confucianism in its basic texts early and late emphasizes reciprocity rather than oppressive subordination, and like Daoism Confucianism waged a critical and often losing war against primal patriarchalism. That Confucianism more often than Daoism became the social vehicle of patriarchal customs in East Asia speaks only to its success in becoming powerful and corrupted by power, not to its basic commitments.

The "primal culture" of Boston is the rationalist egalitarianism of the European Enlightenment mixed with vigorous ethnic and minority communities from all over the world. Has Confucianism anything to say to this? Perhaps it can rework its criticism of Moism and emphasize "love with distinctions" so as to humanize abstract egalitarianism and respect conflicting cultural differences. I shall argue below that the way to do this is with a new ritualization of Boston (Western) modes of social discourse and interaction. An analysis of the dialectical and critical relation Confucianism should have to American culture might very well cast retrospective light on its dialectical and critical relation to primal East Asian culture. It was observed at the conference, for instance, that one major reshaping of Confucianism in the American context is that it places relatively more emphasis on the virtues of public life than on the virtues of filiality, although both are still important. Of those at the conference who identified with the position of Boston Confucianism, a significant number (Judith Berling, John Berthrong, William Theodore de Bary, and Rodney Taylor, as well as myself) were deans consciously identifying ourselves as scholar-officials.

The result of the conference discussion, especially after the feminist critique, was that a significant number of persons, East Asian as well as Western, identified themselves with the Boston Confucian position. Those of us in the religion business know that the enthusiasm of the Christian altar call often does not last long. Furthermore, Confucians in New York, Boulder, Berkeley, Hong Kong, Taiwan, and Seoul might not long want to identify themselves by the proud name of Boston. So "Boston Confucianism" as a school might be very short-lived.

Nevertheless, a large number of scholars for years have attempted to develop Confucianism into a world philosophy rather than one limited to a specific historical culture.[5] The short happy life of Boston Confucianism provides an opportunity for an important rite of passage. Until now, self-confessed East Asian Confucians have had to worry about their ethnic heritage, even in diaspora, and about how Confucianism responds to the modernization of East Asian societies. Non-Asians have had to think of themselves as scholars *of* Confucianism and sympathizers rather than as Confucians in and from non–East Asian cultures. But with the short happy life of Boston Confucianism, it is possible for ethnic East Asians to see Confucianism as a tradition with many cultural embodiments and identities. The first-generation people in diaspora have lived through at least two. Second-, third-, and fourth-generation citizens of Western countries whose ethnic heritage is East Asian have lived in only Western Confucian contexts. Those of us with no ethnic connection to East Asia, who attempt to shape our personal and social lives by Confucian standards in Boston and elsewhere, can now acknowledge that we are Confucians of non–East Asian sorts.

The remainder of this chapter will explore several fundamental issues in understanding this transition in Confucianism effected by the rise, temporary and ironic as it might be, of its Boston school. First will be a sketch of the portable roots of Confucianism, with a discussion of ways of understanding the relation of those roots to the cultures in which they might be planted and the branches into which they might grow. Second will be a sketch of two emphases within the local Boston version of Boston Confucianism, associated with the North of the Charles School and the South of the Charles School respectively (that is, Harvard University and Boston University). Third will be an exploratory discussion of how Boston Confucianism calls for the recovery and uniquely American development of the ancient emphasis on *li* 禮 as ritual propriety; the heart of the argument is a defense of the thesis that American Pragmatism offers a Western philosophic language for expressing the relevance of Confucian ritual theory for the modern world. Fourth will be an experimental exploration of several practical applications of Confucian principles to the Boston cultural situation. Fifth will be a quasi-ironic reflection on several changes in our usual views of Confucianism occasioned by the transitions effected by the Boston School.

Portable Confucianism: Roots and Branches

Although it would be fruitless to attempt to discover the "essence" of Confucianism, as if that were a historically neutral abstraction, it is imperative in any questioning of cross-cultural transfer of influence to state the core of the influence. The best way to identify a tradition is to trace the variegated history of its "core texts and motifs" rather than to specify essential practices or doctrines. The identifying "core" of any tradition is itself the locus of ongoing controversy. Zhu Xi in the twelfth century made an extraordinarily influential modification of what constitute the "core texts" of Confucianism when he chose the "Four Books" rather than the larger list of "classics" that had been standard or other ancient texts.[6] In what follows, I am merely offering a hypothesis here based on my own best reading. The hypothesis attempts a minimalist statement—if leisure exists to transplant more than this, so much the better. Because what I mean by "core" is not a universal essence, it should be stressed that what follows is the core I believe ought to be carried over in the contemporary situation with respect to Boston (and the rest of the West); cores for other transitions, such as to India or Africa, might be different.

The core consists of three elements: primary scriptures, secondary scriptures, and the interpretive context. In the case of Confucianism, my hypothesis is that the primary scriptures are the Four Books, selected by Zhu

Xi in the Song as classics—the Confucian *Analects, The Doctrine of the Mean, The Great Learning,* and *The Book of Mencius*—plus *The Book of Xunzi*. That the Four Books make the list is not surprising; I shall comment on Xunzi later.[7] The secondary scriptures for Confucianism are the major neo-Confucian texts of the Song, Yuan, Ming, and Qing, including among many others the important writings of Zhou Dunyi, Zhang Zai, Shao Yung, Cheng Hao, Cheng Yi, Lu Xiang-shan, Zhu Xi, Wang Yangming, Wang Fuzhi, and Dai Zhen. The interpretive context involves both the historical setting and surrounding texts required to understand how the primary and secondary scriptures took the shape they have; in addition to understanding some Chinese, Korean, and Japanese history, the interpretive context includes texts such as the *I Ching*, the writings of the Daoists, Mohists, and Legalists, and the texts as well as spiritual practices and social organizations of the Chinese Buddhists. In discussing each of these briefly it will be possible to indicate both something of the meaning of the rubrics of primary and secondary scriptures and the interpretive context, as well as reasons for these specific choices for Confucianism as identified for its Boston school.

Primary scriptures are those texts, songs, or rituals that the entire tradition, "generally and for the most part" (as Aristotle would say), accepts as providing its normative principles and motifs of self-understanding. Part of claiming that one's own reconstruction of what is worthwhile in a tradition is correct is the demonstration that one's reconstruction provides a legitimate appropriation of the primary scriptures.[8] Primary scriptures are differently interpreted, of course, with different points emphasized by different schools, some elements suppressed and others exaggerated; the interpretations of primary scriptures can be plainly contradictory to one another, and it is always to be recognized that the role primary scriptures play in one school or another is as much a function of the school as of the scriptures themselves. Good test cases for the "canon" of primary scriptures are cases in which a new movement within a tradition acknowledges itself to be partially heterodox because of something it excludes from the canon or seeks to innovate into the canon.

The Confucian *Analects* are primary scriptures not only because of their founding role in what came to be called "Confucianism" but for two other principal reasons. First, they provide the major themes and motifs of Confucianism, elements developed by nearly every other major thinker. These include humanity, ritual propriety, righteousness, filiality, learning, reciprocity, the importance of developing personal relations that acknowledge differences as well as the equalities of friendship, and a commitment to public life and service; these are usually associated in the *Analects* with incidents or characters that particularize them. Second, the *Analects* provide a particular orientation to the life of the sage, namely, to criticize intellectually and seek to amend practically the current social habits in light of a better way. For Confucius, this took the form of laments about the loss of public and personal virtues compared with the golden age of ritual propriety, and a campaign to restore those virtues through a sensible recovery of ritual propriety.

Because of the centrality of this point for Boston Confucianism, it is worthwhile to note that Confucius's project has an analogue in Plato's. Plato wrote during a period in which the classic values of Greece, for instance as expressed by Pericles, had been undermined. The wars with Persia and the ease of travel to Egypt had shown that there were other ways to have high culture than the Greek. The Sophists had developed a serious philosophy of cultural relativism. And the rise of democracy meant in some quarters that anyone's opinion is as worthy of respect as anyone else's, regardless of education, experience, public spiritedness, or thoughtfulness. Plato's philosophic project is to be read in light of this situation. He invented a subtle metaphysical scheme for describing the nature of real values and showing how they are easily relativized and misunderstood; he demonstrated again and again the dialectical process of discerning what is worthwhile in situations; he developed theories and practical procedures for both educating people to discern the true amidst relativities and bringing the true to bear upon politics. Most importantly, he raised the question of what a just person could do in an unjust world where even the best political efforts would be perverted to unjust ends, and answered that just people need to go into education. Plato invented the Western university just as Confucius invented or at least popularized the style of the Confucian teacher. When Confucianism is brought to a culture that has been prepared by Plato, the frustrated sense of Confucius's life and his failure to win at big-time politics may be understood in terms of his extraordinarily successful alternate strategy.[9]

The Doctrine of the Mean is a primary scripture of Confucianism because it provides the classical expression of the Confucian model of the self as a polar structure stretching between the inner heart of centered readiness to respond to all things according to their value and the ten thousand things of the world. All persons are identical with regard to the readiness to respond in the center, a point identified later in the tradition as universal principle; but each person is uniquely located in perspective on the ten thousand things, needing to respond differentially. The structures of psyche, knowledge, sensibilities, and skills connecting the two poles constitute the self. The Confucian lesson is that these need to be made sincere and subtly transparent so that the centered heart can see the ten thousand things without distortion and act upon them appropriately without perversion. However, the customary structure of the self in psyche, knowledge, sensibilities, and skills is selfish, both distorting vision and perverting action, and the Confucian way is to remedy this selfishness.[10]

The Great Learning is a primary scripture because it shows that the task of education is not limited to the privacy of the soul or even personal life but runs with appropriate shifts in nature through personal social roles, through family structures, community life, and even to the most universal and remote structures of political office. Indeed, true education is based in cosmic realities: the self as described above that should be clear with regard to the manifestation of character, the highest good that is the true home for human nature, and the human community needing renovation that is the true scale of human nature. The juxtaposition of self and society, mediated by cosmic goodness, such that a continuity of obligation exists between personal and public life, are themes surprisingly congenial to Plato, though expressed in unique ways by the Confucian classics.

The Book of Mencius is a primary scripture because of its elaboration of the nature of the centered readiness to respond to the true worths of things, described by Mencius in his discussion of the Four Beginnings (*siduan* 四 端).[11] Throughout the book he elaborates the themes of the original goodness of human nature and its perpetual frustration and perversion. He identifies miseducation and inadequate social structures as the source of the failure of the original goodness to be manifest and properly cultivated. His point focuses the direction of the Confucian project of education.

The writings of Xunzi were not included by Zhu Xi in his canon of primary scriptures, and so I must admit that there is a risk here of heterodoxy; nevertheless, nothing is more orthodox in the Confucian tradition than disputes about the canon. Xunzi has always been deeply honored and his contribution consists in a theory about convention and corruption. If human nature is originally good, why are people ever selfish? His answer is that people are formed by ritual propriety, or by its distorted and perverted forms, or they fail to be formed humanly at all because of a lack of the normative but conventional forms of propriety. Therefore, the content of the Confucian project is to amend, rectify, and inculcate the forms of ritual propriety. From an educational standpoint this concern with propriety is far more important than celebration of the original goodness of human nature or attention to the stern stuff of obligation, both of which are preoccupations of Mencius. Rather, the Confucian focus is best directed, says Xunzi, toward the stylized or conventional social forms that mediate people's relations with one another, with nature, and with institutions such as family, community order, government, and the arts and letters.

By the time of the Song revival of Confucianism, the philosophical stress on ritual piety had diminished, though Zhu Xi published a massively influential book on household ritual.[12] Certain stylized habits of life were by then firmly associated with Confucianism as such, either rightly or because Confucianism had given in to some of the social forms expressive of other cultures, perhaps primal ones, that are not in accord with the spirit of

Confucianism as expressed in the Four Books and Xunzi. The neo-Confucian thinkers did not need to stress much what they thought they already had; and, besides, it is embarrassingly easy for stylized forms of ritual propriety to become hollow forms, so one might do well not to call too much attention to them. The neo-Confucian stress in this period was, rather, on sincerity, perfection of personal knowledge, and purity of will; perhaps something of the Daoists' ridicule of Confucian ritual manners as empty pomposity was taken to heart. Nevertheless, even in stressing sincerity and humaneness, Song and later Confucians were ready to acknowledge the point made by Confucius's and Xunzi's stress on ritual propriety if that stress can be restated.

The most original contribution of Boston Confucianism, I shall argue shortly, is precisely the revival of the call for ritual propriety within Confucianism. To be sure, the humanizing conventions of the American situation, deriving from the Western tradition, especially from the Enlightenment, are vastly different from those of ancient or Ming China. The point of Boston Confucianism is not to reinstate some older set of personal manners—that would be Boston brahminism. The point, rather, is to focus ethical life on the development of social forms and styles that properly humanize people, where humanization is seen within the context of self, society, and goodness as expressed by both the Confucian and Western classics. The long-run argument for the orthodoxy of Boston Confucianism has to be that the inclusion of Xunzi as a portable root for planting in America brings out the best in Confucianism for this situation.

In contrast to the portable primary scriptures, the portable secondary scriptures do not constitute a body of writing that needs to be appropriated and given some positive interpretation. But they do constitute writings that exhibit a complex dialogue with reference to which subsequent Confucians must locate themselves. We do not need to side with Zhu Xi or with Wang Yangming; nor do we need to agree with Zhou Dunyi on exactly what is vacuous. Yet we do need to be aware of the issues that shaped that discussion and have a stance toward them. This is similar to a contemporary Western philosopher having to treat the great thinkers of early modernity such as Descartes, Hobbes, Locke, Hume, Spinoza, Leibniz, and Kant as secondary scriptures; one need not agree with any against the others, but one does have to have a stance toward them. Perhaps contemporary Confucians have to "get over" the neo-Confucians just as postmodern Western philosophers are supposed to "get over" modernity; still, that would be shaping their current work with a stance toward those secondary scriptures. Of course, not all practising Boston Confucians need to be philosophers or scholars, and so they might have little direct knowledge of the Song, Yuan, Ming, and Ching debates; yet their practice would be shaped by those debates and by how they are relevant or not relevant to the present.

The portable interpretive context for Confucianism has to be enough knowledge of Chinese culture and history to be able to situate the primary and secondary scriptures, especially the former. Obviously, there is never enough background knowledge, and scholars will continue to provide hermeneutic readings of the ancient Confucian texts regardless of their transportation beyond the bounds of East Asia and the East Asian diaspora. But it is not too much to expect liberally educated Westerners to learn about the East Asian background so as to be able to situate the Confucian texts. In fact, given the decline in historical knowledge of the Western tradition in Western cultures, there is hardly any greater difficulty in making Confucian texts come alive with college students than with making the ancient Greeks or medieval Christians accessible.

I have stressed in this section elements of Confucianism that need to be portable from East Asian to other cultural grounds, such as the American or even Bostonian. These are roots that need to be planted and to grow for a new and non–East Asian flowering of Confucianism to take place. The theme of roots and branches from *The Great Learning* is a fruitful way to conceive the relation of a fully rooted and flowering culture in Asia to a new vineyard in different cultural soil.

Two Schools of Boston Confucianism

Although a large number of scholars, both of East Asian and of Western extraction, have been attempting to develop Confucianism as a world philosophy, not only as an East Asian one, and although most of these do not live in Boston, I want to lift up a special characteristic of the Boston discussion. The greater metropolitan area of Boston is divided north and south by the Charles River. Boston became a center for creative Confucian studies because of the brilliant work of Tu Weiming at Harvard, north of the Charles. Tu has not only introduced many Western scholars such as myself to the Confucian tradition by his writings and by his extraordinarily gracious genius at public intellectual life, he has developed a rich contemporary sense of Confucianism, fit for Boston and elsewhere.

Perhaps the capstone notion of Tu's contemporary Confucian project is his idea of the fiduciary community. This was first elaborated in his *Centrality and Commonality: An Essay on Chung-yung* (1976b). In the third chapter of that book, bearing the title, "The Fiduciary Community," Tu argues that *The Doctrine of the Mean*, and ancient Confucianism more generally, believed that the good community is not based merely on power relations, although those are present. Rather, it is based as well on symbolic actions that convey the genuine compassion of the king for all people, embracing the lowest citizens in the social scale and visitors from abroad. The symbols for this include taking care of one's family, and exercising "love with distinctions." They also include providing proper support for ministers and officials, and not confusing the administration of the kingdom by appointing relatives, whom one should favor with gifts and recognition but not with office unless they are particularly meritorious. Although the symbols for kingly compassion are drawn from images of parental care and close personal attention, they in fact must convey a humanized impartiality throughout the kingdom that makes the whole a harmonized, personally quickened, fiduciary community. Tu writes:

> In a deeper sense, however, the ruler cannot exercise his power directly on the people; his political influence can only be extended gradually through the mediation of appointed officers. If he fails to identify himself with the welfare of those who are responsible for the execution of his policies, his leadership will be greatly weakened. What he must do, then, is to see to it that his esteem for the worthy, his care for his proximity of blood, and his respect for the great ministers do not hamper his consideration for all officialdom—including the host of subordinate bureaucrats as well. Indeed, this process of inclusion must also involve artisans, farmers, and even strangers from far countries. The ruler's moral persuasion can be truly effective only if it is conducted in the spirit of impartiality. Once the ruler's concern is limited to special interest groups, his efficacy as a leader for the whole country becomes problematical.[13]

The main burden of Tu's analysis, however, is not on the rituals and symbols that convey personalized impartiality, but on the development of the character of the king or sage. In this he directly follows the emphasis of *The Doctrine of the Mean*. Even in his other writings, Tu continues to stress the cultivation of the socially profound self, as evidenced in his biography of the young Wang Yangming (1976a), *Humanity and Self-Cultivation: Essays in Confucian Thought* (1979), and *Confucian Thought: Selfhood as Creative Transformation* (1985). His recent book does not convey the emphasis on humanizing the self in the title, *Way, Learning, and Politics: Essays on the Confucian Intellectual* (1989), but in fact continues that emphasis. Because of Tu's subtle and far-reaching writing and teaching, North-of-the-Charles Boston Confucianism is a philosophy of the transformation of persons to be fully human in the modern world, not just the East Asian world but the world of late modernity and, perhaps, postmodernity. In this, Boston Confucianism appropriates the lineage of Mencius and Wang Yangming, especially as interpreted by Tu's teacher, Mou Zong-san, to whom he dedicated *Centrality and Commonality*.

All that is embraced south of the Charles with an added emphasis: a crucial way to the humanizing of character in all social classes and roles is through the reformation of ritual propriety. Herbert Fingarette began this line of development in America with his *Confucius—The Secular as Sacred* (1972), which deliberately elevated ritual propriety (*li* 禮) to parallel honor with humanity (*ren* 仁) in the interpretation of Confucius. His lever of interpretive argument was the concept of performance in symbolic action, as contrasted with the mere meaning of the symbols. He showed that those things that constitute the human qualities of life, for instance, filiality rather than biological connection, community rather than power relations, friendship rather than pragmatic cooperation, all consist in the performance of symbolic acts. The acts do not symbolize something else as a sign means an object, but in their performance indeed are the humanizing elements of life. Friendship is not described or signified by friendly behavior but consists in it.

South-of-the-Charles Boston Confucianism carries Fingarette's emphasis on ritual propriety a step farther by interpreting it with Charles S. Peirce's pragmatic theory of habits and signs. (Although Peirce was born and raised north of the Charles, he crossed the river to do his best work.) For Peirce, whose roots were wholly Western, human life consists in the exercise of a vast complex of habits. The habits arise out of biological forms, such as the habit of the heart to beat and the lungs to exchange chemicals. But the most interesting habits are those formed by signs that interpret the environment, frame worthy purposes, and allow for the experiencing of things at a distance. Because habits interact with the natural and social environment, they are continually corrected and reformed by what happens. As for Confucius, the significant human levels of life are those that consist in the exercise of the habits formed by the higher signs. The higher signs, which Peirce interpreted with great brilliance in his semiotics, are developed through social interactions; they grow and decay as circumstances dictate. For Peirce, one of the most important aspects of human life is the development of habits that allow us some control over our responses to things, including our responses to the changing of habits. Morals, for Peirce, consist in the development of habits for discerning true values and controlling behavior with respect to what makes life most human. He said that logic is a species of ethics, and ethics is a species of aesthetics; ethics is the exercise of intelligent control to bring about what is good in itself and discerned by aesthetics.[14]

The contribution of the South-of-the-Charles branch of Boston Confucianism is to firmly plant the roots of Confucianism in the soil of American pragmatism with its theory of habits and signs. At the level of decisive humaneness, signs include not only language but gestures, postures, habits of eye contact, manners of entering and leaving conversation, and ways of insisting and deferring. Signs include the social habits making up family and community life, the institutional habits of education, communications media, trade, manufactury, labor, and food production. They include all the ways in which we represent ourselves, our purposes, our work, and our world, ways to which we respond in attempting to act out of our identity.[15]

Boston Confucianism, especially south of the Charles, points out that the specific habits that form personal and social character, habits that are all social in their origin and reinforcement, are often deficient for the exercise of true humanity. They too often pervert or diminish family ties, reducing them to biology plus the dole. They reduce economic activity to rational exploitation of self and other. They reduce politics to contests for power among interest groups. They reduce the arts to expressions of ideology. And sometimes, there simply are no signs at all the habitual exercise of which constitutes a particular human dimension of life. For instance, when the modern Western emphasis on friendship was turned in on the nuclear family, closely associated with the erotic attachment of wife and husband, there were simply no models left for same-gender intimate friendship that do not suggest homosexuality. This particular lack of significant social habits that characterizes the modern West was not true of the ancient or medieval periods in the West and not true of many other cultures that separate the intimacy of sex from the intimacy of friendship.

Thus, Boston Confucianism, by planting the Confucian primary scriptures—especially Xunzi with the emphasis on ritual propriety—in the American soil of pragmatic habit-theory and semiotics, recovers Confucius's project of criticizing the actual society in terms of the ideals expressed in the ritual propriety of humanity. The breadth of the field of signs in the American sense goes far beyond ritual in the ceremonial sense. But then, Confucius and Xunzi had a very broad view of the significance even of ceremony, and the generalization from ritual propriety to a culture of humanizing habits formed by appropriate signs is a natural extension of their insights. By means of this extension, Confucianism is dialectically connected with the entire tradition of Western culture, not merely with the ethnic cultures of East Asia. The program of Boston Confucianism is not merely a call for self-transformation but a critique of the objective nature of the signs that constitute our culture, and a call for their reformation in various ways appropriate to the contemporary situation. Because the self is in fact formed by the objective social habits according to which it must exercise its humanity, South-of-the-Charles Boston Confucianism emphasizes a critique and reformation of objective significant social structures more than an interiorly oriented personal self-transformation. This point is not a contradiction of the North-of-the-Charles focus, only a difference in emphasis.[16] The united claim is that the genuine humanity of personal life in self and society depends upon the cultural availability and prevalence of the proper signs to frame habit; this is to say, genuine humanity depends on properly generalized ritual propriety, and this is something we can do something about, especially through education.

Ritual Propriety and Pragmatism

Although the basic Confucian texts were excellently translated into English thirty years ago by Wing-tsit Chan (1963), Confucianism came to the attention of the broad American philosophic public with Herbert Fingarette's (1972) *Confucius: The Secular as Sacred*. Fingarette's thesis, already mentioned, is that Confucius's philosophy elaborates two essential principles, humanity (*ren*) and propriety (*li*). Humanity seems close to many Western philosophical notions, from Christian love to Heideggerian authenticity, and its Confucian forms have been applied to the Western situation by several thinkers, most notably Tu Weiming (1979, 1985, 1989), Cheng Chungying (1990), Julia Ching (1976), and Antonio Cua (1982).[17]

Propriety or ceremony, however, has been a more difficult notion for Americans than humanity. First of all, even in the indigenous Chinese tradition propriety declined from the status of a major philosophical principle after Confucius and Xunzi. Perhaps this was because it seemed too close to aspects of Legalism that were distasteful to Confucians. By Zhu Xi's time ceremony or propriety had been deposed from high theoretical status to *mere* rules for conventional behavior, rather rigid and rote rules at that. Second, although Confucian propriety has been presented to the West as akin to good manners and polite behavior, there is a deep-seated hostility in North Atlantic cultures since the late eighteenth century to the stylized manners of courtliness. European Enlightenment egalitarianism distrusts manners that have to be learned from others through imitation (Confucius admitted this takes a lifetime). Rather, peasants and poor people are just as excellent as cultivated people if their hearts are sincere, according to the typical American.[18] To a Confucian this is to assert that humanity by itself is sufficient without propriety.

But propriety has a far deeper meaning in the Chinese tradition and its Western parallels are not merely good manners. I shall mention three aspects of its deeper meaning: propriety creates culture, it is conventional, and it is a peculiar kind of harmony. Perhaps the most important insight of Confucius and Xunzi, with almost no parallel in the West, is that the higher institutions of culture consist in the exercise of ritual propriety, broadly considered. With little culture, people can be ruled by a strongman but cannot enjoy good government. With little culture, people can cooperate, but they cannot be friends without the elaborate learned ways of behaving that make up mutual interest, respect, sharing of enjoyment and sorrow, and delighting in one another with faithfulness. With little culture, people can have children and receive life from their own parents, but without learned ritualized behaviors they cannot bring up their children in virtue, or honor their parents in a filial manner. The Confucian problem with barbarians was not that they had the wrong culture but that they hardly had culture at all, and the reason was that they had no or inadequate behaviors of ritual propriety by means of which to embody the higher excellences of civilization.

Of course, ritual behaviors are conventional. It does not really matter what forms are practiced so long as they work to give existence to the cultural virtue in question. Confucius pointed out that regarding ritual hats it makes little or no difference whether they are linen or silk, whichever is most convenient. But in showing deference with regard to the temple, a quick bow while going in the door is a diminishment or routinizing of respect; so it is far better to make a full obeisance before ascending the temple steps (*Analects* 9.3). When Confucian propriety is properly generalized, as I shall argue shortly, language itself appears as a learned, conventional ritualized behavior. Being conventional, languages differ from one another. But the normative question is whether the language in question can convey what is needed. Those languages that support deep civilization are good; those that are so impoverished that friendship, family relations, and good government cannot be expressed are not so good.

The third trait of the Confucian notion of propriety is that it produces a special kind of harmony. "Produces" is not the right word, for the harmony is not a consequent effect of propriety. Rather, the harmony consists in the practice of the rituals at the right occasions by the right people. This was Confucius's most important moral point about propriety—when ritual propriety is observed people are brought into cooperative action that respects the place, needs, and merits of each. Where ritual propriety is not observed, or where a society lacks the rituals that articulate the diverse positions, needs, and merits of its citizens, morality falls back to dependence on the following of moral rules and the happenstance exercise of good will. Unlike moral rules and good will, propriety is lodged in the habits of bones and muscles and in the deepest schemes of imagination. Propriety, of course, is no substitute for the deliberative parts of moral reasoning, nor for sincerity of the heart, just as having eloquent language and habits of speech does not tell one what to say or how to intend. But propriety, especially an eloquent and nuanced language, brings the special harmony that can elude even moral correctness and the good heart.[19]

Propriety is the particular part of the Confucian tradition that I wish here to relate to American pragmatism, although there are other elements that would be equally interesting to relate. In particular, I shall argue that when pragmatism's theory of signs, its semiotic, is used to interpret propriety, a vastly more sophisticated analysis is available to Confucianism than the tradition itself has developed, one that brings Confucianism into intimate connection with the wealth of the Western philosophic tradition without compromising its own heritage. Thus, Confucianism as a philosophy for the Western as well as East Asian world can incorporate significant elements of pragmatism while rejecting other parts, just as the Daoxue movement of neo-Confucianism did with Daoism and Buddhism.

By pragmatism I mean the philosophy of Peirce and his followers.[20] William James, who popularized the term *pragmatism*, did not have a theory of signs and missed Peirce's whole point. Moreover, James popularized the view that pragmatism is the philosophy of "what works," a desperately mistaken distortion of Peirce's original insights.[21] The tradition of pragmatism in America has grown through John Dewey in several directions. The most popular is the Neo-Pragmatism of Richard Rorty, which rejects the speculative side of the philosophy and emphasizes its connections with rhetoric and sophistry (Rorty 1982). My own preference is for the line of development that embraces the speculative side of Peirce and Dewey and learns from Alfred North Whitehead (1929) and Paul Weiss (1974). Whereas Rorty's development of pragmatism hauls the movement back to the modernist-postmodernist strand of late modern thinking, I celebrate its neat evasion of that dead end of philosophy.[22]

Peirce invented pragmatism as a corrective to a line of Western philosophy from Descartes to Kant. Descartes said that mind and body are distinct substances with the consequence that mental representations are of a mysteriously different stuff from the corporeal things they might represent. Kant said that the only way to know that mental representations accurately and certainly represent the material world is by a transcendental argument about what that knowledge would be if it were to be possible. Peirce said, to the contrary of both, that representations are just as much part of nature as anything else except that they exist in interpreters. Interpreters such as human beings are natural things whose interactions are guided by their representations, so that the interpreters construe the world accurately and do not miss the distinctions that are important for the interpreter's welfare and purposes. For Peirce, the point is that the relation between representations and their objects is a special kind of causal relation that has to do with guiding interactions in discerning ways. Rather than focus on the mental property of intentionality, which makes the causal connections between minds and external things unintelligible, pragmatism analyzes intentionality as a special kind (or kinds) of causation having to do with purposive interaction. Peirce's major point about pragmatism as a test for ideas is that the realities of the things with which interpreters interact will correct their representations. For Peirce and Dewey, knowing as having a mental picture is subordinated to learning as the correction of the representations that guide interaction.[23]

Another important contribution of pragmatism is to argue that representations are not mental entities but habits of the behavior of interpreters.[24] The habits have two main connections. On the one hand, the pragmatic theory shows how habits are connected with the things with which interpreters interact, including physical nature, social structures, and other interpreters. The realities of these other things are correctives to habits that do not anticipate them accurately. On the other hand, habits are connected with the human purposes from which interactions take their guidance. Interpretations have many functions. On rare occasions their purpose might be simply and only to know. On most occasions, however, they play performative functions, serving some other purpose which cannot be carried out without some construal of the world and of how to accomplish things. Sometimes purposes are passive and interpretations function to enable sheer enjoyment. Like the Confucians, pragmatists recognize the primacy of the performative or illocutionary functions of interpretation.[25]

The interpretations in any interpreter or community are intricately interwoven and nested the way habits jointly make up a complex life. Semiotics or the theory of signs is the analysis of the structures of interconnected interpretations. Interpretations are made up of signs that interpret, signs as objects interpreted, and signs as the habits of interpreting. Whereas European semiotics (deriving from Saussure, 1959) focuses on signs as interdefined in codes, pragmatic semiotics focuses on how signs come to be in this or that context, how they become determinate or fade into vagueness, how systems of signs presuppose one another, and how changes in one system of signs affects other more or less general systems.

Three particular traits of the pragmatic theory of signs should be lifted up for notice. The first is that it sees any particular interpretation as resting in a vast background of other interpretations, systems within systems; every interpretation has a context and every environment of interpretations can contain an indefinitely large number of focal points.[26] The second is that interpretations are appreciative of the value, worth, and appeal of things, as well as their dignity and place. These value-elements are all part of the reality of things, and pragmatism does not have to accept any fact-value distinction that associates objects with form or structure and value with mental projec-tions. Thus, pragmatism treats experience as fundamentally appreciative, with the values of objects interacting with the purposes of interpreters. Third, the pragmatic theory of signs recognizes that appreciative interpretation spreads across the whole breadth of interpretations from circumambient feelings of the world and its moods to specific purposes and enjoyments, all in continuity.

Thus, the pragmatic theory resonates with the sense of continuity, spontaneity, and aesthetic experience Chang Chungyuan (1963) ascribes to Daoism but that applies equally well to the Confucian sensibilities.

The continuity from background to foreground interpretations in the pragmatic theory is supplemented by an even more important continuity, namely, in the range of interpretive habits. At the fundamental level are the animal habits of organic nature. In English, the ordinary language of "interpretation" is stretched to say that the heart interprets exertion by beating faster, that the stomach interprets hunger by growling, or that an animal interprets sudden large movement by fleeing; nevertheless, these organic habits are low-level interpretations that construe the situation to be a certain way and respond a certain way. The human range of interpretive habits becomes distinctive within the animal world with elementary cooperation, gestures, basic language, and expressive semiotic modes. Together the organic range of interpretations and those involved in elementary human cooperation and society constitute a kind of bio-psychic dance, attuned to and structured by nature's rhythms, but reflecting purpose. At this point conventional signs begin to develop over and above, or as modifying, the natural signs of interpretation. With the more elaborate development of conventional signs social discourse becomes possible with complex languages, cultures, and social organizations. Even though the signs and the habits become more subtle and sophisticated, with conventional elements that may be artful and abstruse, they still are modifications and enrichments of the organic and elementary habits. When societies develop the elaborate sign-systems of high civilization, they have those elements of ritual propriety about which Confucius and Xunzi wrote: the elements that modify cooperation so that it becomes respectful friendship, sex so that it becomes profound love and caring, procreation so that it becomes family life with filiality, and so forth. As the ancient Confucians knew, it does not matter exactly which sign-system carries the functions of ritual propriety, only that a culture have some sign-system that does. This account of the pragmatic approach to signs shows, first, how signs create culture out of nature, second, how signs are conventional and, third, how the signs of high culture constitute the harmonious interactions in which the virtues of high culture consist. In this way, pragmatism picks up on three of the most important elements of the Confucian notion of propriety.

My thesis is that the Confucian theory of ritual propriety can be generalized to include the entire pyramid of signs or organic and social habits, the higher modifying the lower, the lower undergirding and making possible the higher. The ancient Confucians did not believe, as the Daoists suggested, that the higher signs of ritual behavior can be imposed carelessly on baser habits. On the contrary, the uses of ritual propriety are precisely to fulfill the potential excellence of more elementary natural habits by turning power into government, cooperation into friendship, and so forth. The Confucians recognized that the proper uses of propriety require the acknowledgment of and care for the entire range of humanly meaningful nature. They have been optimistic about the power of carefully observed propriety to bring us closer to nature and obviate its distortions.

In this sense, for Confucianism humanity fulfills heaven and earth, and forms a trinity with it; not through being a distinct substance but through shaping interpretively the structured behaviors that constitute a new human reality in civilization. The pragmatic theory of signs offers a rapprochement between the Confucian top-down view of propriety as properly containing all nature and heaven and the Daoist bottom-up view of nature's habits as the touchstone for the authenticity of human culture. The truth lies in recognizing the integrity of the continuum, as expressed in the pragmatic theory.

The moral significance of propriety, or a fully civilized system of signs, is that it makes possible and enables the existence of high culture as harmonies of habits. The achievements of culture have life only in the exercise of the habits whose sign-structures define the culture. Unless there are signs for friendship, family, good government, and so forth, it simply is not possible to have friendship, family, or good government. The moral significance of propriety or a civilized sign-system is its culture-building function.

The sign-system by itself does not solve the problems of moral deliberation, though it makes that deliberation possible at a sophisticated level. Propriety does not tell us what purposes to have except in the negative sense of setting limits to purposes that would be destructive of the practice of civilized behavior. Nor does the fact that a society has a civilized sign-system and practices propriety mean that it is also humane. The rituals can be employed hypocritically and interpretation can be humanly empty. Nevertheless, without the sign-system of high civilization, the civilization itself is impossible.

What pragmatism learns from Confucianism at this point is that much of the moral critique required by our society consists in the analysis of the signs shaping our social habits. More than deliberation about purposes and policies, although those also are to be considered, Confucianism calls attention to the strengths and weakness of the sign-systems that define our civilization itself, our society's practices of propriety. This leads me to put forward for discussion a few brief reflections on Boston Confucianism, that is, on Confucianism enlarged by the pragmatic theory of signs reflecting on the sign-shaped social habits characterizing my American city and analogous areas of Western civilization.

Confucian Principles for Boston Living

What follows are intended to be brief suggestive remarks for developing a Confucian critique of a largely non–East Asian culture. I shall lift up three major Confucian themes defined as problems of propriety and consider how they might apply to the social situation in Boston and its analogues. The themes are, first, how individuals relate to their community and play official and semiofficial roles in the community; although the Confucians call this the relations among ministers and the emperor, I shall call it the theme of civility, where "civility" recalls its roots in the Latin word for city. The second theme is how friendships might be constituted in late-modern societies such as Boston's. The third theme is how families should be organized in such societies. In this way at least certain important elements of the "five relations" (*wulun* 五倫) will have been translated to the modern Western context.[27] Finally, I shall list four new elements to be introduced into the Confucian tradition by its extension to the late-modern West.

A Confucian approach to civility in Boston must recognize and acknowledge the elementary cultural and social habits that a civilizing propriety needs to modify. The first and most important social fact about Boston and most modern cultures is that they are racially, ethnically, and religiously diverse. When ancient Confucians or most East Asians think of their own group, of "us," their fellows are generally racially, ethnically, and religiously homogeneous. For most Americans, although acutely conscious of their racial, ethnic, and religious character because of the always visible alternatives, "we Bostonians" means all the groups that live in Boston, not merely "we Irish American Bostonians" or "we Chinese American Bostonians" or "we African American Bostonians." This sense of diverse groups belonging together and needing to work for the good of all is one of the great achievements of Western culture, and some of the milestones in its development in fact were traversed in Boston. Confucians point out that the "in-principle" commitment to cultural diversity requires concrete positive social habits of deference to the diverse cultures. Boston's contemporary social habits do not include harmonious ways of deferring to the appropriate cultures, and ethnic tensions are rife. Ironically, nearly everyone would like an inclusive and diverse society respecting all the groups together, but Boston's actual social habits frustrate this desire and lead to alienation and sometimes violence. Boston Confucians need to invent rituals for everyday life and government that foster inclusive cultural diversity.

Another social fact with which Confucianism must deal is the Enlightenment tradition of egalitarianism. Egalitarianism is an internally rich ideal, beginning with the equal dignity of all persons as such, including equalities of opportunity, of standing before the law, and of rights of expression and political participation. Although morally sensitive Bostonians are conscious of the fact that egalitarianism is habituated in our expectations far more than in actual practice, compared with many cultures, including those of most East Asian societies, the habits of actual practice often do give rare equality to women, ethnic minorities, and persons from lower classes and unconnected with powerful families. Racial inequalities seem almost intractable but still there is greater opportunity for racial minorities in Boston and like places than in places unaffected by the European Enlightenment. Confucians would point out that even where egalitarian ideals are institutionalized fairly well in social habits, people still need to be recognized as individuals with unique positions and values. The abstractness of equality is a dehumanizing burden, treating people as mere tokens occupying a position in a system, if the social habits of equality are not also framed with the rituals that recognize persons in their different and unique qualities. The Confucian task in an egalitarian society is to develop social habits that recognize and reinforce equality while also addressing the unique persons playing egalitarian roles.

That Boston's modern society is egalitarian, at least in the habits of expectation, does not mean that it does not need a hierarchy of roles in government, business, and other systems such as education. But the hierarchy aims to be functional in structure and meritocratic in terms of qualification to office. Tradition has little weight in American culture for defining offices; offices and roles are constantly being modified, rearranged, invented, or phased out. The meritocracy of qualifications for office is similar in many respects to the ideal of the Chinese Confucian examination system, but extends throughout society, for instance to business. Seniority has to do not with age but with length of time and experience in a position. Although the functional hierarchies and meritocratic placement of position holders are always imperfect, even if it were perfect the Confucian would ask further critical questions. Do the civilizing habits of the society adequately recognize the whole person in the office, and are the offices defined so as to be held by whole people? For instance, a person in a low position at work might be a high official in church or in the family. A person in high responsibility in government or business might be extremely needy in the context of family and a very poor athlete in recreational sports. The civil rituals by which we relate to ourselves and to others in various hierarchical offices need to acknowledge that holding those offices is not the entirety of the person's life. Business relations need not invade privacy, but they ought not deny it either. Confucians in Boston should work for the social rituals that allow people to relate to others in official or semiofficial positions as complex human beings.

I shall now turn from the Confucian theme of civility to that of friendship. The conditions for friendship in Boston reflect the social conditions mentioned above, namely, inclusive cultural diversity in race, ethnicity, and religion, egalitarianism, and a social system with functional hierarchies and a meritocracy. Whereas Chinese Confucianism as well as Western Aristotelianism have emphasized equality as a condition for true friendship, that condition cannot obtain in a society with the late-modern conditions of Boston. Even egalitarianism means that people are to be treated with equal respect who are vastly different in age, talent, interests, and background. With rare exceptions, true friendships in the Boston situation will have to be possible among "unequals," among people of different genders, different ages, different talents and intelligence, and different positions in social hierarchies.

Boston Confucians then need to point out that at the heart of true friendship are the social habits or rituals for enduring through a long time. Friendships are formed only through long endurance of changes in relations among the friends; gender roles change as people age, social positions change with age, talents and responsibilities change, as well as offices in hierarchies. Friends are those who learn to love, respect, and defer to one another through a long period of changes. In this way, they come to relate heart to heart to one another as whole persons. Friendships can begin with the infatuation of a common interest, a shared attitude, or a reciprocal wit; but they need to develop so as to create a subculture of interpersonal habits that arises through participating in one another's lives over time. Confucian ritual strategies need to be developed to sustain friendships through changes in inequalities over time. Confucians rightly warn against the fake rituals of instant familiarity that we associate with salesmen; the manners of "instant informality" are a crass simulacrum of friendship when applied to people who do not really know one another well.

Boston Confucianism needs also to distinguish true friendship from two other relations with which it is easily confused in late-modern Western culture. One is the civil relations of functional interaction within society discussed above, where the social habits with true propriety allow us to recognize people in their wholeness while relating to them according to their functions. Thus, we need rituals for dealing with shopkeepers, bureaucrats, and politicians; but these are not the rituals that necessarily foster true friendship. The second relation to be distinguished from true friendship is collegiality, which is much closer to friendship than civil relations and often its source. Collegiality is the type of relation developed through close proximity, perhaps in working conditions or through living in the same neighborhood. Colleagues relate not only functionally but in sharing much of the rest of their social and personal lives. The rituals of collegiality properly insist that colleagues help one another when in trouble and rejoice and grieve with one another; in traditional societies collegiality is what is meant by "community." But collegiality is a function of the circumstances of proximity. When one changes jobs or moves to a different neighborhood, one can change colleagues with no serious loss. New people enter into one's life to share events, to help, with whom to rejoice and grieve. In such a mobile society as has developed in late modernity, proper Confucian rituals of collegiality are extremely important, but they are not true friendship that endures the changes of circumstances of proximity. True friends stay together through change and separation.

The final Confucian theme to which I would like to relate Boston's circumstances is the family, under which the themes of husband-wife relations, filiality, and younger and older sibling relations are comprised. The general Confucian civilizing reality sought in the propriety of family relations is that each member be prized, supported, and cared for with respect to the ongoing tasks of integrating with excellence the appropriate roles the person has within the family with those the person plays outside the family. This is to say, the family is the matrix within which people can become fully human in all the dimensions of their life, and the care and affection appropriate for the family should consist in the social habits fostering this.

The differences between traditional East Asian and modern American families have often been emphasized by those who claim that Confucianism requires the East Asian structure. Among the differences are these: the traditional East Asian family more sharply distinguishes the sex roles; women tend more to be confined to the home and domestic activities whereas men are more likely to play public roles; seniority is granted greater authority; separate responsibilities are more likely to be given children on the basis of birth order; and sharper separations are made between family members and those who are not kinfolk. Although these differences are real, they still are a matter of degree; families in contemporary China may not be as close to the traditional stereotype as to the modern American stereotype.

Confucianism for a modern American family, especially of the middle class, must cope with the fact that the family is intricately integrated into other public institutions that in traditional East Asia would be internal to the family. Children, for instance, must relate to the school systems and very little to formal education by family members; but where the school system fails, the family in America must make up the difference. Instead of a typical Chinese family business in which people are secure in a position and attain seniority that can be exercised as long as desired, Americans often shift companies, working their way to management responsibilities of some sort, and then retiring to a life of expected leisure supported by retirement plans. American family proprieties or rituals need to accommodate their treatment of each individual according to the shifting roles they play in school and work. A youngish person might be junior in the family but the owner of his business and the boss of older people, including perhaps older relatives. A student might be a failure as a scholar but a helpful and responsible family member. Confucian family propriety cannot address primarily the person in the family role as perhaps is typical in the traditional Chinese family but must also address the person as integrating the familial with the public roles.

About the time of the Moist egalitarian critique of Confucian ideas in China,[28] the prophetic tradition of Israel, followed by the rabbinic institutions and especially by Jesus, attacked the tight kinship system of Jewish life as unjust because of its neglect and persecution of those lacking family. The early

Christian concern for widows, orphans, and strangers led Jesus to denigrate his personal kinship connections and to appropriate kinship language for universal relations (*Mark* 3:31–35): we are all brothers and sisters, children of the one divine father. In both the Jewish and Christian traditions membership in synagogue or church has taken over many of the senses of interpersonal identification typical of kinship families but extended to include those without families. For many people their communal religious identification is as important as their family identification. Confucianism for American Judaism and Christianity needs to recognize in family ritual propriety the identifications members might have with religious communities that exercise some family-like functions.

Having stressed the differences in family conditions between traditional East Asian Confucianism and Boston Confucianism, let me now stress the need for a positive Boston Confucian contribution. American families by and large do not have the civilizing rituals they need to integrate school and home life, to acknowledge women with careers who also are mothers and homemakers, to cope with mature men who can be consumed by job responsibilities or out of work completely, to mediate the passing on of family traditions with what children learn at school and work, to dignify retirement while keeping family ties, and so forth. American families need yet to cope with the fact that so many family members live alone, separated from the family. The modern American family enjoys many advantages of opportunity, and in certain circumstances has obvious problems to be addressed by more and better jobs or better housing arrangements. But even if the advantages were celebrated and the problems overcome, there are insufficient rituals of family life for it to become the home in which people can be cared for and supported in working out the issues of wholeness in their lives. Confucianism in Boston and the modern West has both critical and creative philosophical work to do, in continuity with two and a half millennia of work in East Asia.

In this chapter so far I have argued that Confucianism (and by extension other traditions of Chinese thought) is now a world philosophy with all the intellectual responsibilities this entails. My first line of argument was that Confucianism can learn from and extend the Western tradition of pragmatism, and therefore enter into internal dialectical relations with the Western traditions of philosophy so as to form in part a world tradition of philosophy inclusive of East Asia and the West. The specific argument was that Confucianism properly focuses in its emphasis on ritual propriety the moral implications of the pragmatic theory of signs. The second line of argument was an illustrative survey of cases in which Confucianism in its Boston school can relate to modern American society as critic and cultural creator through ritual propriety, just as it has done for millennia to East Asian societies. Both lines of argument are incomplete and merely suggestive. But I believe they point toward a new dignity and calling, as well as new forms, for Chinese philosophy.

One must take this discussion of Boston Confucianism with a large sense of humor. The fact that Charles Peirce, Tu Weiming, and I are Bostonians is sheerly accidental, and I mean to be speaking for a wide range of people in America and Asia who approach Confucianism as a portable world-philosophy. Wm. Theodore de Bary's development of Confucian studies and practice at Columbia University in New York has been longer lasting and more productive than any of us Confucians from Boston, even if he and his students Judith Berling, Rodney Taylor, and Mary Evelyn Tucker responded to the altar call in Berkeley. Liu Shuhsien and Cheng Chungying share the general program of Boston Confucianism with but brief connections with the City of Boston. But if, with humor, we take Boston Confucianism as a symbol for a larger development, there are four novelties to be introduced into the Confucian tradition in the current discussion.

First, the self-conscious development of a non–East Asian form of Confucianism requires internalizing a historical self-consciousness to a degree unprecedented in the Confucian tradition. Beginning with Confucius, of course, the tradition has been aware of historical distance and change, even when conceptions of the past were mainly legendary. The importation of the primary scriptures of Confucianism to a living tradition in the West, however, requires that the interpretive context be not only the *Yijing* but also Plato's *Republic*, as illustrated above. Just as neo-Confucianism in the Song and Ming learned from the Buddhists and Daoists, Boston Confucianism learns from the pragmatists, and must interpret itself to the Kantians, phenomenologists, and Western logicians. The scale of historical transformation, the degree of change, and the jeopardy of connecting roots with branches is increased now.

Second, to the extent Confucianism flourishes in new forms in the West, there will be people identifying with it, living according to its primary texts and programs, and speaking for it, *who are not serious scholars*. Only a few Confucians in East Asia are serious scholars—ordinary Confucians there imbibe the philosophy with their culture. But in the West until very recently, the few and only people who had any connection with Confucianism at all were the diaspora East Asians and the serious scholars. Like any religious philosophy, Confucianism looks far better when represented only by its learned leaders. But from now on, Confucianism will be represented sometimes by people such as myself who have no pretense at Sinological scholarship and who read the texts in translation. The price of vigorous success is popularization, in this case by some who are Westerners.

Third, success in the West will make multiple religious identity a forced option for Confucians. The nature of religious affiliation is a complex problem that has not been addressed yet. Nor has the question been discussed whether Confucianism is a religion, although it surely is with respect to defining a way of life and shaping "ultimate concern."[29] In East Asia at various times, Confucianism has been affiliated with Buddhism, Daoism, Shintoism, and Shamanism according to diverse models, with some equivocation regarding the meaning of affiliation.[30] In the West, the question will arise whether Confucianism is compatible with Christianity, Judaism, and perhaps eventually Islam. Regarding the first encounter of Confucianism with Christianity, the "Rites" controversy ended in a negative answer to that question.[31] In the present situation, I believe the answer is different.

Fourth and finally, the importance of the virtues of public life for Boston Confucians is made more evident by the emphasis on the recovery of ritual propriety. The Confucian way, especially for South-of-the-Charles Boston Confucians, is to attend to the perfection of all those meaningful social and significatory forms that shape personal and social habits. For it is through these habits and through the signs that shape them that all human relations are mediated, even relations to oneself. What is public office but the care of social structures? What is a scholar-official but a holder of public office who sees that the principal instrument of administration or care is education? By no means is all exercise of public office merely a process of education. But education is perhaps the most effective way of exercising office because it consists in helping people take on signs guiding their habits that they lacked previously or practiced badly. Human beings are hardwired to be responsive to changes in signs. All other exercise of public office involves force, which is inefficient and counterproductive to free human life.

I worry sometimes that Confucianism seems to be inordinately attractive to deans. Deans, of course, attempt to administer by a combination of broadcasts of vision and rewards for good practice; they have little other power. Is Confucianism merely the view that the world is a somewhat loosely run school? I think not, at least in its Boston branch. War is an evil shaped by the ritual signs of enmity, greed, and bitter memory. Poverty is shaped by the ritual signs that define ownership and exchange. Psychological and sexual abuse are behaviors shaped by signs feeding needs and passions. Hopelessness, despair, acting out, neighborhood violence, and self-destructiveness turned into a subculture are all functions of the signs shaping the realities of our culture. The signs, the ritual behaviors, are not about something other than themselves in context: they in their exercise are the very realities of human life. The Confucians have indeed identified the hard realities of life, and offer a way to reform them so that self and society are united in goodness.

Suggestions for Further Reading

For more information on Confucianism and comparative philosophy, see Robert Cummings Neville (2008), *Ritual and Deference: Extending Chinese Philosophy in a Comparative Context*. For a discussion of Confucianism and Christianity, see my essay in Amos Yong and Peter G. Heltzel, eds. (2004), *Theology in Global Context*. Many more suggestions for further reading appear in the notes to this chapter.

Notes

Parts of this essay appear in my (2000), *Boston Confucianism: Portable Tradition in the Late-modern World*, (Albany: State University of New York Press).

1. See Tu Weiming (1991), "The Living Tree: The Changing Meaning of Being Chinese Today" in *Daedalus*. The original topic for that issue was the Chinese Diaspora. But it was changed to reflect the distinction between the center and the periphery, and the changing relations between those two. In either image, the diaspora or the center-periphery, the assumption is that Confucianism has something to do with "being Chinese." The present essay disputes that.

2. A distinction needs to be drawn at this point between scholars and philosophers. A scholar, in the Western sense of that term, aims to understand a philosophy historically in terms of the intimate meanings of its basic texts and the full social reality of the contexts of its development. A scholar need not ask whether a particular philosophy is true, or whether it has application for the present time. Indeed, a good scholar in philosophy needs to be sensitive to and knowledgeable about conflicting philosophies in order to understand their dialectical tensions. A philosopher is concerned with the truth and pertinence of philosophical ideas. Philosophy has a creative element of extending any inherited philosophy into new contexts, and interpreting new contexts in terms of ideas newly pertinent. Of course, philosophers depend on scholars for their understanding of historical philosophies, and some philosophers can also be authentic scholars. Some scholars go beyond historical understanding to authentic philosophy. But whereas true scholarship requires knowledge of the original languages of the texts and intimate acquaintance with their social contexts, philosophers can work from translations and from histories written by others. Indeed, often the critical meaning of philosophies becomes clear only in the endeavor to translate them to some other language and culture.

3. To be sure, the response is far more ancient. Both the early Buddhists and the Nestorian Christians represented important elements of Western thought to which Confucians had to respond. Christian missions to China in the sixteenth and seventeenth centuries also brought Confucians in touch with European renaissance thought. But it was in the nineteenth century that science and other aspects of Western modernity came to be taken with great seriousness, as in the work of Kang Yuwei, for instance.

4. For a general interpretation of ancient Chinese philosophy as disputation regarding social criticism, see A. C. Graham (1989). For an interesting reinterpretation of neo-Confucianism that treats it as a cultural and political movement as well as a philosophic one, see Hoyt Cleveland Tillman (1992); see especially his references to Wang Anshi.

5. One thinks particularly of Wing-tsit Chan, Chung-ying Cheng, Antonio Cua, Liu Shu-hsien, and Tu Weiming, among Chinese authors writing in English, and of Wm. Theodore de Bary among Western scholars. At a presentation of an early draft of this chapter at the neo-Confucian Seminar at Columbia University, Professor de Bary pointed out that the development of Confucianism in America, in English, antedates its most recent flourish in Boston; Tu Weiming, for instance, had received some of his graduate education in the Columbia University program and others of Professor de Bary's students, such as Judith Berling and Rodney Taylor, did not think of themselves as Confucians for the very first time at the Berkeley conference.

6. Tillman (1992), Introduction and *passim*.

7. With greater leisure of transplantation, I would include the *I Ching*, the *Book of Odes*, and the *Book of Rites*.

8. I have analyzed the distinction between primary and secondary scripture, and its relation to tradition, in Neville (1991), 36–46.

9. On Plato as a social revolutionary through education, see Robert S. Brumbaugh (1962), (1982), and (1989). For my comparison of Plato and Confucius, see my (1981), chapter 2.

10. This compressed description of the Confucian model of the self reflects my own reading both of the ancient texts and of their interpretation by neo-Confucians down to the present day such as Tu Weiming. For a more complete description with citations of relevant texts, see Neville (1987a), chapter 2 and (1991a), chapters 7 through 9.

11. *Mencius* 2A6, in Wing-tsit Chan (1963), 65.

12. Zhu Xi (1991).

13. Tu Weiming (1976b), 87.

14. Charles S. Peirce (1839–1914) was a philosopher, mathematician, and scientist; he was unsuccessful in holding academic appointments, was chronically ill with a painful neurological disease, and died in poverty. Nevertheless, he was a philosophical genius on a par with Kant. His important philosophic ideas are found in Peirce (1931–35), especially Volumes 1, 5, and 6; a useful short collection is Philip P. Wiener (1958). I have analyzed Peirce on the points discussed in the text in Neville (1992) and have developed an explicitly Confucian-pragmatic theory of ritual in (1995) *Normative Cultures* (part 5).

15. Neville (1995), chapters 7 through 8.

16. The first two chapters of Tu Weiming's *Humanity and Self-Cultivation* are called "The Creative Tension between *Jen* and *Li*," and "*Li* as Process of Humanization." My own first analysis of Confucian thought (1978) was entirely focused on inner personal transformation.

17. Tu Weiming's last book deals with intellectuals in China more than with Chinese philosophical principles for the West. Cheng's representations of Chinese thought for the West have been deeply influenced by the *I Ching*. See A. S. Cua and Julia Ching for contemporary presentations of Wang Yangming's approach to humanity, the first in a moral, the second in a spiritual mode.

18. See the extraordinarily profound description of this in Alexis De Tocqueville's *Democracy in America*, any edition, Part Two, Book III.

19. Propriety not only has this moral function, but also carries the moral to a religious dimension. Through civilization as embodied in the social practices shaped by proper ritual propriety, the domain of the human becomes equal to and a fulfillment of heaven and earth. See Robert Eno (1990) and the first chapter in A. C. Graham (1989).

20. Charles Hartshorne and Paul Weiss published six volumes of Peirce's philosophical papers, *The Collected Papers of Charles Sanders Peirce*, and Arthur W. Burks edited two more. A new and more nearly complete edition is being published by Indiana University Press but it is not yet far enough along to cover the major philosophical papers. My own books developing pragmatism's theory of nature and signs are a trilogy called *Axiology of Thinking*, consisting of *Reconstruction of Thinking, Recovery of the Measure,* and *Normative Cultures.*

21. John Dewey, also a classical pragmatist, did understand Peirce's theory. Nevertheless, Dewey toured China in 1919 and 1920 lecturing on the elementary advantages of technology, which he believed appropriate for China at that time. See Dewey (1973). The unqualified praise of technology in these lectures contradicts the extremely nuanced and critical approach to technology in Dewey's books for readers of English and that is required for an extension of Confucianism. In comparison, read Dewey (1981) or (1984).

22. Neville (1992). See the introduction and first chapter.

23. See John E. Smith (1978) and Neville (1989).

24. The sketch here of the pragmatic theory of signs as natural habits relating interpreters both to nature and to purposive intentions and intentionality is developed at length in Neville (1989) and (1995).

25. On the performative and illocutionary functions of language, see John Searle (1969) and also Herbert Fingarette (1972) which uses these notions to interpret ritual propriety.

26. Thus, pragmatic semiotics rejects any functionalist approach to interpretation that sees a background as only an aggregate of connected individual interpretations. See Neville (1989), chapter 2.

27. *Doctrine of the Mean*, chapter 20; *Mencius* 3A4; for both see Wing-tsit Chan (1963).

28. Wing-tsit Chan (1963), chapter 9; Graham (1989), II:2.

29. Ultimate concern is the defining point for religiousness according to Paul Tillich (1952), and in some respect that must be right. I have argued that the marks of a religion are rituals that epitomize how people are supposed to relate to life, mythologies or cosmologies that symbolize the universe's character and limits, and spiritual practices aiming at improvement or perfection; see Neville (1991), 156–63; Neville (1996), the introduction and first chapter. See also Eno (1990).

30. See, for instance, Judith Berling (1980).

31. For an extended discussion of the first encounter of Christianity with Confucianism, see Jonathan D. Spence (1984). For an account of the current status of the Confucian-Christian dialogue, see Berthrong (1994). In the long run, of course, Matteo Ricci won the argument.

9

A Feminist Appropriation
of Confucianism

Li-Hsiang Lisa Rosenlee

In feminist discourse, the term *Confucianism* appears more as a term of reproach than a possible theoretical ground for women's liberation. For instance, in Virginia Held's definitive work on care ethics, a traditional Confucian care ethic is said to be unacceptable to feminists.[1] The feminist sentiment of incompatibility between Confucianism and feminist ethics reveals the shared assumption that Confucianism at its core signifies a systematic oppression of Chinese women, in theory as well as in practice, and this sentiment in part is derived from the common understanding of Confucianism as being synonymous with male supremacy, patriarchal family structure, and restricted gender roles for women. Given the fact that Confucianism has been the most dominant intellectual tradition in the Chinese world, the feminist rejection of Confucianism amounts to the proclamation of the superiority of Western theories insofar as the issue of gender parity is concerned. It is true that Confucianism by itself doesn't exhaust the breadth and depth of the whole Chinese intellectual tradition; Daoism and Buddhism, for instance, are prominent in the lives of the Chinese people as well. Some contemporary feminists indeed have explored the possibility of making Daoism, a native religious as well as philosophical tradition, an ally of feminism by pointing out its prioritization of feminine attributes. But this possibility is often accompanied by the assumption that Daoism works within the Cartesian duality where *yin* 陰 and *yang* 陽, femininity and masculinity, are treated as equivalent concepts. This assumption has already been called into question by numerous scholars.[2] The problematic of the feminization of Daoism, however, cannot be dealt with here, for the sake of brevity. In this chapter, we will limit ourselves to a discussion of the intersection between Confucianism and feminism.

To begin with, feminists, sinologists, and the like often suppose, as Margery Wolf did in her critique of Tu Wei-ming's reappropriation of neo-Confucianism, that "Confucian personhood" coincides with the male self, and Confucianism as a whole is fundamentally incompatible with feminism.[3] But, one might argue that to suppose the incompatibility between Confucianism and feminism is to impose a racial hierarchy under the guise of feminism, not to mention the logical fallacy inherent in the wholesale feminist rejection of Confucianism based on some "sexist" remarks found in that tradition. For in either case, the West (whether canonical or contemporary theory) is construed as the sole supplier of ethical theories and the rest of the world is seen as a puzzling moral problem waiting to be solved. In other words, since the indigenous intellectual tradition is seen as inherently sexist and hence fundamentally incompatible with feminist consciousness, women's liberation consequently will have to be justified based on morally superior Western theories. In order to reject such a neocolonial assumption, we will have to reject the wholesale misappropriation of Confucianism found in feminist discourse. More importantly, we will have to go beyond feminists' negative assessment of Confucianism by exploring the possibility of constructing a feminist theory from within the Confucian framework.

However, this is not to say that Confucianism cannot benefit from feminists' critiques, especially the criticism of gender-based divisions of labor in terms of *nei* 內 and *wai* 外 (which will be addressed in detail later). But to admit that there are elements in Confucianism that need rectification is not the same as admitting that Confucianism as a whole is essentially sexist and antifeminist. Likewise, one would not say that Aristotelian virtue ethics, Kantian deontology, or Nietzschean existentialism is essentially sexist and antifeminist because some elements of each need rectification. On the contrary, in the West there is a growing effort made by contemporary scholars to reappropriate the thought of those "sexist" philosophers through the lenses of feminism in order to expand the feminist epistemological horizon.[4] Our feminist exploration of Confucianism here can thus be seen as belonging to the same feminist movement of reappropriating the canons for the sake of women.

In the following, we will concentrate on key Confucian ethical concepts, in particular the relational personhood of *ren* 仁, the virtue of filial piety or *xiao* 孝 as the beginning of humanity, and the complementary correlation of *yin-yang* and *nei-wai*. Our assumption here is that a hybrid feminist theory of Confucianism or Confucian feminism is possible. Not only is Confucianism able to meet the challenges of feminism and to address feminist concerns regarding women's oppression without going beyond its theoretical framework, more importantly it is able to expand the epistemological horizons of feminism. In other words, despite its emphasis on reciprocal inequalities of social roles and its emphasis on the familial virtues of filiality and continuity, Confucianism is presumed to be able to inform feminism with an alternative theoretical ground for women's liberation. A fully articulated Confucian feminism will be reserved as a future project in order to do justice to the diverse landscape of contemporary feminist theories. For now, to provide an outline for this future project shall be sufficient to demonstrate the possibility of the convergence between feminism and Confucianism, or that a possible "feminist space" can be found within the Confucian tradition.

As an analytic category, "gender" has troubled feminists greatly, especially since the existentialists' deconstruction of traditional accounts of the "essence" or "nature" of a woman. The category of "woman" no longer signifies a set of inborn biological facts that supposedly give support to a naturalized gender division of labor, nor does it signify a set of distinctive feminine psychological and/or behavioral traits that somehow compel us to perform certain gender roles. In the existentialists' deconstruction, "woman" signifies a total social construct, a pure phenomenon sustained by one's participation in the process of genderization—that is, a process of acquiring and embodying a set of socially recognizable gender norms. As de Beauvoir boldly declares, "One is not born, but rather becomes, a woman."[5] There is no "woman" as a natural being out there, but rather each woman as a socially and culturally recognizable "woman" is made in accordance with each cultural conception of what constitutes a proper "woman." This existential deconstruction, in part, frees women from the traditional "biological determinism," where women are taken to be natural beings with a set of natural roles, duties, and capacities rooted in their obvious biological differences from men. The existential emphasis on the authentic self defined by its freely chosen projects, instead of by its predetermined essence and social function, opens up a new possibility for women to be free from the patriarchal tradition that defines them. Existential feminism offers a new ethical as well as epistemological ground for women's liberation.

Such a deconstruction however also poses a difficulty for feminists. Namely, how can feminists continue to use the category of "woman" as a collective term to talk about gender oppression across cultural, racial, and class boundaries, since there is no "woman" as such beyond a specific social construct? In the existentialist's world, the phenomenon of being a "woman" is coextensive with one's participation in the process of genderization sanctioned by a specific society as a whole, and nothing more. Hence, in principle, one can only speak of American women, Chinese women, Latino women, etc., but not "woman" as a being that transcends all cultural, racial, or class specificity. There is not, as it were, a Platonic original idea of "woman" to function as the essence underlying each peculiar, cultural conception of "woman," and in virtue of which each cultural conception of "woman" is seen as a particular example of that comprehensive, original idea.

If it is true that a "woman" as a specific cultural phenomenon is made not born, then any cross-cultural attempt to understand women's conditions must also begin with the study of culture. In the case of Chinese women, the concept of "woman" signifies a set of kinship roles and a ritually proper sphere and division of labor within the hierarchical kinship system.[6] Genderization coincides with ritualization and civilization in Chinese society, where a gendered being is also a being that embodies ritual propriety and hence civility. The inquiry into what constitutes a Chinese woman, therefore, should also begin with the concept of culture, instead of a set of transcultural characteristics of the Platonic original idea of "woman."[7]

The need to affirm the cultural differences among women, as it were to preserve a room of one's own, is well articulated by third world feminists such as Chandra Mohanty and Caren Kaplan in response to the mainstream feminist discourse that tends to naturalize the analytic category of "woman," and at the same time totalize both the categories of "third world women" and "Western women."[8] The politics of location has emerged as an important part of postmodern feminist discourse in the cross-cultural study of gender since the term was first coined by Adrienne Rich in the 1980s. Empirical locality is important in discussing gender in a cross-cultural context, but empirical locality signifies more than just one's physical presence in the particular region that one is addressing. One's understanding of the position of Chinese women whether past or present will be limited if one does not have the necessary linguistic skills to navigate the rich cultural resources of China or has never set foot in China. Although by merely being in China, one's observations of the position of Chinese women are not automatically valid, since empirical observations must be guided by a conceptual framework. And as long as one's familiar conceptual framework remains intact, one's empirical observations will reflect more of one's own cultural categories than those of the subjects that one is trying to represent. The instance of Margery Wolf pressing her Chinese informant to describe the attributes of a good woman outside of her kinship roles without a proper understanding of the embodiment of a Chinese woman in her kinship roles is a perfect example.[9] Therefore, to recognize the empirical differences among women requires more of a shift in one's theoretical imagination by which one's familiar cultural categories are no longer the normative reference points. To deconstruct the centrality of Western theories, a critical practice in postmodern feminist discourse, as Caren Kaplan cautions, should not amount to a superficial inclusion of theories from the margins, by which the privileged position of "whiteness" remains intact.[10] What that amounts to is really no more than an act of dominating and marginalizing the "third world women" ironically through their very inclusion in Western feminist discourse.

In Western feminist scholarship, a fair amount of work has been devoted to the analysis of the issues of race and class. But the element of culture in cross-cultural gender studies is relatively neglected, and this is in part due to the neocolonial assumption that women in other parts of the world are merely passive victims of their uniformly "sexist" traditions, which should be discarded without reservation. But without a genuine understanding of culture, feminists also erase the very subject matter and the agency of the subject that they intend to understand. The same pattern of marginalization found between white men and white women is thereby perpetuated in the transnational feminist discourse in which the agency and modernity of "Western women" is contrasted with the victimization of the tradition-bound, helpless "third world women." The imposition of one's cultural framework onto the world of the Other reflects only the limitation of one's conceptual horizon, instead of an approximation of the reality of the Other. Thus, Western authors often adopt the pose of a moral theorist coming to the rescue of the victimized third world women. Through this lens, the global feminist movement can then only be conceived of on a simple "impact-response" model, according to which changes in a "sexist," "traditional" society can only come about by importing Western ethical theories and Western ways of life. This implicit yet imperialistic dichotomy embedded in cross-cultural studies needless to say must be rejected so that the affirmation of the moral agency of others, who then can be thought of as being able to rectify themselves with their own cultural resources, can subsequently take place.

In the case of Chinese society, Confucianism is the most important cultural resource for self-rectification, where rectified Confucianism is also a newly hybrid feminist ethical theory for women's liberation. By concentrating on Confucianism, however, this project does not intend to preclude the possibility of constructing Daoist feminist ethics, or Buddhist feminist ethics, both of which are also important in Chinese cultural narratives. But since most feminist critiques have focused on Confucianism and most sinologists have agreed that Confucianism underpins the foundation of Chinese civilization, it seems fitting that Confucianism be our point of entry into the new world of a hybrid feminist theory in transnational feminist discourse.

In brief, the connection between Confucianism and Chinese sexism can be seen through the convergence of three cultural imperatives: the familial virtue of filial piety, ancestor worship, and the continuity of the family line. They work as a theoretical, ethical ground to justify and sustain social practices, most noticeably concubinage, the acquiring of female child brides and servants, and female infanticide.[11] To a large extent, Chinese sexism can be interpreted as the logical fallout of the emphasis on familial continuity coupled with the assumption that this continuation is possible only through the male line. This in turn is interlocked with the Confucian familial virtue of filial piety, and the ritualized, religious, and civil practice of ancestor worship. The *nei-wai* distinction as a gender distinction, which assigns men to the realm of *wai* (the realm of literary and personal accomplishment, and extrafamilial relations) and women to *nei* (the realm of concealment, practical household management, and familial, kinship relations), helps substantiate the limited functionary roles allotted to women. Besides being groomed to be daughters, wives, and mothers for the sole purpose of perpetuating the patrilineal line, women are also deprived of an access to the *wai* realm of *wen* 文 (culture) and *zheng* 政 (governance), where one's literary talent has an explicit ethical, public use and where one's good name is passed on and remembered beyond the immediate familial realm.

Perhaps the most notable intersection between social practices and the *nei-wai* distinction as a normative distinction between genders is the infamous practice of footbinding, in which the female body is concealed and marked through human means as a sign of *wen*, that is, a sign of culture and civility in the illiterate realm of *nei*.[12] Through binding their own feet and the feet of their daughters, women come to mimic their male counterparts in making and transmitting this unique "culture of ours" through wraps and needles, instead of words and brushes. In other words, in footbinding, women subvert the Confucian way of being civilized, by trimming their raw flesh instead of cultivating their whole person. This subversion reflects the structural limitation that is imposed on women as gendered beings, who have no legitimate access to the realm of *wai*, the realm of literary learning, governance, and personal accomplishment. And it is this desire to be remembered through perpetuating a male heir in the familial realm and through virtuous self-cultivation and accomplishment in the extrafamilial realm that underpins the problem of gender disparity in Chinese society. Women—the illiterate, nameless beings concealed in the realm of *nei*—are not and cannot be fully "personed."[13]

The problem of gender disparity in Chinese society is also a problem of the ritual boundary of the *nei* and the *wai* as gender-based divisions of labor and spheres of activities. The dynamic interplay between the *nei* and the *wai*, on the one hand, robs women of any legitimate access to the *wai* realm of literary learning, and on the other hand, conceals women's achievements, especially in the areas of *wen* (culture) and *zheng* (governance).

Women's incomplete personhood is further accentuated by the Confucian ethical project of self-cultivation that begins with the study and appropriation of the classics, the words of past sages, and the Confucian ideal of *junzi* 君 子 (exemplary persons), who are not only filial and ritually deferential, but more importantly are able to lead the people by their virtuous examples.

By contrast, due to the *nei-wai* distinction, women, the limited beings, are forever incomplete. The Confucian project of self-cultivation and the ideal of *junzi,* although they are not gender specific in their moral content, are nevertheless beyond the reach of women as gendered beings of *nei.* Hence, what needs to be rectified in Confucianism is the gender-based division of labor of *nei-wai,* instead of the whole Confucian framework of the achieved personhood of *ren,* its emphasis on filial piety, or even the importance of familial continuity embodied in the practice of passing on the family name and in the practice of ancestor worship—all are part of the grand notion of filial piety. In other words, in our hybrid Confucian feminism, the *nei-wai* distinction as a gender distinction will need some modifications in order to create a feminist space.

But first of all, let us outline the basic assumptions of our hybrid feminist theory that is Confucian and feminist at the same time. First of all, our Confucian feminism presupposes a relational self situated in a web of relations that are not just external "add-ons" to some "core" self supposed to exist prior to the external relations. Instead, the substantial self is coextensive with the web of relations. One's moral worth in turn is measured against one's practical achievement in sustaining harmonious social relations beginning with the parent-child relation, since it is in the parent-child relation that one first finds oneself in the world. The virtue of filial piety, which emphasizes the reciprocal care between parent and child, is our starting point of being human. The parent is to be affectionate, and the child filial; that is to say, the child must be ritually proper and responsive to the parent's wishes. Without locating oneself in social relations, one is without a substantial existence, and hence one is not fully "personed" in the world. This starting point is Confucian through and through, since it is entirely consistent with the Confucian achieved personhood of *ren,* in which a person becomes a "person" only through embodying specific social virtues which in turn can only be actualized in specific social relations and roles, starting with familial relations and roles.

One possible objection to this is that there is a danger in presupposing an unequal worth among human beings. The danger, of course, lies in the possible human rights abuse inflicted on those who fall below the socially defined minimal qualification for being a person. That is to say, if rights and entitlements depend on the actual contribution of a person measured in accordance with the success of her social relations, there would be no safety net for those who fail to achieve. The discourse on the natural rights of man is indeed a familiar one in Western political theory in modern times. Hobbes's natural equality of man (and woman!) marks the beginning of modern contractual theory in which all men are said to be equal and free without qualification. This Hobbesian equality of man (and woman) however is premised on the inherently conflicting nature of human relations, since the state of nature is a state of war. Alternatively, absolute equality in Western political theory can also be found in Locke's theory, which by and large is rooted in the theory of divine creation. But, if one is to reject the Hobbesian chaotic beginning of human relations or the Lockean metaphysical divine sanction of absolute equality, then the importance of harmonious social relations must consequently be substantiated not just as "part" of the self but as the very "essence" of the self. In other words, a person is a person only if he or she is a person-in-relations. Severance of all social relations, in a sense, makes a person "unpersoned." The parent-child relation in which one first finds oneself in the world must be substantiated prior to other relations that expand one's self in the world.

Although it is true that the virtue of filial piety is prima facie a familial virtue applied to the natural relationship between parents and their offspring, it certainly can be extended to accommodate modern nontraditional families where primary caregivers might be grandparents, foster parents, relatives, or even social workers in an orphanage. The point of emphasizing the importance of filial piety is to transform the conventional lineal relationship between the caring and the cared-for into a reciprocal one, so that there is no "naturalized" duty or obligation required of one toward the other without reciprocity. Filial piety is the gateway to humanity at the minimal level. One's genuine care for others is the starting point of being human, without which one is not entitled to anything in return. There is, in a word, no entitlement without qualification in Confucian ethics. From the Confucian reciprocal standpoint, a perpetually ungrateful, disrespectful child indeed has no substantial humanity and is entitled to no social privilege.

Some scholars argue that some sort of basic respect owed to others is needed in ethics in order to deal with issues such as slavery or the abuse of human rights.[14] Most noticeably, the Kantian universal "respect for persons" is taken to be an indispensable ethical principle despite all the criticism of the abstract nature of the person presupposed in Kantian ethics. But if the end is to assert to some sort of "universal" principle upon which all people are treated with respect and care, the virtue of filial piety can do a better job than the abstract respect for persons in Kantian ethics. A genuine care for others, not just respect for an abstract person, can be achieved and "universalized" by extending the familial virtue of filial affection between parent and child to strangers. This extension is achievable since every person is also a person in the parent-child relation; that is to say, everyone is someone's father, mother, son, or daughter, not an abstract person without social relations. And the basis for this extension is Confucian as well, since the capacity of empathy, according to Mencius, is one of the four basic beginnings of humanity. The genuine affection that one has for one's family can thus be extended to strangers, who are also persons-in-relations. Filial care, in principle, can also be extended to every sentient being that is also situated in the natural relation of parent-offspring as well, and this extension can be used to provide some sort of protection for the world of nature from unnecessary human intrusion. The virtue of filial piety not only asserts the fundamental relatedness of one's being in the world, but more importantly is able to give the Kantian abstract "respect for persons" a concrete content and theoretically extend it from the human world to the world of all sentient beings.

Secondly, in the outline of a Confucian feminism, we propose the centrality of the virtue of *ren* as the culmination of one's achieved personhood. The virtue of filial piety is the starting point of being human, but a person is also a person in an ever-enlarging web of relations. While family is the focused center, community, society, state, and the world at large are the extended fields of the relational self.[15] Or, if you will, family, community, state, and the world at large are a series of concentric circles. The self is enlarged as the circle of one's concerns and relations is enlarged. The circle of concerns for one's family is not separate from or in conflict with one's concern for the state or the world at large. As stated earlier, the private virtue of filial piety is not a separate virtue from political good; instead, it is the building block, the foundation upon which the actualization of extended public good depends. In other words, Confucian ethics assumes the priority of the family, and familial virtue as the necessary condition for the actualization of public virtue. An unfilial son or daughter is also an untrustworthy subject; conversely, one way to ensure the harmony and longevity of the state is to groom trustworthy subjects by grooming filial sons and daughters. Once the foundation is firm, the embodiment of public good will be firm as well. Or, to put it in contemporary political rhetoric, strong family values mitigate social discord.

The virtue of *ren* begins with the virtue of filial piety, which is also the beginning of being human. It is not surprising that not just etymologically, or paronomastically, but also philosophically, the virtue of *ren* and the concept of person are one and the same in Confucian ethics. Beyond being filial and deferential at home, a person of *ren* is also a person of *yi* 義, of *li* 禮, of *zhi* 知, of *shu* 恕, and of *xin* 心. This is so because to be *ren* is also to be a person who embodies specific social excellences appropriate to specific social relations. And since there is no metaphysical ground upon which a person is a person without qualification, the scope of one's social relations is also the scope of one's substantial self. The self must, as it were, extend outward to actualize itself, and at the minimal level, the self must constantly sustain the existing familial relations through which the self first comes into existence. In the course of one's lifetime, as the web of relations is extended from the family to the world at large, so is the range of different social virtues that are required in order to continue to sustain those relations. The virtue of *ren*, though comprehensive in its scope, is not an "original" principle underlying all other particular virtues or existing prior to all others as the necessary condition for their actualization. Instead, the virtue of *ren* as the culmination of one's personhood can only be actualized in each particular relation governed by a particular social excellence appropriate to that relation.

By affirming the virtue of *ren* as the highest achievement of a relational personhood, our Confucian feminism also affirms a practical ethic without the need for a metaphysical grounding. It affirms the priority of human relations. The community in which one is located or, in Heidegger's words, the community into which one is *thrown* must be the starting point and the focused center, while the world at large, or the world of the Other, is the extended field. In this Confucian world, one's care for others will not just be an abstract respect for persons with impersonal laws of reason, but a genuine care with a concrete ritual content. But, the virtue of *ren* will not give rise to a strictly communitarian ethic in which one's circle of concerns is limited to one's community or one's family. For the ethic of *ren* acknowledges the priority of meeting the needs of one's community as the starting point and at the same time stresses extending that genuine care for one's own to the world of others. Hence, taking the virtue of *ren* as the ethical ideal, our Confucian feminism is able to, on the one hand, address the feminist need for a concrete morality taking human relations as a priority, and, on the other hand, is able to meet the ethicist's general demand for a "universal" ethical principle to ensure some sort of basic "human rights," or a sense of "justice" and "fairness" owed to a person as a person without qualification.

Lastly, in our Confucian feminism, we affirm the complementarity and reciprocity of *yin-yang* and *nei-wai* as the basic structure of human relations. We suppose that in a world of concrete human relations, complementarity and reciprocity characterize the very nature of each relation. Unlike the Hobbesian model, the power structure of each particular relation is not that of domination and submission in which the superior has an absolute power over the inferior. In the Confucian world, although it is true that social relations are hierarchical in nature, they are also reciprocal and complementary through and through. For instance, although in the father-son relation, the father and son are socially unequal, the legitimacy of the father's authority over the son depends on the reciprocal care that the father and the son have for each other. If the father is not ritually affectionate toward the son, the son then ceases to be obligated by his filial duty toward the father. In "historical" reality, the legend of sage-king Shun who defied his vicious father in marriage yet was still considered virtuous illustrates the point here. The father is entitled to the son's filial submission only insofar as the father is righteous in his own conduct. Our Confucian feminism assumes no fundamental supremacy embodied in the position of the father regardless of the actual virtuous achievement of the father. That is to say, by affirming the hierarchical nature of human relations, we do not thereby affirm patriarchy as articulated by Western political theorists, such as Locke, who grant an absolute power to the position of the father over his children as well as his wife. The power of the father as a social superior in Confucian ethics is by contrast much tempered by reciprocity. There is no such thing as right without obligation, let alone absolute authority, in Confucian ethics. The point here is that each social relation, although hierarchal in nature, is also reciprocal and complementary.

Our Confucian feminism asserts the basic hierarchical, yet complementary and reciprocal scheme of Confucian human relations in which inequality based on ability or moral authority is the starting point among particulars rather than an absolute equality without qualification. Parents and children are not socially equal and they should not be equal, nor are teachers and students, nor the elderly and the young. The assumption in Confucian ethics is that the socially inferior must observe a basic sense of deference toward the socially superior, so that there is a sense of harmony and continuity in the complex web of human relations where the knowledge of the past is passed on from the elderly to the young, from the parent to the child, and from the teacher to the student. The knowledge of the past signifies more than the literary, intellectual tradition of the past, which can be understood independently of one's appreciation of the past. Here the knowledge of the past also signifies the ritual tradition, and the sense of continuity of one's familial and cultural identity, which can only be learned through embodying particular kinship and social roles. And hence observing basic deference toward the socially superior is essential to the continuity of the ritual and intellectual tradition of the past. Inequality characterizes the basic pattern of social relations, but such a social inequality changes over the course of one's lifetime. One is neither definitely socially inferior nor superior, and each relation is premised on complementarity and reciprocity instead of absolute domination and submission.

In order to meet the challenges of feminism, the hierarchical spousal relation and the gender-based division of labor in terms of the *nei* and the *wai* will need rectification. Within the Confucian merit-based ethical system, there is no necessity that a wife must be subordinated to her husband, since the principle of kinship seniority doesn't apply here. Spouses are not kinsmen by necessity; rather, they become kinsmen through marriage. Hence, the basic deference of the inferior owed to the superior cannot determine the spousal relation. The hierarchal structure found in the spousal relation, in the traditional account, is modeled after the political relation between the ruler and the minister, with the husband being socially superior and wife socially inferior. However, the ruler-husband and minister-wife analogy is inadequate, since unlike the ruler-minister relation, the spousal relation is personal and intimate in nature. And unlike the contractual nature of the political relation, the bond between a husband and a wife (or in the modern sense of partnership) is ideally assumed to last for a lifetime and the life after. The gender-based hierarchy in the spousal relation will lose its justification if women are allowed full access to cultural resources like their male counterparts. In the modern age, an alternative analogy for the spousal relation would be friendship, which is one of the Confucian five relations. Although it is true that the basic scheme for all human relations in the Confucian world is hierarchical in nature including friendship, the assumed hierarchy in friendship is not gender-based.

The hierarchy in friendship is mostly based on moral authority. The association among friends is strictly voluntary, and the duration of that association depends on an assumed common goal. Such a free association in which people are bound together for a self-defined common goal best approximates lifelong partnership in the modern age. This rectification of the relation between husband and wife and the gender-based division of labor is made within the Confucian framework without resorting to any metaphysical basis for absolute equality. In other words, the problem of gender disparity derived from the gender-based division of labor in terms of the *nei* and the *wai* distinction and the hierarchical spousal relation can be addressed by using resources available within the Confucian tradition. With this rectification, the theoretical justification for women's liberation is no longer limited to the liberal argument of individual rights accompanied by an implicit theist assumption of an absolute equality for all. Our Confucian feminism affirms the Confucian tradition while taking into account feminist concerns for gender parity. The result of creating the hybrid identity of Confucian feminism is a qualified inequality among the unequals based on moral authority instead of gender per se. Once the gender-based hierarchy and division of labor is taken away from the spousal relation, what is left is a more flexible rearrangement of the division of labor within one's household in which a woman can be in charge of all or part of the *wai* and a man all or part of the *nei*, or vice versa, depending on the common goal set in that particular relationship by its participants.

Once the gender-based division of labor is eradicated, women will no longer be confined to the limited realm of *nei*, and hence would also be able to achieve the highest cultural ideal of *junzi*, who are not only ritually proper at home but also are fully cultured, leading the masses by their virtuous examples. But eradicating the gender-based boundary of the *nei* and the *wai* would directly challenge the normative gender identity and consequently the sense of civility in the Chinese world. The difficulty here is not so much whether such a change should be made; rather, the question is whether such a change can be justified by the Confucian tradition itself, or whether any change in gender relations can only be made possible by importing Western ethical theories. To put it another way, the question here is whether Confucianism is perceived as a sexist ideology through and through, and hence, as far as the issue of women's oppression is concerned, no rectification can be found within Confucianism.

Confucianism as a living tradition thrives on incorporating others into its expanding self; its adaptability has been proven again and again in history. For instance, the first wave of expansion of Confucianism occurred in its incorporation of the theory of *yinyang wuxing* 陰陽五行 during the late Qin and early Han, enabling it to survive politically first in the Qin under its anti-Confucian policies and subsequently in the Han in competition with the popular *Yinyangjia* and *Daojia*.[16] The second wave of expansion, as commonly known, occurred during the Song period, resulting in the rise of *daoxue* 道學 and *lixue* 理學—that is "neo-Confucianism"—which in reality is more of a mixed plate of Confucianism, Daoism, and Buddhism. Now the new challenge that lies ahead for Confucianism is feminism. The making of Confucian feminism, as Tu Weiming puts it, would be the third wave of expansion of Confucianism, whose survival again is on the line.[17] The goal of making Confucian feminism, of course, is more than simply keeping Confucianism alive in the contemporary world. It is an affirmation of the dynamic nature of Confucianism, so that one can be a Confucian and a feminist without apology, just as one can be an Aristotelian and a feminist, a Kantian and a feminist, or an existentialist and a feminist at the same time, despite some explicitly sexist statements made in that specific intellectual tradition.

This project in essence intends to seek reconciliation between feminism and Confucianism by proposing a hybrid ethical theory in which Confucianism is not just a convenient scapegoat for the oppression of Chinese women. Instead, Confucianism is seen as a dynamic working of different voices and indeterminate meanings in orthodox teachings that afford the Chinese people sufficient conceptual tools to engage in internal critiques of the social abuse of women without resorting to a total rejection of their Confucian roots. In other words, one need not be a Marxist, a liberal, an existentialist, or a radical separatist to be a feminist of some sort, since it would no longer be an oxymoron to be a feminist and a Confucian at the same time. By sorting out the cultural elements of being a woman within the cultural boundaries of China, we also seek to add to the epistemological portrait of the roots of women's oppression whose model of liberation is no longer limited to the Kantian autonomous subject, the Cartesian non-gendered *cogito*, liberal individual rights, or Marxist material equality. Now it is also possible to take Confucian relational, virtue-based personhood as a viable goal for women's liberation. As the epistemological portrait of the roots of women's oppression is enriched by the study of Confucianism, so is the range of the possibility for women's liberation in feminist theoretical imagination.

Suggestions for Further Reading

See James Tiles (2000), *Moral Measures: An Introduction to Ethics West and East* for an overview of comparative issues in ethics. For an excellent general introductory text to Confucianism, see Roger T. Ames and David L. Hall (1987), *Thinking Through Confucius*. For a discussion of Confucian personhood and moral development, see Tu Weiming (1985), *Confucian Thought: Selfhood as Creative Transformation*.

For a general discussion of Chinese feminism, see Tani E. Barlow (2004), *The Question of Women in Chinese Feminism*. For a conventional feminist critique of Confucian patriarchy, see Margery Wolf (1994), "Beyond the Patrilineal Self: Constructing Gender in China," in *Self as Person in Asian Theory and Practice,* ed. Roger T. Ames, Wimal Disanayake, and Thomas P. Kasulis. See also Wolf (1985), *Revolution Postponed: Women in Contemporary China*. Chenyang Li, ed. (2000), *The Sage and the Second Sex: Confucianism, Ethics, and Gender* provides an alternative account regarding the compatibility of Confucianism and feminism. My (2006), *Confucianism and Women: A Philosophical Interpretation* provides a philosophical account of the roots of gender oppression in the Confucian context and a preliminary account of Confucian feminism.

For a good analysis of a role-based concept of gender in the Chinese context, see Barlow (1989), "Asian Perspective: Beyond Dichotomies" in *Gender and History* 1, no. 3. See Lisa Raphals (1998), *Sharing the Light: Representations of Women and Virtue in Early China* for an excellent intertextual analyses in early Chinese texts regarding gender, including women's instruction texts. A must-read on the topic of gender and the *yin-yang* relationship is Allison Black (1989), "Gender and Cosmology in Chinese Correlative Thinking," in *Gender and Religion: On the Complexity of Symbols*, ed. Caroline W. Bynum, Steven Harrell, and Paula Richman. An interesting analysis of the power of names and the nameless nature of a woman's being in Chinese society may be found in Rubie Watson (1986), "The Name and the Nameless: Gender and Person in Chinese Society," *American Ethnologist* 13.

Fred Blake (1994), "Foot-binding in Neo-Confucian China and the Appropriation of Female Labor," in *Signs* (Spring) provides a preliminary, philosophical reading of footbinding. An excellent, alternative account of footbinding is Dorothy Ko (2005), *Cinderella's Sisters: A Revisionist History of Footbinding*. Other titles dealing with the practice of footbinding include Beverley Jackson (1997), *Splendid Slippers: A Thousand Years of an Erotic Tradition*; Ko (2001), *Every Step a Lotus: Shoes for Bound Feet*; Ko (1997), "The Body as Attire: the Shifting Meanings of Footbinding in Seventeenth-Century China," *Journal of Women's History* 8, no. 4; and Howard Levy (1966), *Chinese Footbinding: The History of a Curious Erotic Custom*.

Finally, numerous resources address issues in feminism relevant to a cross-cultural inquiry, including Inderpal Grewal and Caren Kaplan, eds. (1994), *Scattered Hegemonies: Postmodernity and Transnational Feminist Practices*; Virginia Held (2006), *The Ethics of Care*; Chandra T. Mohanty, Ann Russo, and Lourdes Torres, eds. (1991), *Third World Women and the Politics of Feminism*; and Martha Nussbaum (1999), *Sex and Social Justice*.

Notes

A similar version of this chapter was first published in my (2006), *Confucianism and Women: A Philosophical Interpretation* (Albany: State University of New York Press).

1. Virginia Held (2006), 21–22.

2. For more discussion on this, see Li-Hsiang Lisa Rosenlee (2006), chapter 3. Also see Lisa Raphals (1998), chapters 6 through 7. Also, Allison Black (1989).

3. Margery Wolf (1994).

4. Contemporary scholars' interest in reappropriating those philosophers is attested to by a series of publications of feminist interpretations of canonical philosophers such as Plato, Aristotle, Descartes, Hume, etc. Despite Aristotle's and Kant's definitive sexist statements made in their writings, there is no shortage of Aristotelian and Kantian scholars such as Michael Slote and Martha Nussbaum defending the compatibility of Aristotelian and Kantian ethics with the feminist concerns of gender equality. In some cases, scholars such as Martha Nussbaum even defend the superiority of those canonical ethics compared with the distinctive feminist ethics of care advocated by Nel Noddings, Eva Kittay, and Virginia Held, for instance. For detail, see Held (2006). Also see Nussbaum (1999), where she prioritizes the principle of equality over human relatedness.

5. Simone de Beauvoir (1989), 267.

6. For more detail, see Rosenlee (2006), chapters 4 through 5.

7. On the Chinese concept of woman, see Tani E. Barlow (2004), chapter 2.

8. See Inderpal Grewal and Caren Kaplan (1994) and Chandra T. Mohanty (1991).

9. Wolf (1985), 112.

10. Grewal and Kaplan (1994), 144.

11. See Rosenlee (2006), chapter 6.

12. For footbinding see Rosenlee (2006), chapter 6; also see Dorothy Ko (2005), (2001), (1997); Beverley Jackson (1997); Fred Blake (1994); and Howard Levy (1966).

13. For the namelessness of Chinese women, see Rubie S. Watson (1986).

14. See for instance, James E. Tiles (2000). Despite his critique of the abstract nature of Kantian ethics, Tiles took Kant's respect for person as one of his three proposed measures of morality. The problem with Kantian ethics is not just limited to Kant's penchant for abstract personhood; in particular Kantian ethics imports a great deal of moral theology by making God the regulative ideal for morality. For more critique of Kantian ethics, see Rosenlee (2003).

15. For the relational Confucian personhood, see Roger T. Ames and David L Hall (1987).

16. These were schools focused on *yingyang* and Daoist studies, respectively.

17. Tu Weiming (1985).

10

Confucian Trajectories
on Environmental Understanding

Michael C. Kalton

The great traditions of human understanding seem to timelessly transcend the flux of history. But any historian of traditions such as Buddhism, Christianity, or Confucianism can bear witness as to how they have continuously transformed themselves, drawing from the depths of their resources fresh and trenchant responses to the emergent questions of their times. Now the world as a whole faces an urgent new question: Are we humans sustainable? Can we adjust our ways of making a living so that we do not make the earth unlivable for our companion species in the interdependent community of life, and hence unlivable for ourselves as well?

This overriding question shadows the skies under which we now live. As China presses to join Japan, Korea, Singapore, and Taiwan in the ranks of development, East Asia moves to assume a major role in the globalized economic process so interwoven with that alarming new question. And in its own Confucian heritage East Asia has perhaps the most promising foundation in the world for meeting this, the most urgent question of our times.

I use the word *foundation* advisedly. No tradition anticipated that human beings would wrestle with the question of their own viability and future as a species; consequently, no premodern tradition—in fact, no tradition up until the present generation, has really addressed what we now think of as environmental questions. Although some cultures have lived more sustainably than others, none until the present has self-consciously posed our kinds of questions about human impact on the very livability of our world for innumerable other creatures and ultimately for ourselves as well. Nonetheless, our inherited traditions provide frameworks for thinking and understanding that strongly condition our responses to new questions. It is in this respect that the Confucian tradition offers an especially apt and rich framework as we wrestle with the emergent environmental crisis.

Human Beings and the World

We human beings belong to the world; the world belongs to the universe. The blood that flows through our veins, and the thoughts that flow through our brains as well, cannot be alien to the constitution of this universe. At least such was the assumption of those who grew up as heirs of Confucius. As a famous text of the eleventh century, Zhang Zai's *Western Inscription,* put it: "*Qian* [Heaven] is called the father and *Kun* [Earth] is called the mother. I, this tiny being, am commingled in their midst. Therefore what fills up all between Heaven and Earth, that is my body, and that which directs Heaven and Earth is my nature. All people are from the same womb as I, all creatures are my companions."[1] Heaven and Earth signify the universe; as progeny of the universe, we share its nature and form a single extended family.

So what are the genes we inherit from the universe? What traits run through this family? A civilization in close contact with the life-sustaining round of planting, flourishing, and harvest looked to the cycle of the four seasons as the main revelation of the character of the universe. Whatever else it might be, they concluded, the central feature of the universe was the ongoing, unending production and nurturing of life. From such a process we have emerged and in such a process we participate; its dynamics make up the deepest level of nature in general and of our natures in particular. In fact, the seemingly sporadic, humane "life-givingness" that marks humans at our best might be regarded as a derivative of this fundamental character of the universe. Thus, Zhu Xi (1130–1200) framed his *Diagram of the Explanation of Humanity* with the statement: " 'Humanity is the mind of Heaven and Earth whereby they produce and give life to creatures,' and this is what man receives as his own mind."[2]

One of the formative narratives in the Confucian tradition was initiated by Mencius, the seminal Confucian thinker of the fourth century BCE. At the time a debate raged regarding human nature. Mencius lived in times of social upheaval, treachery, and warfare. Looking at such evidence, some philosophers concluded that from birth we are evil, others that we are a mixture of good and evil. Mencius defended the unlikely proposition that, in spite of all indications to the contrary, human beings are fundamentally good, that is, life-giving creatures:

"Look at that barren mountain outside of town," he said. "Once it was covered with trees and with grass. But people cut the trees and their animals ate the grass. Every night the life-giving force would work, producing new sprouts and reviving the plants. But the next day would bring more cutting and more grazing, until finally the life-giving force could not keep up, and the mountain became bare. People think it has always been like that, but that is not so."

Mencius then went on to apply this to the human case:

"People are like this. Everyday they get bent out of shape and depleted by difficult social interactions. When they sleep at night, the life-giving force restores them, so at early dawn they are almost human again. But the next day brings more bending and depletion, until finally they cannot recover. They may seem evil, but that is not their original nature."[3]

This is a powerful story, in part because each of us can easily recognize ourselves in it. We are not evil. But we do get bent out of shape. It has also been an exceptionally powerful story historically, for it captured essential elements of a developing worldview and gave them a shape that carried forward mightily over the next two thousand years. Mencius told this story to make a point about human beings, and this eventually became the well-known Confucian doctrine of our good *benxing* 本性, our "original nature." But equally important, it tells us how to think about the universe: the universe gives life. Unbalanced activity—overcutting trees, overgrazing grass, overstressed human interactions—can tilt the slope toward irreversible destruction, but that is not the deep way of things. The story thus established an "original nature" for the universe as well as an original nature for humans. In fact, our original nature is what it is only because it continues, in a human manifestation, the original nature of the entire universe.

Mencius himself made this connection in a second great story. To elucidate the dispositions in the depth of our heart-mind, he told his story of the child about to fall into the well. "Who," he asks, "will not feel alarm and an urge to save a small child about to fall into a well?" This life-giving impulse reveals our deepest nature, even though it can be blocked and distorted in many ways before we act on it. Mencius described it as commiseration, the beginning of humanity (*ren* 仁).[4] Mencius also described *ren*, the core Confucian idea of goodness, as "what it means to be human."[5] The Chinese character for *ren*, itself a combination of the characters for "human" and for "two," supports Mencius's definition from a typically Confucian point of view: properly relating to other human beings both makes us human and manifests our humanity.

Mencius went on to fill out his account of human nature, not only in terms of life-giving commiseration, the beginning of humanity, but in terms of other qualities of great importance to Confucians. We have, he observed, three other deep, inborn dispositions: a sense of modesty and deference, a sense of shame and dislike for evil, and a sense of approving and disapproving right and wrong. Each of these is the beginning of a fundamental human quality, namely propriety, righteousness, and wisdom.[6]

The "Four Beginnings" (*siduan* 四端) Mencius cited as the full description of human nature might have lost contact with the barren mountain story. But in spite of the human and social focus that is typical of the Confucian tradition, the story continued to unfold in a way that emphasized the systemic connection between humans and the universe. After the great unification of the Chinese empire, Han dynasty (206 BCE–220 CE) thinkers sought to understand the harmonious unity of all things. Their question was how to formulate a government that reflected and worked in harmony with cosmic forces. Their answer was to combine Mencius's account of human nature with the *Book of Changes*. The classic *Book of Changes* describes the first hexagram, Heaven, with four characteristics: origination, flourishing, benefiting, and firmness. This description of the fundamental character of the universe was taken as a reference to the natural world's most basic process, the cycle of the four seasons. In spring, the life force begins to move and originate a new cycle of life and growth; in summer, life grows and flourishes; in autumn, there is harvest and all life is benefited and sustained; in winter, crops are stored firmly and securely, and the life force likewise is stored in the frozen earth.

The *Book of Changes* here presents a description of the four seasons, told, like Mencius's story of the barren mountain, in terms of the life-giving process of the universe. Han dynasty thinkers saw a deep parallel and brought the two narratives together. They drew a correspondence between the qualities of the four seasons and the four aspects in human nature as described by Mencius. Then they elaborated government protocol and ritual so that each season would reflect and emphasize the appropriate correlated aspect of human nature. Spring, in the cycle of seasons, and *in*, in human nature, manifest the most fundamental nature of the cosmos and of humans. The life force of spring runs throughout all the other seasons; the life-giving of humanity runs throughout all the qualities of human excellence.

Song dynasty (960–1279) Confucian thinkers, spearheading a great movement of Confucian revival and revitalization, returned to this cosmic narrative of human nature with a new question.[7] The Confucian position in Chinese society waned after the collapse of the Han dynasty in 220 CE, and during centuries of Buddhist predominance, the center of the question shifted from the government and court to the deep cultivation of the individual's heart-mind. Hence, they sought a deeper understanding of the inner life of the heart-mind, the focus of Buddhist self-cultivation. Could Confucians match the depths of Buddhist cultivation practice?

In developing their response to the Buddhist challenge, early Song Confucians returned to the narratives of Mencius and the *Book of Changes* to understand how the forces of the universe animate and are manifested in the life of human consciousness. Zhang Zai (1020–1077) in the *Western Inscription* spoke of Heaven and Earth (i.e., the universe) as our father and mother: our physical bodies and our natures are an extension of their physical body and their nature.[8] Cheng Hao (1032–1085) spoke of all things in the universe being as a single body; he describes lack of *ren* as paralysis, cutting off the connection of the vital flow of life through the members of this single body.[9] Zhu Xi, the great synthesizer of early Song thought, preferred a related image, that of a single circulatory system of veins running through everything; lack of *ren* is like a blockage in the blood flow.[10]

Along with these images of our embodied continuity with the universe, it became common to speak of the universe in ways that easily transfer to descriptions of the human heart-mind. Song thinkers were thus attracted to the language of the *Book of Changes*, which says of the *fu* 復 hexagram (meaning "return" and representing spring): "In *fu* we see the heart-mind of Heaven and Earth."[11] Heart-mind (*xin* 心) here does not mean to attribute consciousness to the universe; Zhu Xi explicitly rejects that interpretation. Rather, it represents what the *Book of Changes* in another famous passage describes as the *dade* 大德, or the fundamental character or disposition of the universe, to produce and give life (*shengsheng* 生生).[12] Now there is readiness to speak of this quality of the universe itself as *ren*, "humanity." As Zhu Xi says: "Humanity is the heart-mind of Heaven and Earth whereby they produce and give life to creatures, and this is what man receives as his own heart-mind."[13] The Confucian view is thus developed here in a way that shows how cultivating our heart-mind can unite us with the vital flow of life in the universe. This describes the perfection of the heart-mind, the goal of all self-cultivation.

Mencius told a great environmental story of origins more than two thousand years before there was any such concept as "the environment." He told of the life force of an ecosystem, and he used the way human beings defeat and overcome that life-giving force as his model for why we find it hard to see and activate the life-givingness within ourselves. Too much tree cutting, too much grazing, and life can no longer revive. These are shortsighted and overly self-centered economic activities. Maybe such shortsighted and overly self-centered economic activities are also the way we distort our own life-giving nature as we interact within the human community, as well. Mencius's story, without modification, all too easily applies to modern life.

And Mencius's second story of the baby falling into the well hits home, too. We are indeed alarmed and distressed to see human babies falling into the well of death in impoverished nations. And we are increasingly distressed likewise to see the babies of our fellow creatures perish in the wave of extinction that accompanies our modern way of life. Mencius was right about our feelings. His story has application today, even well beyond his original intention.

If we are living Mencius's story of the barren mountain, and if our heart-mind is experiencing the alarm of seeing life destroyed, it might have something to do with our own modern story. In the eighteenth century, Adam Smith, the founder of modern economics, gave us that story in his book, *The Wealth of Nations*. He explained how wealth and well-being could originate from each individual seeking to maximize his or her own profit. The "invisible hand" of the market would coordinate this individual, self-seeking activity so that it would give life to the whole community. This story leaves modern people with the notion that human nature, on its deepest level, is self-centered. And as we go about maximizing our personal profit, unabashed self-interest is viewed as unproblematic, because, so we are told, the market transforms this into a force that takes care of the whole community. In this view, the market functions somewhat like Mencius's life-giving force—except that while market produces wealth for (some) humans, it opens the nonhuman world to pitiless exploitation.

The difference between the kind of story Adam Smith tells and the one Mencius tells has become critical. Adam Smith's story of the origination of well-being looks only at human society. It does not make us at home on the earth, nor does it join our interest with the interest of our fellow living creatures. Rather, it makes the human community into something like a conquering army, here to control everything for our own self-interest, and to carry off the wealth. And so the economy does its accounting in the style of conquerors, counting only costs to ourselves and ignoring costs to other forms of life and to the air, water, and soil that we have taken over. That is why market forces drain life from the larger community of living beings even as they produce wealth for some members of the human community.

Thus, the great and urgent question of our times has become sustainability: How long can this system continue? How can we change it, so we will be at home on the earth, and so that the earth will continue to be the source of life for us and other creatures? All answers to this question now agree on one point: human economic practice must take into serious account the well-being of the wider community of life. We now understand clearly that life and the whole earth is a single interconnected system. But because of our self-centered economics, we are blocking the proper flow of life-giving forces through this system.

The Confucian version of the human story accurately portrays this situation: we exist in a single interconnected system of life, and when we take care of only our own physically separated individual well-being, the system gets blocked up, even paralyzed. Even as the market myth seems at the height of worldwide triumph, disillusion and doubt are widespread. Riots in the streets accompany the WTO wherever it meets. People know free market profit maximizing will not allow life to flow through the earth, and they doubt whether it will even provide for short-term life flow through the human community. The protest arises from concern both for ourselves and for the whole community of the earth. Mencius and the later Confucians who developed his ideas were right about our original nature (*benxing*). More than any time in the past, direct evidence shows that the deep feelings of our heart-mind reach out beyond the individual self, beyond the human family, expanding into and fostering the life of the whole to which we belong.

But are these feelings strong enough? Self-interest seems to have become systematized economically as the strongest force on earth. We can see many ways we could change so that the situation would not be "either/or," our economic interest or the environment. But we seem paralyzed by self-interest. Those moved by environmental concern often still assume self-interest is the deepest force in human nature and they despair. They say we will change only when it is absolutely clear we must change for our own self-interest, and by then it will be too late. Confucians, as we shall see, refocus and supplement this one-sided view.

How to Live

While human beings may belong to the natural universe, we inhabit a niche of such unique subjectivity and flexibility that the question of guidance for a proper ethos, a fitting way of life, emerges as a central component of virtually every society. Creatures that live by instinct, or by a narrower range of appetite and a weaker ability to modify their environment in predictable ways, must function on a more automatic level of responsiveness. The community of life evolves in concert with the more or less predictable activities of its members and weaves them into a web of interdependent relationships. But humans evolved a twofold prowess that set them apart. We evolved a communicative prowess that leads to a form of knowledge that accumulates and grows exponentially over generations. And we matched this with the manipulative abilities of opposable thumbs, a combination that has yielded the technological prowess that in the short term means we can no longer be contained within the system of mutual constraints that demands and rigorously selects members of the community in terms of their fit. Instead of the sharing the common imperative of adaptive fit, we pride ourselves on adapting the world to our desires. In the long run, of course, there is no escaping such systemic constraint, since we, too, are dependent on the intricate web of life. But in the short run, we seem relatively free: show us a constraint, and it will be regarded as a problem to be overcome. Consequently, humans have to invent rules and guidelines, coming up with an ethos, a somewhat arbitrary but shared way of life. We alone of the world's species have needed to create ethics in order to flourish in our lives together. And as the environmental crisis has now made clear, we need a more inclusive ethic as well, an environmental ethic, in order to flourish along with other species in the community of life as a whole.

Many societies have looked to a divine lawgiver as the source of moral norms. The obligation to obey such norms has been separated from other sorts of humanly legislated codes as a distinctive area of life called "morality." Confucians have taken a different tack, using a conceptual structure that emerges from the dynamics of the natural world. In fact, environmental ethics, or environmentalism, brings to the contemporary world the closest approximation of the sense of natural guidance that has been central to East Asian traditions for millennia. In this worldview, the universe to which we belong emerges and self-differentiates not by divine fiat, but in accord with its own inner pattern (*dao* 道) in a "self-so" or spontaneous way (*ziran* 自然).[14] An oak tree bears acorns, and acorns grow into oak trees in a self-so way in accord with the natural pattern (*dao*) already within them.

And just as there is a fitting *dao* for an oak tree, so too is there a *dao* for all creatures, including humans. Every creature is endowed with its own interior nature that guides and informs its behavior accordingly. All of these *dao* or natures enjoy a mutual fit, for they are all diverse emergent manifestations from a single source. This is evident in the shared East Asian concept of a single *dao* running through all things. Song Confucians, who often substituted the term *li* 理 for *dao*, made a cornerstone of their metaphysics and cosmology of the proposition, "*Li* is one, but manifested diversely."[15]

The East Asian concept of *dao*, or its close counterpart *li*, are intuitions grounded in the interdependent fit so evident in the workings of the complex natural world around us. If everything works harmoniously in terms of everything else, there must be some inner unifying pattern running through it all—an organic wholeness most easily grasped in the paradigmatic unity of a single living body. By a self-so dynamic, members function to bring about the well-being of the complex whole to which they belong.

Against the background of this shared understanding of the universe as a single, living system, Confucian thought took up the question of the complex world of human life, where humans seem too easily to get out of touch with the guidance that naturally informs every life and every situation. The ideal of self-cultivation was thus framed in terms of the spontaneous appropriateness of response, which characterizes the natural world. The ideal figure, the sage, is in such perfect touch with the guidance inherent in every situation that he responds appropriately in an entirely spontaneous, self-so manner. The situation of every person is no different from that of the sage, except that we must struggle with the blockage that somehow obscures guidance and distorts responsiveness.

The remarks concerning the need for ethics with which we opened this section point to a caveat regarding this way of stating the ideal: because of our language-based cumulative learning and the power of our manipulative techniques, we no longer enjoy the self-so fitness that emerges from the coevolutionary dynamics of the life community. The reality of an all-encompassing and deeply pragmatic normative guidance is real enough in the long run, and we must indeed find and practice a way of life that works, that is, fits. The contemporary term for this is "sustainability"; Confucians called it "the mandate." But the thoughtless perfection of the bird that eats when hungry and drinks when thirsty is far too simple a model to encompass the complexity that goes with human society. We must cultivate a sensitivity and responsiveness to appropriate guidance in a mode proportioned to the scope of our powers—which are likewise the scope of our problem.

Confucians responded to this by a continual emphasis on the importance of self-cultivation and careful attention to its various modes. Of course the mode of cultivation must fit the nature of the problem or hindrance involved, so the pivot of this entire endeavor becomes the manner in which one grasps the nature of the problems we humans confront.

The Problem

Virtually all religious traditions, and their secular counterparts as well, agree that humans confront major problems. However, each religious tradition develops its distinctive character in the enunciation of the nature of these problems. Buddhists profoundly analyze the root dynamics of suffering, Christians wrestle with sin and forgiveness, Muslims with submission. Confucians, taking as their paradigm the spontaneously life-giving dynamics of the world of nature, question deeply what it is that deflects human responses from the life-giving mark. They assume no fundamental and fatal flaw: humans, like other creatures, exhibit varying degrees of excellence and limitation, but Heaven and Earth do not produce fundamentally flawed forms of life. If something distorts our fitting response to our situation, it must be sought in tensions inherent in the dynamics of the system itself.

How then can one describe this problem? What separates or cuts us off from a naturally endowed life-giving responsiveness? Mencius spoke only of the impact of negative social experiences, but Song Confucians sought a deeper explanation. Zhu Xi reflected a new direction by paying attention to the dynamic life of the flow of feelings in our heart-mind. He said: "Therefore those who can bear seeing others suffer and are without commiseration are just blocked up by selfishness and have not yet recognized the *li* of their mind that runs through the self, Heaven and Earth, and all creatures. Thus the essence of seeking humanity is simply a matter of not losing one's original heart-mind [*benxin* 本心]."[16]

So something in our heart-mind includes concern for "Heaven and Earth, and all creatures," and something obstructs that concern and blocks it up. Selfishness locks our concern into our small individuality, so it cannot flow into the great whole to which we belong. As Song dynasty Confucian thinkers pondered this tension between individuality and belonging to a larger whole, they elaborated an understanding that naturally expressed itself in terms of paired contrasting concepts. One side of the pair reflected mainly the ideal of holistic unity and the single flow of life. These were concepts such as the "supreme ultimate" (*taiji* 太極), principle (*li*), original nature (*benxing*), and *dao*-mind (*daoxin* 道心). The other side of the pair reflected mainly our physicality, and hence the individual separateness that could easily lead us astray into selfishness. These were concepts such as material force (*qi* 氣), material nature (*qizhixing* 氣質性), and human mind (*renxin* 人心).

The Mencian story that highlights the life-giving force flowing through all things is naturally holistic, encompassing all creatures in a pervasive systemic unity. But even if society and the whole natural world form one great interdependent system, the system is made up of physically distinct individual units. Ideally, the individual would harmonize "naturally" with the whole. But with individual distinctness, there is always the possibility of the individual putting his or her own interests first. Due to their central concern for self-cultivation, Song Confucian thinkers developed Mencius's story into a philosophy that saw systematic reality in terms of the tension between holism and individual existence. They often explained that Mencius, in his situation, had need to concentrate mainly on the holistic side of things, the "good" feelings of the original nature that are in unified flow with the heart-mind of Heaven and Earth. But for self-cultivation to have the desired effect, it was also necessary to pay careful attention to the potential problems of individuality as well.

Song Confucian concern with regard to the tension between holism and individuality is reflected in their discussions and attitudes regarding human feelings. The emergence of feelings in response to situations is the concrete, real manifestation of the deepest dispositions of our nature. Just as our nature reflects both our connectedness with all things (our *benxing*) and our individuality (our *qizhixing*), we can see the same aspects in our actual feelings. The famous Four Beginnings discussed by Mencius and paired with the life-giving process of the four seasons by Confucians of the Han dynasty, were clearly holistic in scope and function, as we have seen in our discussion of humanity (*ren*). But the classic *Book of Rites* presented another list of feelings, the so-called Seven Feelings (*qiqing* 七情): desire, hate, love, fear, grief, anger, and joy.[17] Clearly, these could overlap with the feelings discussed by Mencius. But while Mencius's formulation clearly regarded the holistic side—that is, the side of the feelings that integrates us with others—the seven feelings could also easily operate in a self-centered way. Thus, to the contrastive pairs of principle force and material force, *dao* mind and human mind, and original nature and physical nature, Song dynasty Confucians added a contrastive pair of feelings, the four beginnings and seven feelings.

The Song Confucian concern for cultivation of the heart-mind invited further psychological definition and reflection on the tension between the system and the individuality inherent in the nature of our existence. Mencius laid the foundation for understanding our common shared life and the feelings that join us appropriately with all creatures. Later, in the Song dynasty, Confucian thinkers filled out this story with a solid account of individuality, metaphysically and cosmologically grounded in the concept of the "physical nature." Individuality was not regarded as evil, but it was considered the aspect of existence that easily leads to blocking up our proper connection with other creatures; this proclivity to self-centeredness is the origin of distorted responsiveness. Ideally, feelings should do full justice to both these dimensions of our existence.

The Song Confucians thus developed a keen and theoretically grounded awareness regarding the tensions inherent in the kinds of feelings that animate the lives of our heart-minds. It is well known that Korean Confucians during the Chosŏn dynasty (1392–1910) developed this level of the Confucian dis-course with unmatched care and sophistication. Every nuance of the relative dynamics of the four beginnings and the seven feelings was examined and argued in the course of the famous Four-Seven Debate, which became the hallmark discourse of Korean Confucian thought. T'oegye (1501–1570) and Yulgok (1536–1584) are the most prominent names in this controversy, but the question is so compelling that it was taken up and argued anew by each generation who thought seriously about the feelings that guide us.

The question explores community, individuality, and the origination of our feelings. T'oegye and Yulgok discussed it in terms of *li* and *qi*, the philosophical concepts Song Confucians used to account for the communal and individual sides of existence. There is only one existence, and it is both communal and individual, both *li* and *qi*, both shared and separate. How then do these two aspects of our reality function in the arising of our feelings? Are both sides always included in the same way? Are there some feelings, such as those spoken of by Mencius, that originate in a special way in the commonality of our existence, even though our individual heart-mind is the vehicle of their manifestation?

The concepts of *li* and *qi* enabled a probing investigation of these questions. With such sophisticated conceptual tools, T'oegye and Yulgok achieved one of the great discussions of the origins and scope of the life of our heart-mind.[18] T'oegye's effort above all was to explicate how *li*, the communal, interconnected aspect of our reality, could be a primary activating source in the movement of our feelings. He wanted to explain how that connection was so powerful it could mobilize forceful feelings that lead beyond our separateness and individuality. His formula for the origination of such feeling was: "*Li* gives issue and *qi* follows it." For T'oegye and Yulgok, this was a gripping philosophical problem. In our own time, it is being put to an empirical test: Can we transcend our individualism and anthropocentrism to act for the well-being of the human community and for the community of life beyond the human species, or will we wait until the threat is so imminent that we are finally moved, perhaps too late, by our powerful feelings for self-preservation?

The assumption that the latter is true, that self-interest is the final arbiter of human activity, lies at the heart of much contemporary despair in the face of the growing environmental crisis. While the Confucian analysis offers no easy optimism, it does present a more complete and potentially useful view of the human situation. Indeed, contemporary systems theorists are also paying serious attention to the critical role of the evolution of symbiotic and altruistic dynamics. No longer does "survival of the fittest" imply only self-centered struggle and competition; the fitness of cooperation in an interdependent systemic network has full recognition among contemporary systems thinkers. Confucians, however, have also spent several thousand years dedicated to finding ways to cultivate human character in the light of these realities.

Self-Cultivation and Keeping the Life Community Intact

The Confucian understanding of the dynamics of the human heart-mind is both more realistic and more hopeful than the shortsighted contemporary focus on the primacy of self-interest. Their analysis of the human problem, the inherent tension of individual lives lived interdependently within a holistic system, historically attended mainly to human society as the encompassing system. Now we see clearly that the relevant community of life must include all systems, all organisms, that the life of even microbes within our soil is parent and support to our own lives. This advance in ecological understanding only underlines the crux of the problem and emphasizes the importance of what Confucians have to offer regarding practical self-cultivation.

Confucians framed their approach to self-cultivation with a saying taken from a work compiled more than 2,500 years ago, the classic *Book of Documents*: "The human mind is perilous, the *dao* mind is subtle; be discerning, be undivided. Hold fast the mean!"[19] By "human mind" they meant the feelings attached to maintaining our personal well-being—the seven feelings of the T'oegye-Yulgok debate. They regarded this as "perilous" because, however necessary such feelings might be, they can easily lead to an inappropriately self-centered dynamic. The "*dao* mind" refers to feelings that relate us appropriately to the larger community to which we belong—the equivalent of Mencius's Four Beginnings. It is subtle in the sense that such feelings can easily be missed or overwhelmed, drowned out in the insistent noise of strong feelings that would have us take care of ourselves first and foremost. The "mean" or centeredness to which we should hold fast is not an average tradeoff between these two, but rather a center like a bull's-eye, right on the mark, whatever is appropriate to any given situation.

Confucians attended carefully to the interplay of these sorts of feelings because they were aware that feelings form the first line of our response to any situation. Human conduct is motivated, directed in some way or other. Feelings not only move us, they move us in some direction, that is, they constitute the first line of guidance. In situations of conflict or confusion, we have a second line of guidance: we can slow down and think about what to do and why. But thought, with the task of sorting out appropriate and inappropriate feelings and inclinations, is itself already deeply influenced by feelings. In view of this, Confucians advocated the cultivation of a calm, focused, self-possessed state of mind much less subject to the strong pull of individually oriented self-centered desires. They introduced a meditative practice, "quiet sitting," as an aid to such cultivation.

Confucian focus on cultivating selected sorts of feelings—those that attune us in a life-giving way to the living web of interdependence to which we belong—stemmed from an acute awareness that we are endowed only with the seeds of various sorts of feelings. That is why Mencius spoke of the four feelings he identified as four beginnings, or the core guidance system for acting as full human beings, the human *dao*. Neglect them and they remain rudimentary inclinations lost in the welter of other pulls on our mind-and-heart; cultivate them and they become humanity, rightness, propriety, and wisdom.

Feelings we deliberately nurture tend to thrive and grow strong while those neglected tend to become more muted. But since we feel and respond only within a matrix of living relationships, it is an oversimplification to think that cultivation of the feelings has only to do with one's personal efforts. Mencius explained that the humans of his society showed little sign of the life-giving feelings inherent in human nature because they got bent out of shape day after day by dealing with life in a dissolving society. His perceptive analysis identified two poles, the most public and the most personal sectors of social life, as sources of the self-organizing dynamics of society. In many passages he argued as if the good or bad example of the king and high ministers would sway the whole community; in many others he sounded as if everything hinges on the quality of our most immediate personal relationships in the bosom of the family. High-profile figures clearly shape the tone and practice of society. But so, too, does our personal character shape family life. The quality of family life ramifies into the local community, which sends ripples into a yet wider area in the upward dynamic we associate with the power of grassroots movements.

How, then, do such dynamics affect contemporary society? What kinds of feelings are brought forth and ingrained by social currents in the responsive life of our modern minds-and-hearts? How fare the *dao*-minded and human-minded sides of our inclinations and feelings, and with what environmental consequences? And finally, how can personal cultivation impact this in a way that makes any difference?

Looking first from the perspective of dynamics originating at the most public pole, the top-down dynamic, a striking phenomenon is the emergence of a global consumer ethos. Propelled by the media, the United States occupies much the same example-setting position in contemporary global consciousness that Mencius saw the king occupying in an earlier political and social order. Images of American affluence fill the television and movie screens of nations around the world, showing them the good life that can be had if only they can develop their own economies. Advertising and marketing conflate consumption and well-being so that even people who "have everything" will feel a need to acquire more, the latest model, the largest, the smallest. Obesity now ranks with AIDS as a global pandemic that threatens to swamp health care systems, giving us a grim symbol of how shortsighted is the consumer vision of "the good life." At the same time our other forms of consumption undermine the health of the life community, so we find that our increasing affluence is accompanied by a wave of extinctions. The human mind, in the form of an insufficiently reflective, short-term focus on personal convenience and comfort and on maximizing a single species in the community of life, enjoys a trajectory of unprecedented self-aggrandizement.

The ancients observed that "the *dao* mind is subtle," less evident, seemingly more easily overwhelmed than the human mind. But the self-transcending *dao* mind too is an inborn and necessary component of our feelings, and it likewise enjoys enlarged dynamics in the contemporary world. The same media that purvey the dream of affluence also bring images and news of suffering and disaster. An international network of NGO's has emerged to respond to lively concerns regarding health, human rights, and the environment. The heart-mind of empathetic commiseration moves people to respond and reach across borders as never before, breaching political, ethnic, and species distinctions. Green political parties have emerged as a force, especially in Europe, and now some governments, such as the Netherlands, are taking a world leadership role on environmental causes. Regarding the environment, the most common publicly invoked motive is self-interested fear for human well-being. But many people are also strongly motivated by an earth-centered valuing of life, a feeling that finds strong encouragement in environmental literature and, on a more popular level, in a variety of nature shows. The growth of the subtle *dao* mind is evidenced in the growing numbers of people who proclaim passionately that we are but *part* of the system and must support its integral life.

These top-down dynamics in our public life shape individuals, who in turn both share and shape each other's feelings and attitudes. This interaction creates a corresponding bottom-up dynamic influencing the formation of the social heart-mind. This public-personal loop can easily form a kind of dynamic and mutually reinforcing feedback in which individuals simply reinforce the shape of the groups by which they are shaped. Confucians, however, also saw personal cultivation as a potentially transforming, rectifying force that could ramify along social networks, from individual to family and friends, from family and friends to community, from communities to nations and beyond to the whole world.[20] But how can individuals achieve the relative independence from systemic influence to reshape a disordered society and rectify interpersonal relationships?

Addressing this issue pushed Song Confucian analysis of the life of the feelings to a deeper level. They observed that in the course of constantly engaged activity we tend to lose our depth of personal reflection and self-possession. Moreover, turmoil and unreflective haste generally facilitate the dominance of the powerful, individual-centered feelings of the human mind over the deep, life-giving responsiveness of the *dao* mind. Without time to find our deeper wellsprings of direction, we flow with the unsorted values of the world around us, rather than with the best, the most life-giving responsiveness available within us.

This insight led Song Confucians to make maintaining a self-possessed, focused mind a central feature of Confucian self-cultivation. Such cultivation advocated slowing down when circumstances permitted, even to the point of deliberately slowing speech and gait and cultivating a deep personal quiet in the practice of meditation. The name they gave to keeping this state of mind as a means to enhance their most profound and life-giving responsiveness was "maintaining reverence."

The pace of life these premodern Confucians wished to slow down, even in the urban centers of political power and wealth, was molasses-slow by contemporary standards. Means of transportation and communication imposed their own implacable limits on the flow of activity; no circumstances existed that could call a phrase such as "instant gratification" into common usage. If "maintaining reverence" was difficult in such circumstances—as was frequently observed by masters of such self-cultivation—what might be said of its relevance and applicability in our rapidly accelerating contemporary world?

We certainly do experience the difficulties that led Confucians to advocate "maintaining reverence." Shelves of self-help books reflect the loss of centeredness and grounding that results from filling up every available moment with noise and activity. Studies are now devoted to charting what is happening to our young people's decreasing attention spans and their ability to learn and evaluate new material. Many lament the diminishment of meaningful political discourse in a barrage of rapid-fire sound bites. We are becoming habituated to increasing speed; even the action movies of a few years ago now seem plodding by comparison. But the heightened level of excitement accompanying accelerated stimuli is not matched by a more profound level of response. Speed keeps consciousness on the surface; we still need reflective time for significance to sink in.

Our modern way of making a living steadily accelerates the pace of life. Industrial processes feed technology to produce more goods ever more efficiently. As technology advances in terms of doing more and accomplishing it more quickly, it both saves time and allows us to fit more and more into the saved time, leading to daily routines crammed with activity. In the workplace, technology allows us to produce more and so we are expected to produce more. At home, we expect tasks to take less time so we plan more and more things to fit into our day. Multitasking, first at work, and then throughout daily life, has become a characteristic of economically advanced societies.

Our increased productivity requires increased consumption, a self-reinforcing feedback loop in which we feel pressured for time to consume our products and then pressured likewise for time to earn the money to pay for them by more production, which again we must consume. This feedback loop of production and consumption demands the lubrication of advertising to keep its momentum: we must be shown more and more products that we "need" in order to live well, and our desire to consume must be nurtured to a fine and responsive attunement by the advertising industry.

This human production and consumption takes place in the midst of a community within which we are but a single species. Technology has dramatically expanded the speed and scope of human ability to intervene in the world, so our reach now affects everything. The community of life, especially in its more complex forms, cannot adapt to the rate of our exploitation or its unintended side effects. Generations of fish are in the net before they can reproduce. Forest habitat disappears. Rivers lose spawning beds to waters cascading from deforested hillsides, and the waters into which they flow become dead zones depleted of oxygen because of the unprecedented algae blooms fed by the runoff of fertilizers intended to speed and increase plant growth in the fields growing our food.

Because we maintain our lives only in an interdependent relational community of life, Confucians emphasized the need to slow down in order gain the reflective self-possession that would free the life-giving responsiveness appropriate to conducting ourselves in this community of interdependent lives. Our own immediately felt needs seem evident and invite quick action. Understanding the needs and situation of others, and perceiving how our own necessities deeply intertwine with those of others, is a wisdom born from deeper reflection and carried out in a more thoughtful practice. While the focus of Confucian thought was mainly on rectifying problems that disrupt human society, we now see and experience the further need for this personal cultivation in order for human society to fit appropriately with the larger community of life. To thrive within a community affected by one's actions requires familiarity, understanding, and concern. Confucians called the frame of mind conducive to such a way of living "maintaining reverence." Such reverence, a combination of attention, caring, and respect, is exactly the human quality upon which the well-being of the earth community now seems to depend.

This slowing down, giving reverence time to grow and function, might be regarded as a quality of life issue today. Increasing numbers of people, overstimulated by the intensity of our consumer society, want to stop moving so fast; they feel a lack of connection and want more time to care about what there is to care about right around them: the people, the places, the world of nature and its myriad forms of life. Beginning at a personal level, this quest already sends ripples of reorganization through society. "Simple living" is not only a magazine title but a movement. An Internet search for the phrase yields 236 million results. Norwegians decided to reverse the "time is money" syndrome and seek more time rather than annual raises. Similar considerations have moved a number of European countries to shorten the work week, even as vacations and holidays have expanded. This slowing down contradicts the competitive global dynamics of ever-increasing production and consumption, but it responds to a deep human need. When France tried in 2006 to again lengthen its reduced work week in the name of global competition, the country was wracked by such rampant social protest the measure had to be rescinded.

Such quality of life issues and movements are not yet the kind of deep cultivation Confucians meant by "maintaining reverence," but they belong to the same inclination, seeking a less hurried pace to enable a more deeply aware and responsive mode of living. In these developments we see *dao* mind not as just some moral duty, but an attractive pull of our feelings, reflecting a dimension of our responsive life without which neither we nor the community of life can thrive. But it takes *time* to cultivate this side of life, time to spend with family and friends, time to participate in the community, time to take walks in the woods or by the river, time to reflect on one's actions and interactions, time to grow in sensitivity to appreciation for the whole community of life. The Confucian emphasis that we must take the time to appreciate with reverent responsiveness this net of relationships within which we are sustained and through which we sustain others has, if anything, gained in meaning. It has also gained in urgency.

Conclusion

The Confucian tradition, arising amid conditions of political and social dissolution in ancient China, made community its central concern. The *dao* that Confucians investigated and pursued was seen as informing the self-organizing (*ziran*) dynamic of life-giving relationships in the natural world, including human society. When we allow self-centered dynamics to distort the function of community, they observed, we break down the natural or "original" flow of life through the community. Self-concern has its place, but it easily becomes a distorting focus that destroys the larger web of relationships. We well know the path leading from self-interest to competition and thence into the dynamics of hostility, defense, and aggression.

Such, in fact, were the dynamics prominent in the social milieu of Mencius. But he saw that a more fundamental or "original" condition—wholeness—precedes disintegration. The denuded mountain, he says, was not originally barren, but full of life. Humans are not originally barren islands of self-concern; they are full of a connective life that naturally ramifies into a community of care. Our deepest feelings, he maintained, move us with empathetic concern for the well-being of others.

Now that our technologically enhanced prowess enables us to modify the world so rapidly and on such a large scale, it becomes imperative that those interventions be informed not only by a concern for the well-being of a single species, ourselves, but for the entire living community. We are threatened with denuded, barren mountains of our own making; we know they were not originally like that. And we sometimes feel almost hopeless confronted with the globe-spanning power of a self-interest-driven, profit-maximizing economic system. But that also is of our own making, and if we consider the evidence of growing concern for environmental destruction, we know that Mencius was right: we are not originally, fundamentally, like that.

The problem we confront calls for cultivating and nurturing in our personal and our public life a reordered, a more life-giving kind of concern. The seeds are there, but they need to be nurtured. Confucians know much about such nurturing. They emphasized slowing down, a practice that rectifies an unworthy status quo by enabling a more self-possessed and life-giving participation in the affairs of the community. Much in the life of our technologically powerful, demanding, and fast-paced societies drains away the thoughtfulness and depth with which we would ordinarily respond to the world. If anything, as the pace of life accelerates, the kind of cultivation the Confucians developed, and the reasons for it, become ever more relevant.

Confucians called the technique of maintaining a state of calm, focused self-possession "maintaining reverence." The term *reverence* suggests the way this condition tends to subordinate our feelings of self-regard, promoting instead a sensitive responsiveness to the larger whole from which we draw life and to which we belong. Words such as "awe" and "reverence" are often used in religious contexts, describing human encounter with matters of ultimate concern, sacred matters. Confucians have suggested that the sacred is found when the flow of activity in daily life finds its true character of nurturing and supporting life. Living this way, we "join in the transformative, nurturing activity of Heaven and Earth, and in so doing form a third with them."[21] These words take on a new and practical meaning in the contemporary world, for the human reach now touches the entire community of life, which can and will thrive if, and only if, we can live and work with the reverence that renders us once again life-giving.

Suggestions for Further Reading

For an excellent overview of Confucian views on nature and the environment, see Mary Evelyn Tucker and John Berthrong, eds. (1998), *Confucianism and Ecology: The Interrelation of Heaven, Humans, and Earth*. For discussions of contemporary China's contemporary environmental challenges, policies, and possible trajectories, see Elizabeth C. Economy (2005), *The River Runs Black: The Environmental Challenge To China's Future*, or Robert P. Weller (2006), *Discovering Nature: Globalization and Environmental Culture in China and Taiwan*. For a broader look at environmental thinking in Asia, see J. Baird Callicott and Roger T. Ames (1989), *Nature in Asian Traditions of Thought: Essays in Environmental Philosophy*.

Notes

1. Translated in Michael Kalton (1988), 51.

2. Translated in Kalton (1988), 146. Zhu Xi begins here with a quote taken from Cheng I.

3. Paraphrase of *Mencius* 6A8. Author's translation; chapter and passage numbers refer to all standard editions.

4. *Mencius* 2A6.

5. *Mencius* 1B15.

6. *Mencius* 6A6.

7. Song Confucians explicated a metaphysical framework of Daoist proportions and a sophisticated theory and method of cultivating the inner life of the heart-mind that could rival the Buddhists. This revitalized "neo-Confucianism" predominated throughout East Asia down to the modern era. "Neo" is a Western scholarly addition, a recognition of the scope and significance of these developments. They, however, simply regarded themselves as Confucians, faithful restorers carrying forward the tradition of Confucius. I therefore will not discriminate, but use the term *Confucian* inclusively, and designate certain historical thinkers or developments by dynasty, as was the common Confucian practice.

8. Translated in Kalton (1988), 51–52.

9. *Yishu* 2A, 2a. Author's translation; chapter and passage numbers refer to all standard editions.

10. *Zhuzi Yulei* 95.8b–9a. Author's translation; chapter and passage numbers refer to all standard editions. Zhu Xi's name, along with the two Cheng brothers, is attached to the "Cheng-Zhu school" of thought, the major or "orthodox" Song school of Confucian thought.

11. *Book of Changes*, Hexagram 24. Author's translation from the *Yijing*; chapter and passage numbers refer to all standard editions.

12. *Book of Changes*, Appended Remarks, Part 2, Chapter 1.

13. *Zhuzi Yulei* 105.71a.

14. In the modern lexicon of East Asia this term is now used to translate the Western word *nature* or *natural*.

15. The dictum originated in a discussion of Cheng Yi and Yang Shi regarding *The Western Inscription*. Cheng's letter is translated in Wing-tsit Chan (1963), *A Sourcebook of Chinese Philosophy*, 550–51.

16. *Zhuzi Yulei*, 95.8b–9a.

17. *Book of Rites*, Chapter 9. Author's translation; chapter and passage numbers refer to all standard editions.

18. For a translation of the extensive exchange of letters in which the debate was carried on, see Kalton (1994), *The Four-Seven Debate*.

19. *Book of Documents*, Part 2, 2.15. Author's translation; chapter and passage numbers refer to all standard editions.

20. This process is presented in the first chapter of the *Great Learning*, and from the Song dynasty onward became a centerpiece of Confucian thought.

21. *Doctrine of the Mean*, Chapter 22. Author's translation; chapter and passage numbers refer to all standard editions.

Appendix I

List of Names

The following is a list of names that appear in this book, including for the reader's reference the native characters. Names printed in bold also appear in the glossary.

Chinese Names

Carsun Chang or Zhang Junmai 張君勱 (1886–1969)
Chen Liang 陳亮 (1143–1194)
Cheng Hao 程顥 (1032–1085)
Cheng Yi 程頤 (1033–1107)
Confucius or **Kongzi** 孔子 (551–479 BCE)
Dai Zhen 戴震 (1723–1777)
Dong Zongshu 董仲舒 (c. 179–104 BCE)
Fan Zongyan 范仲淹 (989–1052)
Gao Yihan 高一涵 (1884–1968)
Gaozi 告子 (c. 420–350 BCE)
Han Yu 韓愈 (768–824)
Huang Zongxi 黃宗羲 (1610–1695)
Laozi 老子 (c. sixth century BCE)
Li Ao 李翱 (fl. 798)
Liu Shu-hsien 劉述先 (b. 1938)
Liu Zongyuan 柳宗元 (733–819)
Lu Xiangshan 陸象山 (1139–1193)
Lu Xun 魯迅 (1881–1936)
Mou Zongsan 牟宗三 (1909–1995)
Mozi 墨子 (473–390 BCE)
Mencius or **Mengzi** 孟子 (371–289 BCE)
Ouyang Xiu 歐陽修 (1007–1072)
Ruanyuan 阮元 (1764–1849)

Shao Yong 邵雍 (1011–1077)
Sima Guang 司馬光 (1019–1086)
Su Shi 蘇軾 (1037–1101)
Tu Weiming 杜維明 (b. 1940)
Tang Junyi 唐君毅 (1909–1978)
Wang Anshi 王安石 (1021–1086)
Wang Bi 王弼 (226–249)
Wang Fuzhi 王夫之 (1619–1692)
Wang Yangming 王陽明 (1472–1529)
Weng Fanggang 翁方綱 (1733–1818)
Xu Fuguan 徐復觀 (1903–1982)
Xunzi 荀子 (c. 310–238 BCE)
Xun Yue 荀悅 (148–209)
Yang Xiong 揚雄 (53 BCE–18 CE)
Zhang Zai 張載 (1020–1077)
Zhou Dunyi 周敦頤 (1017–1073)
Zhuangzi 莊子 (c. fourth century BCE)
Zhu Xi 朱熹 (1130–1200)

Japanese Names

Arai Hakuseki 新井白石 (1657–1725)
Chikamatsu Monzaemon 近松門左衛門 (1653–1725)
Fujiwara Seika 藤原惺窩 (1561–1619)
Fujiwara Teika 藤原定家 (1162–1241)
Hayashi Razan 林羅山 (1583–1657)
Hirata Atsutane 平田篤胤 (1776–1843)
Hishikawa Moronobu 菱川師宣 (d.1694)
Hoshina Masayuki 保科正之 (1611–1672)
Ihara Saikaku 井原西鶴 (1642–1693)
Itō Jinsai 伊藤仁斎 (1627–1705)
Itō Tōgai 伊藤東涯 (1670–1738)
Kada no Azumamaro 荷田春満 (1669–1736)
Kaibara Ekken 貝原益軒 (also Ekiken, 1630–1714)
Kamo no Mabuchi 賀茂真淵 (1697–1769)
Kumazawa Banzan 熊沢蕃山 (1619–1691)
Maruyama Masao 丸山真男 (1914–1996)
Matsudaira Sadanobu 松平定信 (1758–1829)
Motoda Eifu (Nagazane) 元田永浮 (1818–1891)
Motoori Norinaga 本居宣長 (1730–1801)
Nakae Tōju 中江藤樹 (1608–1648).

Ogyū Sorai 荻生徂徠 (1666–1728)
Ōjin 応仁 (c. fifth century)
Tokugawa Ienobu 德川家宣 (1666–1712)
Tokugawa Ietsugu 德川家継 (1709–1716)
Tokugawa Ieyasu 德川家康 (1542–1616)
Tokugawa Tsunayoshi 德川綱吉 (1646–1709)
Tokugawa Yoshimune 德川吉宗 (1684–1751)
Wani 王仁 (c. fifth century) K. **Wang In***
Yamaga Sokō 山鹿素行 (1622–1685)
Yamazaki Ansai 山崎闇斎 (1619–1682)
Yanagisawa Yoshiyasu 柳沢吉保 (1658–1714)

Korean Names

An Hyang 安珦 (1243–1306)
Chang Hyŏn-kwang 張顯光 (1554–1637)
Ch'oe Ch'iwon 崔致遠 (b. 875)
Ch'oe Han-ki 崔漢綺 (1803–1877)
Ch'oe Ikhyŏn 崔益鉉 (1833–1906)
Cho Hanbo 曹漢輔 (c. fifteenth century)
Chŏng Che-tu 鄭齊斗 (1649–1736)
Chŏng Chiun 鄭之雲 (1509–1561)
Chŏng Mong-chu 鄭夢周 (1337–1392)
Chŏng Tojŏn 鄭道傳 (1337–1398)
Chŏng Yagyong 丁若鏞 (1762–1836)
Chumong 朱蒙 (58–19 BCE)
Han Wonjin 韓元震 (1682–1751)
Hŏ Mok 許穆 (1595–1682)
Hong Taeyong 洪大容 (1731–1783)
Kang Hang 姜沆 (1567–1618)
Kim Ch'ong-hŭi 金正喜 (1786–1856)
Kim Pusik 金富軾 (1075–1151)
Kobong 高峰 (1527–1572)
Koi 古爾王 (234–286)
Kongmin 恭愍王 (1330–1374)
Kŭnchogo 近肖古王 (r. 346–375)
Lee Chae-hyŏn 李齊賢 (1287–1367)
Lee Chin-sang 李震相 (1818–1885)
Lee Hangro 李恒老 (1792–1868)
Lee Hyŏnil 李玄逸 (1627–1704)
Lee Kan 李柬 (1677–1727)

Lee Ŏn-chŏk 李彥迪 (1491–1553)
Lee Saek 李穡 (1328–1396)
Park Chi-wŏn 朴趾源 (1737–1805)
Park Ch'o 朴礎 (1367–1454)
Park Kyu-su 朴珪壽 (1807–1876)
Park Ŭn-sik 朴殷植 (1859–1925)
Sŏ Kyŏngdŏk 徐敬德 (1489–1546)
T'aejo 太祖大王 (r. 53–146)
Tan'gun 檀君 (c. 2333 BCE)
T'oegye 退溪 (1501–1570)
Ugye 牛溪 (1535–1598)
Yu In-sŏk 柳麟錫 (1842–1915)
Yulgok 栗谷 (1536–1584)
Yun Hyu 尹鑴 (1617–1680)
Wang In 王仁 (c. fifth century)

Appendix II

Historical Periods of China, Japan, and Korea

Below is a list of the historical periods of China, Japan, and Korea. Relevant periods are annotated with information regarding Confucianism's history. Names and terms printed in bold also appear in the glossary.

China

Three Sovereigns and Five Emperors 三皇五帝 (c. 2070BCE)

Xia 夏 (2200–1751 BCE)

Shang 商 (1751–1045 BCE)

Zhou 周 (1045–249 BCE)

Western Zhou 西周 (1045–771 BCE)

Eastern Zhou 東周 (770–256 BCE)

Spring and Autumn Period 春秋 (722–481 BCE)

Warring States Period 戰國 (480–221 BCE). The lifetimes of the famous "Warring States philosophers," **Confucius** (551–479), **Mencius** (371–289), and **Xunzi** (c. 310–298 BCE).

Qin 秦 (221–206 BCE)

Han 漢 (206 BCE–220 CE). Beginning in the Han, Confucianism becomes entrenched as offical state ideology and remains a political force until the founding of the republic in 1911.

Western Han 西漢 (206 BCE–9 CE)

Xin 新 (9–23)

Eastern Han 東漢 (25–220)

Three Kingdoms 三國 (220–280). This initiates the Wei-Qin period (220–420), which sees the rise of neo-Daoism (*xuanxue*) and the arrival of Buddhism, both of which influence Confucian thinking.

Western Jin 西晉 (226–316)

Eastern Jin 東晉 (317–420)

Southern and Northern Dynasties 南北朝 (386–589)

Sui 隋 (581–618)

Tang 唐 (618–907). Scholars such as Han Yu (768–824), Li Ao (fl. 798), and
    Liu Zongyuan (733–819) defend Confucianism against Buddhist and
    Daoist influences.

Five Dynasties and Ten Kingdoms 五代十國 (907–960)

Song 宋 (960–1279). Lifetime of **Zhu Xi** (1130–1200) and the rise of
    neo-Confucianism.

Northern Song 北宋 (960–1127)

Southern Song 南宋 (1127–1279)

Liao 遼 (916–1125)

Jin 金 (1115–1234)

Yuan 元 (1260–1368)

Ming 明 (1368–1644). Lifetime of noted neo-Confucian **Wang Yangming**
    (1472–1529).

Shun 順 (1644)

Qing 清 (1644–1911). Rise of the School of Han Learning or *hanxue*,
    which emphasizes the practical application of Confucianism and was
    critical of much Song and Ming neo-Confucian scholarship.

Japan

Jomon 縄文 (dating back to c. 10,000 BCE)

Yayoi 弥生 (c. 900 BCE–250 CE)

Yamato 大和 (250–710). In the fifth century, the Korean scholar **Wang In** is
    said to have introduced Confucianism into Japan.

Nara 奈良 (710–794)

Heian 平安 (794–1185)

Kamakura 鎌倉 (1185–1333)

Kemmu Restoration 建武の新政 (1333–1336)

Muromachi 室町 (1336–1573). From the mid-fifteenth to mid-sixteenth
    centuries, Confucianism becomes a topic of study at the **Ashikaga
    Gakkō**.

Azuchi-Momoyama 安土桃山 (1573–1603). Following the Japanese invasion
    of Korea in the 1590s, Japan receives an influx of Korean and Chinese
    neo-Confucian texts, which are distributed among Zen temples for study.
    Zen priest Fujiwara Seika (1561–1619) becomes the first prominent
    "convert" to Confucianism.

Edo 江戸 (1600–1827). The Tokugawa government begins its long association
    with Confucian advisors. Starting in the Edo period, Confucianism

becomes entrenched as a cultural force in Japan, and remains so to this day, alongside Buddhism and Shintoism.

Meiji 明治 (1868–1912)

Taisho 大正 (1912–1926)

Showa 昭和 (1926–1989)

Heisei 平成 (1989 to present)

Korea

Kojosŏn 古朝鮮 (2333 BCE–57 CE)

Three Kingdoms (57 BCE–668 CE)

Koguryŏ 高句麗 (37 BCE–668 CE). The National Confucian Academy is founded in 372 in Koguryŏ.

Paekche 百済 (18 BCE–660 CE). During the reign of King Kŭnchogo (346–375), the Paekche scholar **Wang In** introduces the Confucian classics to Japan.

Silla 新羅 (57 BCE–935 CE)

United Silla 統一新羅 (668–935). Lifetime of noted Confucian philosopher Ch'oe Ch'iwon (b. 875).

Koryŏ 高麗 (918–1392). In this, Korea's medieval period, Kim Pusik (1075–1151) writes a Confucian history of the Three Kingdoms period.

Chosŏn 朝鮮 (1392–1910). In this active period of Korea's intellectual history, great debates such as the **Four-Seven Debate** and the **Ho-Rak Debate** occupy Confucian scholarship.

Glossary

Analects. See ***Lunyu***.

Ashikaga Gakkō 足利学校 (Japanese). The oldest institute of higher learning in Japan, it promoted Confucian studies, especially from the mid-fifteenth to mid-sixteenth centuries.

bakufu 幕府 (Japanese). Government, often refers to the shogunate. See ***shogun***.

Book of Changes. See ***Yijing***.

Book of Documents. Also *Book of History* or *Classic of History*. See ***Shujing***.

Book of Mencius. See ***Mengzi***.

Book of Rites. Also *Classic of Rites*. See ***Liji***.

Book of Songs. Also *Classic of Poetry*. See ***Shijing***.

Book of Xunzi. See ***Xunzi***.

cheng 誠 (Chinese). Commonly translated as integrity or sincerity; a concept closely associated with the classic text ***Zhongyong***.

Confucius and **Confucianism**. See ***Kongzi***.

daimyo 大名 (Japanese). Heads of powerful regional families in feudal Japan.

dao 道 (Chinese). One of the most fundamental and most disputed terms in Chinese thought, often translated as "way." It has been interpreted to mean, among other things, a metaphysical entity, a cosmological or social order, or an ethical code.

Daoism or ***daojia*** 道家 (Chinese). A major indigenuous philosophy of China, along with Confucianism, Moism, and Legalism. Central texts include the *Daodejing* 道德經 and *Zhuangzi* 莊子. The legendary founder Laozi 老子 is said to have been a contemporary of Confucius.

daotong 道統 (Chinese). A term meaning "transmission of the *dao*" coined by neo-Confucian scholar Zhu Xi to express the continuity between the classical Confucianism of the Warring States period and the Confucian revival of the Northern Song dynasty.

daoxue 道學 (Chinese). The name given by neo-Confucian scholars of the Song dynasty to their own teachings; translated as "learning of the way."

daren 大人 (Chinese). In modern Chinese, this means simply adult; in Confucianism, it means a person of distinction who is, however, not yet a "consummate" person. Compare to *ren* 仁.

Daxue 大學 (Chinese). The *Great Learning*, originally one chapter of the *Book of Rites*, selected by Zhu Xi as one of the Four Books (see *sishu*), or primary texts of Confucianism.

de 德 (Chinese). Traditionally translated as virtue, not only in the sense of the quality of one's character but also in the sense of one's capacity for effective or appropriate action.

Doctrine of the Mean. See *Zhongyong*.

fa 法 (Chinese). Laws and regulations. Often used to translate the Buddhist term *dharma*.

fajia 法家 (Chinese). Known as Legalism, a pragmatic political philosophy, one of the major indigenous philosophies of China, along with Confucianism, Daoism, and Moism.

Five Classics. See *wujing*.

five constants. See *wuchang*.

five relations. See *wulun*.

focus and field. According to William James (1842–1910), the self is characterized by a "focus-field" structure in which focal awareness is surrounded by a dimly felt experiential field. We tend to identify the "self" with the focal aspect, but selfhood comprises the whole field of experience. This focus-field model for selfhood is influential not only in Anglo-American pragmatism and process philosophy but in contemporary Confucian scholarship as well.

Four Beginnings. See *siduan*.

Four Books. See *sishu*.

Four-Seven Debate. Perhaps the most famous debate in Korean Confucian intellectual history, it concerns the relationship between the Seven Feelings (*qiqing*) and the Four Beginnings (*siduan*). The main contenders were **Kobong**, **T'oegye**, **Ugye**, and **Yulgok**.

gewu 格物 (Chinese). The "investigation of things," which aims at an enlightened understanding of the world and worldly experience. A term originally from the *Daxue*.

gong 公 (Chinese). An ethical term, concerning the community and community interests.

Great Learning. See *Daxue*.

han 漢 (Chinese). The largest ethnic grouping in modern China. Also the name of a Chinese dynasty. For a timeline of Chinese dynasties, see Appendix II.

hanxue 漢學 (Chinese). The School of Han Learning, a school of Confucianism in the Qing dynasty; also known the School of Evidential Learning. Now associated with sinology in general.

he 和 (Chinese). Harmony, largely in the sense of a harmonious mingling of individual elements without an erasure of distinctions.

Heart-mind. See *xin*.

Ho-Rak Debate. Named after the two areas in Korea, Honam and Rakha, where the two factions of debating scholars lived. The debate concerned whether or not humans and animals share the same "original nature."

hungu 勳舊 (Korean). A faction of neo-Confucian political reformers of Korea's early Chosŏn period who supported Chŏng Tojŏn's emphasis on institutional reform.

junzi 君子 (Chinese). Originally means a ruler or aristocrat, but Confucianism uses *junzi* in a normative sense to mean an exemplary or an accomplished person.

kami 神 (Japanese). The deities and ancestral spirits of the Japanese *shintō* tradition.

keguan 客觀 (Chinese). The "guest's-eye view" which seeks harmony and benefit for all; in modern Chinese it means "objective" or "fair." Compare with *zhuguan*.

keji 克己 (Chinese). Self-discipline, in the sense of overcoming selfish desires; an important component in the development of an exemplary person in Confucianism.

Kobong 高峰, a pen name for Ki Taesŭng 奇大升 (1527–1572). (Korean). His correspondence with **T'oegye** forms part of the **Four-Seven Debate**. See also **Ugye** and **Yulgok**.

kogaku 古学 (Japanese). The "ancient learning" schools of the Tokugawa period in Japan, which advocated the direct study of ancient texts as opposed to the commentaries of neo-Confucians.

kokugakusha 国学者 (Japanese). Refers to the nativist scholars of Japan, who rejected foreign teachings such as Confucianism.

Kongzi 孔子 (Chinese). "Master Kong," or Confucius as he is known in the West, lived from 551 to 479 BCE and can rightfully be considered one of the most influential thinkers in Chinese history. His teachings form the basis of Confucianism.

Laozi. See **Daoism**.

Legalism. See *fajia*.

li 利 (Chinese). Often means personal advantage, but can also mean benefit in general.

li 理 (Chinese). Confucian term meaning order, pattern, rationale, or principle.

li 禮 (Chinese). Ritual propriety in Confucianism, associated with utmost appropriateness in all one's roles and relations; one of the five core Confucian values (see **wuchang**).

Liji 禮記 (Chinese). *Book of Rites*. One of the Five Classics (**wujing**) of Confucianism, predating the *Analects* (**Lunyu**), it deals with ritual practice and personal conduct.

Lunyu 論語 (Chinese). The Confucian *Analects*, a collection of teachings attributed to Confucius; one of the Four Books (**sishu**) selected by Zhu Xi as a primary text of Confucianism.

Lushi Chunqiu 呂氏春秋 (Chinese). *Spring and Autumn Chronicles*. One of the Five Classics (**wujing**) of Confucianism, it chronicles historical events of pre-Qin China.

Mencius or **Mengzi** 孟子 (Chinese). May refer to the Confucian philosopher (372–289 BCE), as well as the book attributed to him. Mencius is known for arguing that human nature is originally good by virtue of the Four Beginnings, which are the roots of characteristics such as humaneness, righteousness, propriety, and wisdom. See also **siduan** and **Xunzi**.

Mind-heart. See **xin**.

minben 民本 (Chinese). Loosely meaning "the people are the basis of the state," it appears in many ancient texts, expressing the idea that the state's people have final authority because the will of *tian* and the will of the people are the same.

ming 命 (Chinese). Command, decree, fate, or destiny. See also *tianming* at the **tian** entry.

ming 名 (Chinese). Refers to names and the act of naming. In the *Analects* 13.3, Confucius stresses the importance of naming properly (*zhengming* 正名).

minjung 民衆 (Korean). Loosely translated as "the people" or "the masses," a term associated with South Korea's struggle for democracy in the 1970s and '80s. Some minjung activists, though not all, were opposed to Confucianism, which they considered conservative and backward.

Moism or *mojia* 墨家 (Chinese). Founded by **Mozi** 墨子 (473–390 BCE), Moism is one of the major indigenous philosophies of China, along with Confucianism, Daoism, and Legalism.

nei 內 (Chinese). The realm of concealment, practical household management, and familial kinship relations, often associated with the activities of women. See also **wai**.

Neo-Confucianism. The revival of Confucianism in the Song Dynasty. See also **daoxue**.

Neo-Daoism. See **xuanxue**.

New Confucianism. The contemporary period of Confucian scholarship, arguably beginning with the 1958 essay "A Manifesto on Chinese Culture to the World" by philosophers Tang Junyi, Mou Zongsan, Xu Fuguan, and Zhang Junmai.

qi 氣 (Chinese). Literally "air" or "breath," *qi* is a complicated term referring to the active principle or "vital energy" in all things; sometimes *qi* is understood in terms of the Western distinction between matter and energy, but in the Chinese tradition not only living beings but also elements such as stone and wood have *qi*.

qiankun 乾坤 (Chinese). "Heaven and earth," or the universe. Similar to *tiandi* (see **tian**).

qing 情 (Chinese). Human emotions and feelings.

qiqing 七情 (Chinese). The Seven Feelings as first listed in the *Book of Rites*, including desire, hate, love, fear, grief, anger, and joy. The extent to which these overlap with the Four Beginnings discussed by Mencius is the subject of the famous Four-Seven Debate in Korean Confucianism.

rangakusha 蘭学者 (Japanese). The "Dutch learning scholars" of Japan, who studied European knowledge in general.

ren 人 (Chinese). A common term for "person" or "human being." Compare to **ren** 仁.

ren 仁 (Chinese). One of the five core Confucian values (see **wuchang**). It connotes a "consummate person" or "authoritative conduct" in terms of Confucian standards of personal development; it has been commonly translated as "benevolence" or "humanity."

sarim 士林 (Korean). A faction of neo-Confucian political reformers of Korea's early Chosŏn period, noted for their idealism.

School of Evidential Learning. Also **School of Han Learning**. See **hanxue**.

Seikyō yōroku 聖教要録 (Japanese). The *Essential Teachings of the Sages* by Yamaga Sokō, which marks the beginning of Japan's ancient learning movement (**kogaku**).

sheng 生 (Chinese). Birth, growth, and life; also creativity, transformation, and change.

Seven Feelings. See **qiqing**.

Shijing 詩經 (Chinese). *Book of Songs*. One of the Five Classics (**wujing**) of Confucianism, it is the oldest existing collection of Chinese poetry.

shintō 神道 (Japanese). The indigenuous religion of Japan; literally, the "way of the gods."

shogun 将軍 (Japanese). Originating as a military title in the Heian period, the shogunate (as opposed to the imperial family) became the de facto governing body of feudal Japan.

shu 恕 (Chinese). Deference toward others, implying an ability to put oneself understandingly in another's shoes.

Shujing 書經 (Chinese). *Book of Documents* or *Classic of History*. One of the Five Classics (**wujing**) of Confucianism, it is a collection of documents related to ancient Chinese history.

siduan 四端 (Chinese). The Four Beginnings, which according to Mencius are innate in human nature and indicate its original goodness. They are: commiseration as the beginning of humaneness (**ren** 仁), shame as the beginning of righteousness (**yi** 義), modesty as the beginning of propriety (**li** 禮), and a sense of right and wrong as the beginning of wisdom (**zhi** 知).

sishu 四書 (Chinese). The Four Books selected by Zhu Xi in the Song Dynasty as the primary texts of Confucianism, including the Confucian *Analects*, the *Doctrine of the Mean*, the *Great Learning,* and the *Book of Mencius.* See **Lunyu, Zhongyong, Daxue**, and **Mengzi.**

Spring and Autumn Chronicles. Also *Spring and Autumn Annals.* See **Lüshi Chunqiu.**

taiji 太極 (Chinese). The "supreme ultimate," a basic cosmological principle of neo-Confucianism.

tian 天 (Chinese). Commonly translated as "heaven," but also means simply sky. Connotes nature, natural order, and the place of humanity within this order. Appears in compounds such as *tiandao* 天道 "way of heaven," *tiandi* 天地 "heaven and earth," and *tianming* 天命 "decree of heaven" or "fate."

T'oegye 退溪, a pen name for Yi Hwang 李滉 (1501–1570) (Korean). His correspondence with **Kobong** forms part of the **Four-Seven Debate.** See also **Ugye** and **Yulgok.**

Ugye 牛溪, a pen name for Sŏnghon 成渾 (1535–1598) (Korean). His correspondence with **Yulgok** forms part of the **Four-Seven Debate.**

wai 外 (Chinese). The realm of literary and personal accomplishment, and extrafamilial relations, often associated with the activities of men. See also *nei.*

Wang In 王仁 (Korean, or Japanese **Wani**). In the fourth or fifth century, Wang In is credited with introducing Confucian texts from Korea into Japan under the emperor Ōjin.

Wang Yangming 王陽明 (1472–1529) (Chinese). Ming-dynasty Confucian scholar, associated with *xinxue* 心學 or the "school of heart-mind." Along with **Zhu Xi**, one of the most important neo-Confucian philosophers.

wanwu 萬物 (Chinese). The "ten thousand things" or "myriad things," referring generally to all of worldly existence. Also written *wanyou* 萬有.

wen 文 (Chinese). Often translated as "culture," *wen* also refers to a greater order giving pattern and meaning to both nature and human culture.

wu 物 (Chinese). Commonly translated as "things," but can also be used in a more dynamic sense to mean "events." See also *gewu, shiwu,* and *wanwu.*

wujing 五經 (Chinese). The Five Classics of the Confucian canon, including the *Book of Rites,* the *Spring and Autumn Chronicles,* the *Book of Songs,* the *Book of Documents,* and the *Book of Changes.* See **Liji, Lushi Chunqiu, Shijing, Shujing,** and **Yijing.**

wuchang 五常 (Chinese). The "five constants," or core values of Confucianism, including humaneness or "authoritative conduct" (***ren*** 仁), appropriate conduct (***yi*** 義), propriety (***li*** 禮), wisdom (***zhi*** 知), and trustworthiness or "standing by one's word" (***xin*** 信).

wulun 五倫 (Chinese). The "five relations" of ruler and subject, parent and child, elder brother and younger brother, husband and wife, and friend and friend.

xuanxue 玄學 (Chinese). The teachings of the neo-Daoists of the Wei-Qin period (220–420), translated as "abstruse learning."

xiao 孝 (Chinese). Filial piety, or "family feeling." Appropriate family feelings form the foundation of ethical conduct in Confucianism.

xin 心 (Chinese). Alternatively translated as "heart-mind" and "mind-heart." The "original heart-mind" or *benxin* 本心 is subject to the same debates surrounding ***xing*** 性.

xin 信 (Chinese). One of the five core Confucian values (see ***wuchang***), commonly translated as "trustworthiness." The character itself shows the graph for "person" (人) standing next to "speech" or "words" (言), so it might be more precisely translated as "standing by one's words" or "making good on one's words."

xing 刑 (Chinese). Penal law or punishment.

xing 性 (Chinese). Human dispositions and tendencies, or "human nature." A debate in Confucianism, dating back to two of its earliest thinkers Mencius and Xunzi, concerns whether or not human disposition is innately good. Compounds include *benxing* 本性 or "original nature," and *xingshan* 性善 or "good nature."

Xunzi 荀子 (Chinese). May refer to the Confucian philosopher (c. 310–238 BCE), as well as the book attributed to him. Unlike **Mencius**, Xunzi did not believe that human nature is innately good.

yamato 大和 (Japanese). The dominant ethnic group of Japan, also the name of one of Japan's historical periods. For a timeline, see Appendix II.

yang. See ***yin*** and ***yang***.

yi 義 (Chinese). One of the five core Confucian values (***wuchang***), commonly translated as "morality" or "righteousness." However, "appropriateness" conveys the sense of *yi*'s meaning without invoking the conceptual associations most Westerners attach to morality.

Yijing 易経 (Chinese). *Book of Changes.* One of the Five Classics (***wujing***) of Confucianism, it deals with ancient cosmological and philosophical beliefs concerning the meaning of change and transformation, and the dynamic balance of opposing forces such as ***yin*** and ***yang***.

yin 陰 **and** ***yang*** 陽 (Chinese). *Yin* and *yang* are complicated terms often associated with pairs of opposites: hot and cold, earth and sky, female and male, etc. In relation to ***qi***, they express the dynamic balance of forces sustaining the world. They often appear in the phrase *yinyang wuxing* 陰

陽五行, which expresses a cosmological principle based on the relations between *yin* and *yang* and the "five phases" or "five modes of conduct" (五行), water, wood, earth, fire, and metal.

Yulgok 栗谷, a pen name for Yi I 李珥 (1536–1584) (Korean). A prominent neo-Confucian scholar of the Chosŏn period, whose correspondence with **Ugye** forms part of the **Four-Seven Debate**. See also **Kobong** and **T'oegye**.

zheng 正 (Chinese). Proper conduct, which is appropriately sensitive to context. Appears in the compound *zhengming* 正名, or "naming properly," discussed in *Analects* 13.3.

zheng 政 (Chinese). Government, especially in the Confucian sense of "governing properly."

zhi 知 (Chinese). One of the five core Confucian values (see **wuchang**), commonly translated as "knowledge" or "wisdom." However, when used actively in the sense of "to know," *zhi* also means "to realize" or "to make manifest."

zhong 忠 (Chinese). "Doing one's best" or "doing one's utmost." In *Analects* 4.15, *zhong* and **shu** are identified as the two elements uniting all of Confucius's philosophy.

Zhongyong 中庸 (Chinese). The *Doctrine of the Mean*, notably translated by Roger T. Ames and David L. Hall as *Focusing the Familiar*. It is one of the Four Books (**sishu**) selected by Zhu Xi as the primary texts of Confucianism.

zhuguan 主觀 (Chinese). The "master's-eye view," which may seek personal benefit; in modern Chinese it means "subjective." Compare to **keguan**.

Zhu Xi 朱熹 (1130–1200). Also known as Zhuzi 朱子 or "Master Zhu." Song-dynasty Confucian scholar associated with *lixue* 理學 or the "school of principle." Along with **Wang Yangming**, one of the most important neo-Confucian philosophers.

ziran 自然 (Chinese). An important concept in Chinese philosophy, *ziran* is often translated as "naturalness." It connotes that the world, and all things in it, are "self-so." In Confucianism, *ziran* is associated with the idea that one must not perform rituals perfunctorily but instead must be natural and sincere.

Zuo Zhuan or **Zuozhuan** 左傳 (Chinese). A book of history attributed to Zuo Qiuming 左丘明, a fifth century BCE contemporary of Confucius.

Bibliography

Ames, Roger T., and David Hall (1987). *Thinking Through Confucius*. Albany: State University of New York Press.

———, trans. (2001). *Focusing the Familiar: A Translation and Philosophical Interpretation of the* Zhongyong. Honolulu: University of Hawai'i Press.

Ames, Roger T., and Henry Rosemont Jr., trans. (1998). *The Analects of Confucius: A Philosophic Translation*. New York: Ballantine Books.

Angle, Stephen C. (2002). *Human Rights and Chinese Thought*. Cambridge: Cambridge University Press.

Barlow, Tani E. (2004). *The Question of Women in Chinese Feminism*. Durham: Duke University Press.

Bauer, Wolfgang (1976). *China and the Search for Happiness: Recurring Themes in Four Thousand Years of Chinese Cultural History*. Translated by Michael Shaw. New York: The Seabury Press.

Berlin, Isaiah (1969). *Four Essays on Liberty*. New York: Oxford University Press.

Berthrong, John H. (1998b). *Transformations of the Confucian Way*. Boulder: Westview Press.

———, and Evelyn Nagai Berthrong (2000). *Confucianism: A Short Introduction*. Oxford: Oneworld Publications.

Bol, Peter K. (1992). *"This Culture of Ours": Intellectual Transition in T'ang and Sung China*. Stanford: Stanford University Press.

Boodberg, Peter (1953). "The Semasiology of Some Primary Confucian Concepts." *Philosophy East and West* 2, no. 4: 317–32.

Bresciani, Umberto (2001). *Reinventing Confucianism: The New Confucian Movement*. Taipei: The Taipei Ricci Institute for Chinese Studies.

Chan, Joseph (1999). "A Confucian Perspective on Human Rights for Contemporary China." *The East Asian Challenge for Human Rights*, ed. Joanne Bauer and Daniel Bell. Cambridge: Cambridge University Press.

Chan, Wing-tsit (1955). "The Evolution of the Confucian Concept of *Jen*." *Philosophy East and West* 4, no. 4: 295–319.

———. (1963). *A Source Book in Chinese Philosophy*. Princeton: Princeton University Press.

Chang, Carsun, et al. (1958). "A Manifesto for A Reappraisal of Sinology and Reconstruction of Chinese Culture." *The Development of Neo-Confucian Thought*, ed. Chang. New York: Bookman.

Chang, Kwang-chih (1964). "Some Dualistic Phenomena in Shang Society." *Journal of Asian Studies* 24, no. 1: 45–61.

Chang, Wejen (1998). "The Confucian Theory of Norms and Human Rights." *Confucianism and Human Rights*, ed. Wm. Theodore de Bary and Tu Weiming. New York: Columbia University Press.

Chen Duxiu (1960). "The Way of Confucius and Modern Life." *Sources of Chinese Tradition.* Vol. 2. Compiled and translated by Wm. Theodore de Bary, Wing-tsit Chan, and Chester Tan. New York: Columbia University Press.

Cheng, Chung-ying (1998). "Transforming Confucian Virtues into Human Rights." *Confucianism and Human Rights*, ed. Wm. Theodore de Bary and Tu Weiming. New York: Columbia University Press.

———, and Nicholas Bunnin, eds. (2002). *Contemporary Chinese Philosophy.* Oxford: Blackwell Publishers.

The Chinese Classics (1970). Hong Kong: Hong Kong University Press.

Ching, Julia (1976). *To Acquire Wisdom: The Way of Wang Yang-ming.* New York: Columbia University Press.

Choi, Jungwoon (1999). "The Kwangju People's Uprising: Formation of the 'Absolute Community.' " *Korea Journal* 39, no. 2: 238–82.

Chŏng T'ojŏn. *Pulssi chappyŏn* [Criticism of Buddhism]. Trans. Charles Muller. http://acmuller.net/jeong-gihwa/bulssijapbyeon.html.

Chŏng Yagyong. *Chungyong kang'ŭibo* [A Supplement to the Discussion of the *Zhongyong*]. Trans. Wonsuk Chang. Unpublished translation from *Yŏyudang chŏnsŏ* [Collected Works of Yŏyudang].

Chua, Beng-Huat (1995). *Communitarian Ideology and Democracy in Singapore.* London: Routledge.

A Concordance to the Kuo-yu (1973). Taipei: Chinese Materials and Research Aids Service Center.

Cua, A. S. (1983). "Li and moral justification: A study in the Li Chi." *Philosophy East and West* 33, no. 1: 1–16.

———. (1985). *Ethical Argumentation: A Study in Hsun Tzu's Moral Epistemology.* Honolulu: University of Hawai'i Press.

de Bary, Wm. Theodore (1959). "Some Common Tendencies in Neo-Confucianism," *Confucianism in Action*, ed. David Nivison and Arthur Wright. Stanford: Stanford University Press.

———. (1983). *The Liberal Tradition in China.* New York: Columbia University Press.

———. (1998a). "Introduction," *Confucianism and Human Rights*, ed. de Bary and Tu Weiming. New York: Columbia Univiversity Press.

———. (1998b). *Asian Values and Human Rights: A Confucian Communitarian Perspective.* Cambridge: Harvard University Press.

———, Irene Bloom, and Richard Lufrano, eds. (1999–2000). *Sources of Chinese Tradition.* 2 vols. 2nd ed. New York: Columbia University Press.

———, Donald Keene, George Tanabe, and Paul Varler, eds. (2001). *Sources of Japanese Tradition.* 2 vols. 2nd ed. New York: Columbia University Press.

———, and Tu Weiming, eds. (1998). *Confucianism and Human Rights.* New York: Columbia University Press.

Beauvoir, Simone de (1989). *The Second Sex*. New York: Vintage Books.

Descartes, René (1970). *Meditations on First Philosophy*. *The Philosophical Work of Descartes*. Vol. 2. Trans. E. S. Haldane and G. R. T. Ross. Cambridge: Cambridge University Press.

Dewey, John (1916). *Democracy and Education*. *John Dewey: The Middle Works*. Vol. 9. Ed. Jo Ann Boydston. Carbondale: Southern Illinois University Press.

———. (1927). *The Public and its Problems*. *John Dewey: The Later Works*. Vol. 2. Ed. Jo Ann Boydston. Carbondale: Southern Illinois University Press.

———. (1928). "Philosophies of Freedom." *John Dewey: The Later Works*. Vol. 3. Ed. Jo Ann Boydston. Carbondale: Southern Illinois University Press.

———. (1938). "Democracy and Education in the World Today." *John Dewey: The Later Works*. Vol. 13. Ed. Jo Ann Boydston. Carbondale: Southern Illinois University Press, 1991.

———. (1939). "Creative Democracy—The Task before Us." *John Dewey: The Later Works*. Vol. 14. Ed. Jo Ann Boydston. Carbondale: Southern Illinois University Press, 1991.

Donnelly, Jack (1999). "Human Rights and Asian Values: A Defense of 'Western' Universalism." *The East Asian Challenge for Human Rights*, ed. J. Bauer and D. Bell. Cambridge: Cambridge University Press.

Duncan, John (2002). "The Problematic Modernity of Confucianism." *Korean Society: Civil Society, Democracy and the State*, ed. Charles K. Armstrong. London and New York: Routledge.

Eisenstadt, S. N. (1996). *Japanese Civilization: A Comparative View*. Chicago: University of Chicago Press.

Elman, Benjamin A. (1994). *From Philosophy to Philosophy: Intellectual and Social Aspects of Change in Late Imperial China*. Cambridge: Harvard University Press.

Fazzioli, Edoardo (1986). *Chinese Calligraphy: From Pictogram to Ideogram*. New York: Abbeville.

Feinberg, Joel (1986). *Harm to Self*. Oxford: Oxford University Press.

Fung, Yu-lan (1952–53). *A History of Chinese Philosophy*. 2 vols. Trans. Derk Bodde. Princeton: Princeton University Press.

———. (1964). *A Short History of Chinese Philosophy*. Ed. Derk Bodde. New York: The Macmillan Company.

Graham, A. C. (1989). *Disputers of the Tao: Philosophical Argument in Ancient China*. La Salle: Open Court.

Granet, Marcel (1977). "Right and Left in China." In *Right and Left: Essays on Dual Symbolic Classification*, ed. Rodney Needham. Chicago: University of Chicago Press.

Grewal, Inderpal, and Caren Kaplan, eds. (1994). *Scattered Hegemonies: Postmodernity and Transnational Feminist Practices*. Minneapolis: University of Minnesota Press.

Gross, David (1992). *The Past in Ruins: Tradition and the Critique of Modernity*. Amherst: University of Massachusetts Press.

Habermas, Jürgen (1996). "Popular Sovereignty as Procedure." *Between Facts and Norms*. Cambridge: MIT Press.

Han, Sangjin (1997a). "Human Rights and Growth in East Asia." *Korea Focus* 5, no. 1: 1–13.

————. (1997b). "Political Economy and Moral Institution: The Formation of the Middling Grassroots in Korea." *Humboldt Journal of Social Relations* 23, no. 1–2: 71–89.

————. (1999a.) "Popular Sovereignty and a Struggle for Recognition from a Perspective of Human Right." *Korea Journal* 39, no. 2: 184–204.

————. (1999b). "Confucianism and Postcolonialism in the East Asian Context of Development." *The Review of Korean Studies* 2: 23–44.

————. (2006). "Toward A Communitarian Concept of Human Rights: The Agenda for Intercultural Dialogue." Paper presented at the conference *The Global Futures of World Regions*, organized by the Korean Sociological Association, September 28–29.

————. (2007). "Why Intercultural Dialogue? What Do We Gain for Human Rights in North Korea?" *Human Rights in North Korea*, ed. S. J. Han and K. D. Park. Seoul: Sejong Institute.

Han, Sang-Kwon (1996). *Society and the Institution of Appeal in Late Chosen Dynasty*. Seoul: Ilzokak.

Hansen, Chad (1992). *A Daoist Theory of Chinese Thought: A Philosophic Interpretation*. Oxford: Oxford University Press.

Hansen, Valerie (2000). *The Open Empire: A History of China to 1600*. New York: W. W. Norton.

Held, Virginia (2006). *The Ethics of Care*. Oxford: Oxford University Press.

Hong Tae-young. *Ŭisan mundap* [Dialogues at Ui Mountain]. Trans. Jeongyeup Kim. Unpublished manuscript.

Honneth, Axel (1995). *The Struggle for Recognition: The Moral Grammar of Social Conflicts*. Cambridge: Polity Press.

Hsiao Kung-chuan (1979). *A History of Chinese Political Thought*. Trans. F. W. Mote. Princeton: Princeton University Press.

Huang Siu-chi (1977). *Lu Hsiang-shan: A Twelfth Century Chinese Idealist Philosophy*. Westport: Hyperion Press.

Huntington, Samuel (1996). "Democracy's Third Wave." *The Global Resurgence of Democracy*, ed Larry Diamond and Marc F. Plattner. Baltimore: Johns Hopkins University Press.

IMKH: Institute for Modern Korean History, ed. (1990). *The Collection of Historical Materials on the Kwangju People's Uprising* (in Korean). Seoul: Pulbit.

Ivanhoe, Philip J. (2000). *Confucian Moral Self Cultivation*. 2nd ed. Indianapolis: Hackett.

Judge, Joan (1998). "The Concept of Popular Empowerment (Minquan) in the Late Qing: Classical and Contemporary Sources of Authority." *Confucianism and Human Rights*, ed. Wm. Theodore de Bary and Tu Weiming. Columbia University Press.

Kalton, Michael (1988). *To Become a Sage*. New York: Columbia University Press.

————, Oaksook C. Kim, Sung Bae Park (1994). *The Four-Seven Debate: An Annotated Translation of the Most Famous Controversy in Korean Neo-Confucian Thought*. Albany: State University of New York Press.

Keightley, David N. (1988). "Shang Divination and Metaphysics." *Philosophy East and West* 38, no. 4: 367–97.

KHMC: Kwangju 5.18 Historical Materials Compilation Committee, ed. (1997). *The Collected Materials on the Kwangju Pro-Democracy Movement of May 1980* (in Korean). Kwangju.

Kim Pusik. *Samguk sagi* [History of the Three Kingdoms]. Trans. Wonsuk Chang. Unpublished manuscript.

Knoblock, John (1988–1994). *Xunzi: A Translation and Study of the Complete Works.* 3 vols. Stanford: Stanford University Press.

Ko, Dorothy (1994). *Teachers of the Inner Chambers: Women and Culture in Seventeenth-Century China.* Stanford: Stanford University Press.

Kuo, Eddie C.Y. (1996). "Confucianism as Political Discourse in Singapore: The Case of an Incomplete Revitalization Movement." *Confucian Traditions in East Asian Modernity: Moral Education and Economic Culture in Japan and the Four Mini-Dragons,* ed. Tu Wei-Ming. Cambridge: Harvard University Press.

Kwang, Han Fook, Warren Fernandez, and Sumiko Tan, eds. (1997). *Lee Kwan Yew: The Man and His Ideas.* Singapore Press Holdings.

Kwon Tai-Hwan and Cho Hein (1997). "Confucianism and Korean Society." *Democracy in Asia,* ed. Michèle Schmiegelow. Frankfurt: St. Martin's Press.

Lau, D. C. (1970). *Mencius.* London: Penguin.

———. (1979). *Confucius: The Analects.* Harmondsworth: Penguin.

———. (1996). *A Concordance to the Xunzi.* Hong Kong: Commercial Press.

Lau, D. C., and Chen Fong Ching, eds. (1994). *A Concordance to the* Lüshi chunqiu. Hongkong: Commercial Press.

Lee Ŏjŏk. "First Letter to Manggidang." Trans. Michael Kalton. Unpublished translation from *Hoejaejip* [Collected Works of Hoejap].

Lee, Peter H., ed. (1993–96). *Sourcebook of Korean Civilization.* 2 vols. New York: Columbia University Press.

Legge, James, ed. (1960). *The Chinese Classics.* Hong Kong: Hong Kong University Press.

———, ed. (1985). *The Chinese Classics.* Taipei: Southern Materials Center.

Li, Chenyang (1999). *The Tao Encounters the West.* Albany: State University of New York Press.

Liu Shu-hsien (1998). *Understanding Confucian Philosophy: Classical and Sung-Ming.* Westport: Praeger.

———. (2003). *Essentials of Contemporary Neo-Confucian Philosophy.* Westport, CT, and London: Praeger.

Makeham, John, ed. (2003). *New Confucianism: A Critical Examination.* New York: Palgrave Macmillan.

Maruyama, M. (1974). *Studies in the Intellectual History of Tokugawa Japan.* Princeton: Princeton University Press.

Mote, Frederick W. (1989). *Intellectual Foundations of China.* 2nd ed. New York: McGraw-Hill.

———. (1999). *Imperial China 900–1800.* Cambridge: Harvard University Press.

Nagel, Thomas (1995). "Personal Rights and Public Space." *Philosophy and Public Affairs* 24, no. 2: 83–107.

Neville, Robert C. (2000). *Boston Confucianism: Portable Tradition in the Late-Modern World.* Albany: State University of New York Press.

Nivison, David S. (1966). *The Ways of Confucianism*. Ed. Bryan Van Norden. La Salle: Open Court.

Peerenboom, Randal (1998). "Confucian Harmony and Freedom of Thought." *Confucianism and Human Rights*, ed. Wm. Theodore de Bary and Tu Weiming. New York: Columbia University Press.

Pye, Lucian (1985). *Asian Power and Politics*. Cambridge: Cambridge University Press.

Ren Jiyu, ed. (1979). *Zhongguo zhexue shi* [A History of Chinese Philosophy]. 4 vols. Beijing: People's Publishing House.

Russell, Bertrand (1922). *The Problem of China*. London: George Allen & Unwin.

Schwartz, Benjamin (1985). *The World of Thought in Ancient China*. Cambridge: The Belknap Press of Harvard University.

Slingerland, Edward, trans. (2003). *Confucius: Analects with Selections from Traditional Commentaries*. Indianapolis: Hackett.

Sŏ Kyŏngdŏk. *T'aehŏsŏl* [Discussion of the Vast Tenuousness]. Trans. Jeongyeup Kim. Unpublished translation from *Hwadamjip* [Collected Works of Hwadam].

Tang Junyi (1988a). "Zhongguo zhexuezhong ziranyuzhouguan zhi tezhi" [The distinctive features of natural cosmology in Chinese philosophy]. *Zhongxi zhexue sixiang zhi bijiao lunwenji* [Collected Essays on the Comparison between Chinese and Western Philosophical Thought]. Taipei: Xuesheng shuju.

———. (1988b). *Complete Works*. Taipei: Xuesheng shuju.

Taylor, Charles (1992). "The Politics of Recognition." *Multiculturalism*. Princeton: Princeton University Press.

Tillman, Hoyt Cleveland (1982). *Utilitarian Confucianism: Ch'en Liang's Challenge to Chu Hsi*. Cambridge: Harvard University Press.

———. (1992). *Confucian Discourse and Chu Hsi's Ascendancy*. Honolulu: University of Hawai'i Press.

———. (1994). *Ch'en Liang on Public Interest and the Law*. Honolulu: University of Hawai'i Press.

Tu Weiming (1976a). *Neo-Confucian Thought in Action: Wang Yang-ming's Youth (1472–1509)*. Berkeley: University of California Press.

———. (1976b). *Centrality and Commonality: An Essay on Chung-yung*. Honolulu: University of Hawai'i Press.

———. (1979). *Humanity and Self-Cultivation*. Berkeley: Asian Humanities Press.

———. (1984). *Confucian Ethics Today: The Singapore Challenge*. Curriculum Development Institute of Singapore.

Tu Weiming, Milan Hejtmanek, and Alan Wachman, eds. (1992). *The Confucian World Observed: A Contemporary Discussion of Confucian Humanism in East Asia*. Honolulu: University of Hawai'i Press.

Tu Weiming and Mary Evelyn Tucker, eds. (2003–04). *Confucian Spirituality*. 2 vols. New York: Crossroad.

Twiss, Summer (1998). "A Constructive Framework for Discussing Confucianism and Human Rights." *Confucianism and Human Rights*, ed. Wm. Theodore de Bary and Tu Weiming. New York: Columbia University Press.

Wieger, Leon (1965). *Chinese Characters*. New York: Dover.

Wilhelm, Richard, and Cary F. Baynes, trans. (1977). *Book of Changes*. Princeton: Princeton University Press.

Wolf, Margery (1985). *Revolution Postponed: Women in Contemporary China*. Stanford: Stanford University Press.

Xia Yong (2004). "Minben yu minquan: zhongguo quanli huayu de lishi jichu" [*Minben* and people's rights: historical foundation of Chinese rights discourse]. *Zhongguo shehui kexue* [Social Sciences in China] 5.

Xu Fuguan (1975). *Zhongkuo renxing lun shi: xian-Qin pian* [A History of the Chinese Theory of Human Nature: The Pre-Qin Period]. Taipei: Commercial Press.

Xu Shen (1966). *Shuowen jiezi zhu*. Shanghai: Guji zhubanshe.

Yao, Xingzhong (2000). *An Introduction to Confucianism*. Cambridge: Cambridge University Press.

Yao, Xinzhong, ed. (2003). *Encyclopedia of Confucianism*. 2 vols. London and New York: RoutledgeCurzon.

Yu, Anthony C. (2005). *State and Religion in China: Historical and Textual Perspectives*. Chicago and La Salle: Open Court.

Zhang Longxi (1999). "Translating Cultures: China and the West." *Chinese Thought in a Global Context: A Dialogue Between Chinese and Western Philosophical Approaches*, ed. Karl-Heinz Pohl. Leiden: Brill.

Zhao, Tingyang (2005a). "Human Rights as the Credit Rights: A Non-Western Theory of Universal Human Rights." Unpublished manuscript.

———. (2005b). "The Concept of All-under-Heaven: A Semantic and Historical Introduction." Unpublished manuscript.

Zhu Xi (1991). *Further Reflections on Things at Hand*. Trans. and with commentary by Allen Wittenborn. Lanham: University of America Press.

Contributors

Roger T. Ames is Professor of Philosophy and editor of *Philosophy East and West*. His recent publications include translations of Chinese classics: *Sun-tzu: The Art of Warfare* (1993); *Sun Pin: The Art of Warfare* (1996) and *Tracing Dao to its Source* (1997) (both with D. C. Lau); the *Confucian Analects* (1998) and the *Classic of Family Reverence: A Philosophical Translation of the* Xiaojing (forthcoming) (both with H. Rosemont); *Focusing the Familiar: A Translation and Philosophical Interpretation of the* Zhongyong, and *A Philosophical Translation of the* Daodejing: *Making This Life Significant* (with D. L. Hall) (2001). He has also authored many interpretive studies of Chinese philosophy and culture: *Thinking Through Confucius* (1987), *Anticipating China: Thinking Through the Narratives of Chinese and Western Culture* (1995), and *Thinking From the Han: Self, Truth, and Transcendence in Chinese and Western Culture* (1997) (all with D. L. Hall). Recently, he has undertaken several projects that entail the intersection of contemporary issues and cultural understanding. His *Democracy of the Dead: Dewey, Confucius, and the Hope for Democracy in China* (with D. L. Hall) (1999) is a product of this effort. Almost all of his publications are now available in Chinese translation, including his philosophical translations of Chinese canonical texts. He has most recently been engaged in compiling the new *Blackwell Sourcebook of Chinese Philosophy*, and in writing articles promoting a conversation between American pragmatism and Confucianism.

John Berthrong, educated in Sinology at the University of Chicago, has been the Associate Dean for Academic and Administrative Affairs and Associate Professor of Comparative Theology at the Boston University School of Theology since 1989. Active in interfaith dialogue projects and programs, his teaching and research interests are in the areas of interreligious dialogue, Chinese religions and philosophy, and comparative philosophy and theology. His published and forthcoming books are *All under Heaven: Transforming Paradigms in Confucian-Christian Dialogue* (1994, with a Chinese translation from Renmin Chupanshe 2006), *The Transformations of the Confucian Way*

(1998), and *Concerning Creativity: A Comparison of Chu Hsi, Whitehead, and Neville* (1998). He is co-editor with Professor Mary Evelyn Tucker (1998) of *Confucianism and Ecology: The Interrelation of Heaven, Earth, and Humans.* In 1999 he published *The Divine Deli,* a study of religious pluralism and multiple religious participation in North America. He also collaborated with Evelyn Nagai Berthrong on *Confucianism: A Short Introduction* (2000), which has been translated into Italian and Russian. He most recently co-edited, with Liu Shu-hsien and Leonard Swidler (2004), *Confucianism in Dialogue Today: West, Christianity, and Judaism,* and has *Expanding Process: Exploring Philosophical and Theological Transformations in China and West* forthcoming in 2008 from SUNY Press.

Wonsuk Chang is a Senior Researcher at the Academy of Korean Studies. His books and articles on comparative philosophy, Chinese philosophy, and Korean philosophy have appeared in *Philosophy East and West, Wiener Beiträge zur Koreaforschung,* and *Tong'yang chŏlhak yŏn'gu* [Journal of Eastern Philosophy], including "Reflections on Time and Related Ideas in the *Yijing*" (2009), "Translating Terms from Korean Confucian Philosophy" (2008), "Comparative Study between Process Thought and Korean Philosophy Today" (2007), and "Yugaŭi ŭisasot'onggwa sanghopaeryŏ" [Communication and mutual care ethics in Confucianism] (2006). His is currently translating Korean philosophical material into the English language and editing a sourcebook in Korean philosophy.

Youngjin Choi is Professor of Korean Philosophy at Sungkyunkwan University and president of the Korean Society for Philosophy East-West. He has written many articles on Korean Confucianism and related issues, including "*21 Segiui dongyangcheolhak*" [Eastern thoughts in the 21st century] (2005), "*Joseonjo yuhaksasangsaui yangsang*" [The modes of history of confucianism in Joseon period] (2005), "*Hanguksahoeui yugyojeok jeontonggwa gajokjuui*" [Confucian tradition and familial relations in Korea] (2006), and "*Dongasia geunseyuhage iseo cheon, seong, do e daehan insik*" [Ideas on heavens, natural disposition, and the way in modern East Asian Confucianism] (2004).

Sangjin Han is Professor of Sociology at Seoul National University and specializes in critical social theory, the comparative study of democratic development, intercultural dialogue on human rights and communitarian well-being, middle-class politics and civil society, and third way development. He has lectured at Columbia University in New York, Ecole des Hautes Etudes en Sciences Sociales in Paris, and Beijing University in China. He served as chairman of the Presidential Committee on Policy Planning for the Republic of Korea and president of the Academy of Korean Studies, among others.

He is the author of *Habermas and the Korean Debate, Contemporary Society and Human Rights, Theory of the Middling Grassroots, Korea's Third Way*, and *Bureaucratic Authoritarianism in Korea*.

Leah Kalmanson is a Ph.D candidate in the Department of Philosophy at the University of Hawai'i at Mānoa. Her article "Levinas in Japan: The Ethics of Emptiness and the Doctrine of No-Self" is forthcoming from *Continental Philosophy Review* (2010), and she is currently co-editing an essay collection *Levinas and Asian Thought*.

Michael C. Kalton graduated from Harvard University in 1977 with a joint degree in East Asian Languages and Civilization and Comparative Religion. Since 1990 he has been Professor of Interdisciplinary Studies at the University of Washington, Tacoma. The interdisciplinary character of the program allowed him room to expand from his work in Korean Neo-Confucian thought into contemporary environmental concerns and into systems theory, especially Complex Adaptive Systems, systems that learn and evolve. He sees a deep and creative synergy between premodern Neo-Confucian thought and self-cultivation and these areas of contemporary thought and concern; investigating this potential cross-fertilization has become his major research focus. His major publications on Korean Neo-Confucianism include *To Become a Sage: The Ten Diagrams on Sage Learning by Yi T'oegye* (1988), and *The Four-Seven Debate: An Annotated Translation of the Most Famous Controversy in Korean Neo-Confucian Thought* (1994).

Robert Cummings Neville is Professor of Philosophy, Religion, and Theology at Boston University where he is also dean emeritus of the School of Theology. He has been president of the International Society for the Study of Chinese Philosophy, the American Academy of Religion, the Metaphysical Society of America, the American Theological Society, and the Highlands Institute for American Religious and Philosophical Thought. Among his recent books are *Ritual and Deference* (2008), *On the Scope and Truth of Theology* (2006), *Religion in Late Modernity* (2001), and *Boston Confucianism* (2000). Neville is a graduate of Yale University and has taught there and at Fordham University, SUNY College at Purchase, SUNY Stony Brook, as well as Boston University.

Peter Nosco (PhD Columbia University) is Professor of Asian Studies at the University of British Columbia. He specializes in the intellectual and social history of early modern Japan and has published on Japanese Confucianism and its rivals including Japanese nativism and Christianity. Most recently he has written on "The Experiences of Christians during the Underground Years and Thereafter" (2007) in a special issue of *The Japanese Journal of Religious*

Studies (vol. 34, no. 1) on the theme of Christians in Japan, which he co-guest edited with Mark R. Mullins.

Li-Hsiang Lisa Rosenlee is an Associate Professor of Philosophy at the University of Hawai'i, West Oahu. She is the author of "Confucianism and Women—A Philosophical Interpretation" (2006) in addition to numerous articles published in various journals such as *Philosophy East and West*, *International Philosophical Quarterly*, *Journal of Chinese Religion*, *Asian Philosophy*, and *China Review International*. Her latest project is on the comparative study of maternal thinking, care ethics, and Confucianism, which will appear in the anthology *Liberating Traditions: Essays in Feminist Comparative Philosophy*.

Sor-hoon Tan is Associate Professor of Philosophy at the National University of Singapore. She has published in international journals and contributed to edited works on Chinese philosophy, pragmatism, and comparative philosophy. She is author of *Confucian Democracy: A Deweyan Reconstruction*, editor of *Challenging Citizenship: Group Membership and Cultural Identity in a Global Age* (2005), and co-editor of *The Moral Circle and the Self: Chinese and Western Approaches* (2003), *Filial Piety in Chinese Thought and History* (2004), and *Democracy as Culture: Deweyan Pragmatism in a Globalizing World* (2008).

Index

Ames, Roger, and David Hall, 15, 82, 99, 101n12, 105, 118, 188; and Henry Rosemont, 107
An Hyang, 37, 213
Analects, 2, 6n1, 34, 53, 55, 59, 79, 97, 106, 116, 150, 219, 222, 224, 226; and desire, 115; and family relations, 78, 82, 108; and government, 113, 115, 147; and harmony, 74; and *li* (ritual), 108, 110, 111, 159; and *qi* cosmology, 71; and *ren*, 107, 108, 117; and the self, 88, 109
Arai Hakuseki, 60, 65, 212
Ashikaga: the school or *gakkō*, 54, 216, 219; government, 54

Berthrong, John, 3, 83, 101n12, 145, 148, 173n31, 209
Book of Changes. See *Yijing*
Book of Documents (*Shujing*), 47, 203, 210, 223, 224
Book of Rites (*Liji*), 80, 117, 172, 201, 210, 220, 222–224
Book of Songs (*Shijing*), 117, 219, 223, 224
Buddhism, 10–13, 28, 29, 35–40, 53–57, 64, 147, 150, 160, 169, 170, 175, 179, 187, 191, 195, 199, 215–217, 220

Carsun Chang, 105, 211
Chan, Wing-tsit, 107, 108, 158, 172n5
Chang Hyŏn-kwang, 44, 213
Chen Liang, 23, 26, 211

cheng, 20, 21, 89, 219
Cheng brothers, 23, 54, 58; Cheng Hao, 12, 22, 25, 150, 195, 211; Cheng Yi, 12, 22, 23, 25, 134, 150, 210n5, 211; Cheng-Zhu teachings 56, 58, 210n10
Cheng Chungying, 158, 169
Chikamatsu Monzaemon, 59, 212
Cho Hanbo, 39, 213
Ch'oe Ch'iwon, 35, 36, 213, 217
Ch'oe Han-ki, 45, 213
Ch'oe Ikhyŏn, 50, 213
Chŏng Che-tu, 45, 213
Chŏng Chiun, 40, 213
Chŏng Mong-chu, 37, 213
Chŏng Tojŏn, 37, 38, 213, 221
Chŏng Yagyong, 2, 45, 47, 49, 91, 96, 213
Chosŏn period, 3, 21, 33–36, 38, 40, 43–45, 47–51, 139–141, 143n68, 201, 217, 221, 223, 226
Christianity, 14, 87, 89, 99, 145, 147, 148, 154, 158, 168, 170, 171, 171n4, 173n31, 191, 199
Chumong, 35, 213
Confucius and Confucianism: compared to ancient Greeks, 1, 41, 69, 81, 83n1, 87, 92, 95, 145, 146, 151, 154; defining key terms, 1, 68, 88, 89, 98, 108, 109; and family relations, 4, 14, 15, 68, 70, 71, 74, 78–82, 84n23, 85n34, 108, 145, 155, 157, 167, 168, 175, 179, 181–184, 197, 204; and government, 11, 57, 61, 80, 109–113,

Confucius and Confucianism (continued)
116, 121, 122, 130, 132–134, 137, 139,
159, 162, 163, 180; interpreting the
Confucian tradition, 2, 34, 67, 68, 70,
83n2, 91, 169; neo-Confucianism, 2,
9–12, 22, 33, 34, 36–40, 44–52, 54–
58, 66, 101n12, 131, 160, 169, 172n4,
176, 210n7, 216, 222, 224 (see also
Song dynasty); New Confucianism,
3, 6, 13, 19, 29, 99, 222; and self-
cultivation, 4, 13–16, 19–21, 23,
25–28, 33, 38, 43, 52, 57, 68, 77,
78, 88, 93, 97, 98, 107–109, 111,
115–117, 152, 155, 158, 172n16, 180,
181, 195, 199–209, 210n7. See also
individual Confucian philosophers,
disciples, texts, and core terms (such
as ren, li, yi, zhi, xin, and xiao)
Cua, Antonio, 82, 110, 158, 172n5,
172n17

Dai Zhen, 12, 22, 150, 211
dao (in Confucianism), 2, 9, 10, 12–15,
17, 19, 20, 28, 36, 39, 40, 72, 83n2,
90, 98, 116, 135, 198, 219; dao mind,
44, 47, 96, 200, 201, 203–205, 208;
daotong, 22, 23, 67, 219; daoxue 11,
22, 23, 25, 26, 160, 187, 220
Daoism, 10–13, 17, 28, 29, 35, 36, 38,
39, 40, 53, 58, 145, 146, 147, 150,
153, 160, 162, 163, 169, 170, 175,
179, 187, 216, 219; Daodejing, 84n11,
219; neo-Daoism, 11, 215, 225
daren, 74, 220
de, 72, 80, 111, 220
de Bary, William Theodore, 52, 65, 105,
118, 128, 130, 131, 134, 148, 169,
172n5
Descartes, Rene, 95, 96, 153, 160
Dewey, John, 5, 96, 97, 101n12, 105–
108, 112, 114, 118, 160, 161, 173n21
Doctrine of the Mean. See Zhongyong
Dong Zongshu, 11, 211

Edo period, 44, 58, 63, 216; city, 56,
58, 63

fa, 26, 55, 15n1, 90, 220
Fan Zongyan, 23, 24, 211
Five Classics, 10, 59, 222–225
five constants, or five constant virtues,
45, 46, 48, 49, 52n9, 222, 223, 225,
226
five relations. See wulun
focus and field, 4, 71, 72, 74, 79, 93, 94,
98, 99, 183, 184, 220
Four Beginnings, 16, 40–43, 47, 152,
194, 201, 203, 220, 222, 223, 224
Four Books, 2, 22, 59, 149, 150, 153,
220, 222, 224
Four-Seven Debate, 3, 29, 40, 41, 45, 52,
201, 217, 220, 221, 223, 224, 226
Fujiwara Seika, 55, 65, 212, 216
Fujiwara Teika, 55, 212

Gao Yihan, 130, 211
Gaozi, 97, 211
gewu, 26, 27, 220
gong, 26, 88, 220
Graham, A. C., 3, 94, 95, 172n4, 173n18
Great Learning, 2, 47, 59, 78, 150, 152,
154, 210n20, 220, 224

Han dynasty, 10, 11, 21, 24, 28, 37, 53,
187, 194, 201, 211, 215, 220; Han
culture 34, 35, 83, 99;
hanxue or School of Han Learning, 10,
12, 29, 216, 221
Han Wonjin, 45, 46, 213
Han Yu, 11, 97, 216
Hayashi Razan, 55, 56, 65, 212
he, 4, 74, 111, 221; harmony, 110, 111,
118, 121, 125, 147, 158, 159, 183,
185, 194, 221
heart-mind. See xin
Hinduism, 14
Hirata Atsutane, 62, 212
Hishikawa Moronobu, 59, 212
Hŏ Mok, 43, 45, 47, 213
Ho-Rak Debate, 3, 44, 45, 47, 48, 217,
221
Hong Taeyong, 48, 213
Hoshina Masayuki, 56, 212

Huang Zongxi, 12, 211
hungu, 38, 44, 221

Ihara Saikaku, 59, 212
Islam, 14, 104, 147, 170, 199
Itō Jinsai, 58, 212, 63

Judaism, 14, 167, 168, 170; Judeo-
   Christian tradition, 87, 89, 99
junzi, 4, 68, 70, 108, 111, 180, 181, 186,
   221

Kada no Azumamaro, 59, 212
Kaibara Ekken, 57, 66, 212
Kamo no Mabuchi, 62, 212
Kang Hang, 55, 213
Kant, Immanuel, 87, 153, 160, 169,
   172n14, 176, 182, 183, 187, 189n4,
   189n14
keguan, 82, 221, 226
Keightley, David, 4, 68, 69
keji, 108, 109, 221
Kim Chŏng-hŭi, 48, 213
Kim Pusik, 36, 213, 217
Kobong, 40–42, 213, 220, 221, 224
kogaku, 58, 221, 223
Koguryŏ kingdom, 35, 36, 217
Koi, 35, 213
Kojosŏn, 35, 217
kokugakusha, 62, 221
Kongmin, 35, 213
Koryŏ period, 34, 36, 37, 140, 217
Kumazawa Banzan, 56, 66, 212
Kŭnchogo, 36, 213, 217

Laozi, 38, 39, 146, 211, 219. *See also*
   Daoism
Lau, D. C., 107, 108
Lee Chae-hyŏn, 37, 213
Lee Chin-sang, 44, 213
Lee Hangro, 50, 213
Lee Hyŏnil, 44, 213
Lee Ik, 47
Lee Kan, 45, 46, 48, 213
Lee Ŏn-chŏk, 39, 40, 214
Lee Saek, 37, 214

Legalism, 10, 158, 219
Legge, James, 89
li 利, 82, 221
li 理, 2, 23, 27, 39, 66n1, 66n3, 147,
   198, 200, 201, 202, 221; order,
   pattern, principle, or rationale, 17, 18,
   20, 21, 23, 25, 26, 50, 39–44, 46, 47,
   49, 72–75, 78, 96, 198, 221
li 禮, 4, 18, 68, 70, 74, 78, 80, 81, 89,
   106, 108–112, 118, 149, 156, 158,
   183, 222, 224, 225; propriety or ritual
   propriety, 4, 40, 41, 46–48, 68, 70, 74,
   78, 80, 89, 97, 100n8, 108, 110, 111,
   150–153, 156–160, 162–164, 166–170,
   173n19, 173n25, 178, 194, 203, 222,
   224, 225; rites, 16, 59, 108, 110, 121,
   135, 136, 170. *See also Book of Rites*
Li Ao, 11, 211, 216
Liu Shu-hsien, 105, 172n5, 211
Liu Zongyuan, 11, 211, 216
Lu Xiangshan, 26, 27, 211
Lu Xun, 93, 112, 211,
Lushi Chunqiu, 111, 222, 224

Maruyama Masao, 60, 212
Matsudaira Sadanobu, 60, 65, 212
Meiji period, 63, 217
Mencius, 2, 10, 12, 15, 22, 29, 37,
   59, 82, 91, 100, 119n29, 146, 150,
   155, 211, 215, 219; and the Four
   Beginnings, 40, 152, 182, 194, 203,
   223, 224; and government 109, 137,
   204; and human nature or *xing*, 16,
   17, 19, 42, 97, 98, 138, 192, 193,
   197, 222, 225; and natural and social
   order, 194–197, 200–202, 208, 209
minben, 122, 126, 136–141, 141n6,
   144n70, 144n72, 222
mind-heart. See *xin*
ming 名, 91, 94, 98, 135, 222
ming 命, 4, 75, 88, 91–94, 98, 222
Ming dynasty, 10, 12, 13, 17, 22, 25, 27–19,
   44, 45, 50, 150, 153, 169, 216, 224
minjung, 103, 143n69, 222
Moism, 148, 222; Mozi, 83n2, 93, 211,
   222

Motoda Eifu, 63, 212
Motoori Norinaga, 62, 212
Mou Zongsan, 14, 29, 105, 211, 223

Nakae Tōju, 56, 212
nei, 176, 180, 181, 184–186, 222
neo-Confucianism. See Confucianism
neo-Daoism. See Daoism

Ogyū Sorai, 58–60, 65, 66, 91, 213
Ōjin, 53, 213, 224
Ouyang Xiu, 23–25, 36, 211

Paekche kingdom, 35, 36, 53, 217
Park Chi-wŏn, 48, 49, 214
Park Chʼo, 38, 214
Park Kyu-su, 49, 214
Park Ŭn-sik, ix, 50, 214
principle, pattern, order, or rationale. See li 理

qi, 16, 17, 39, 66n3, 71, 88, 97, 98, 200–202, 223, 225; vital energy, 38–44, 46, 47, 223
qiankun, 89, 223
Qin dynasty, 10, 187, 215, 222; Wei-Qin period, 10, 11, 215, 225
qing, 28, 223
Qing dynasty, 10, 17, 21, 22, 25, 29, 44, 48, 49, 141n6, 150, 216, 221; Qing School of Evidential Learning, 12
qiqing, 40, 201, 220, 223; Seven Feelings, 40–43, 47, 201, 203, 220, 223

rangakusha, 62, 223
ren 人, 74, 88, 98, 223
ren 仁, 1, 2, 4, 14, 15, 18, 19, 66n4, 68, 70, 74, 76, 78, 79, 85n30, 89, 196–109, 111, 117, 156, 158, 176, 181, 183, 184, 193, 195, 201, 223–225
rites, propriety, or ritual propriety. See li 禮
Ruanyuan, 48, 211
Russell, Bertrand, 81

sarim, 38, 44, 223
Seven Feelings. See qiqing

Shang dynasty or kingdom, 9, 68–70, 83, 84n4, 215
Shao Yong, 12, 22, 25, 212
sheng, 78, 89, 94, 95, 223
shintō, 56, 62, 170, 217, 221, 223
shu, 14, 15, 82, 83, 183, 223, 226
Silla kingdom, 35, 36, 217
Sima Guang, 23–25, 36, 212
Sima Niu, 1, 94, 100n8
Sŏ Kyŏngdŏk, 38, 214
Song dynasty, 9, 10, 12, 13, 17, 21–29, 38, 54, 150, 152, 153, 169, 187, 194, 195, 198, 200, 201, 205, 210n7, 210n10, 216, 220, 222, 224, 226; Northern Song, 11, 12, 21–25, 36, 216, 219; Southern Song, 2, 11, 22, 23, 26, 216
Spring and Autumn period, 12, 215
Su Shi, 23, 25, 212

Tʼaejo, 36, 214
taiji, 200, 224
Tang dynasty, 10, 11, 21, 28, 37, 53, 216
Tang Junyi, 4, 70–73, 75–80, 105, 212, 223
Tanʼgun, 35, 214
Three Kingdoms period (Korea), 34–36, 217
tian, 4, 13, 14, 75, 76, 88–91, 98, 99, 100n8, 137, 138, 222–224; tianming, 13, 136, 137
Tʼoegye, 40–46, 52, 56, 201–203, 214, 220, 221, 224
Tokugawa government and society, 55–57, 59–63, 65, 66, 213, 216, 221
Tokugawa Ienobu, 60, 213
Tokugawa Ietsugu, 60, 213
Tokugawa Ieyasu, 55, 213
Tokugawa Tsunayoshi, 59, 66, 213
Tokugawa Yoshimune, 59, 60, 213
Tu Weiming, 5, 13, 21, 27, 29, 83, 99, 105, 108, 118, 145, 154, 155, 158, 169, 172n5, 176, 187, 188, 212

Ugye, 40, 43, 214, 220, 224
Unified Silla period, 34, 36, 217

wai, 180, 181, 184–186, 224
Wang Anshi, 23–25, 172n4, 212
Wang Bi, 11, 84n11, 212
Wang Fuzhi, 12, 150, 212
Wang In, 36, 53, 213, 214, 216, 217, 224
Wang Yangming, 5, 12, 22, 27–29, 45, 50, 51, 55–58, 62, 134, 150, 153, 155, 172n17, 212, 216, 224, 226; Wang Yangming School, 44, 45
wanwu, 71, 89, 224
Warring States period, 9, 12, 15, 21, 22, 215, 219
wen, 180, 224
Weng Fanggang, 48, 212
wu, 18, 224
wulun, 164, 225; five relations, 164, 186

Xia dynasty or kingdom, 9, 68, 215
Xia Yong, 137
xiao, 4, 14, 68, 70, 79, 80, 85n34, 176, 225. *See also* Confucianism: and family relations
xin 心, 16, 26, 30n7, 36, 78, 95, 115, 183, 195, 225; heart-mind, 195–197, 200–202, 205, 201n7, 224, 225; heart-and-mind, 92, 98, 114, 114; mind-heart, 12, 13, 16–18, 20, 21, 26–28, 225; *xinxue* 12, 28, 224
xin 信, 58, 66n4, 225
Xin dynasty, 215
xing 刑, 111, 112, 225
xing 性, 4, 16, 17, 19, 40, 76–78, 84n23, 88, 94–98, 225
Xu Fuguan, 19, 105, 212, 223
Xun Yue, 11, 212
Xunzi, 3, 5, 10, 12, 24, 29, 85n32, 91, 109, 146, 212, 215, 219, 222; and Boston Confucianism, 150, 153, 157; and human nature or *xing*, 15, 17, 19, 152, 225; and natural and social order, 20; and ritual in civilization and culture, 18, 157, 158, 162

Yamaga Sokō, 58, 213, 223

Yamato, 54, 216, 225
Yamazaki Ansai, 56, 65, 213
Yanagisawa Yoshiyasu, 59, 213
Yang Xiong, 11, 24, 212
Yen Yuan, 92
yi, 68, 70, 78, 80, 82, 85n30, 89, 106, 111, 119n28, 183, 224, 225
Yijing, 1, 25, 54, 65, 69, 72, 88, 93, 169, 219, 224, 225; *Book of Changes*, 1, 25, 54, 72, 88, 90, 95, 194, 195, 219, 224, 225
yin and *yang*, 17, 39, 46, 69, 175, 176, 184, 188, 225, 226
Yu In-sŏk, 50, 214
Yuan dynasty, 10, 12, 25, 54, 150, 153, 216
Yulgok, 40, 43, 44, 52, 201–203, 214, 220, 226
Yun Hyu, 43, 45, 47, 214

Zhang Zai, 12, 22, 25, 150, 192, 195, 212
zheng 正, 80, 226; *zhengming*, 62, 222
zheng 政, 80, 111, 180, 226
zhi, 92, 106, 116, 183, 224–226
zhong, 14, 15, 66n4, 82, 226
Zhongyong, 2, 33, 47, 75, 78, 99, 135, 219, 224, 226; *Doctrine of the Mean*, 59, 150, 151, 154, 155, 224, 226
Zhou Dunyi, 12, 22, 25, 39, 150, 153, 212
Zhou dynasty or kingdom, 9, 12, 16, 21, 35, 58, 67–69, 84n2, 91, 215; Duke of Zhou, 90, 113, 116; *Rites of Zhou*, 24, 36, 37
Zhuangzi, 17, 19, 146, 212, 219
zhuguan, 82, 226
Zhu Xi, 2, 11, 12, 22–29, 40, 42, 46, 47, 49, 54, 55, 57–59, 61, 91, 101n12, 134, 149, 150, 152, 153, 192, 195, 200, 212, 216, 219, 226
Zi Xia, 94, 100n8
Zigong, 93

Printed in Great Britain
by Amazon